The End All Around Us

Millennialism and Society
Series Editor: Brenda E. Brasher

Millennialism and Society had its genesis in the 1996–2002 annual meetings of the Center for Millennial Studies at Boston University. Those meetings brought together an international array of scholars to discuss the texts and traditions of religious revelation or apocalypses concerning the end of the world as we know it, whether in a tumultuous final judgement or a utopian eternal paradise. As apocalyptic texts advance an argument that massive change on earth is possible, even desirable, because it is part of a divine plan, the scholars' goal was to attain a richer, more nuanced understanding of our most ancient ideas of social change, including their influence on societies today.

Taken together, *Millennialism and Society* as a series represents a sustained effort on the part of this scholarly network to advance our understanding of what is a frequently unruly element of our cultural heritage.

Gender and Apocalyptic Desire
Edited by Brenda E. Brasher and Lee Quinby
Senior Advisers: Cynthia Eller and Rosalind I. J. Hackett

War in Heaven/Heaven on Earth
Theories of the Apocalyptic
Edited by Stephen D. O'Leary and Glen S. McGhee
Senior Adviser: Frederic J. Baumgartner

The End that Does
Art, Science and Millennial Accomplishment
Edited by Cathy Gutierrez and Hillel Schwartz
Senior Advisers: Jeffrey Stanley and Matt K. Matsuda

The End All Around Us
Apocalyptic Texts and Popular Culture

Edited by
John Walliss and Kenneth G. C. Newport

LONDON   OAKVILLE

Published by

UK: Equinox Publishing Ltd., Unit 6, The Village, 101 Amies St.,
London SW11 2JW
USA: DBBC, 28 Main Street, Oakville, CT 06779

www.equinoxpub.com

First published 2009 by Equinox Publishing Ltd.

British Library Cataloguing-in-Publication Data
A catalogue record for this book is available from the British Library.

ISBN   978 1 84553 261 1   (hardback)
           978 1 84553 262 8   (paperback)

Library of Congress Cataloging-in-Publication Data
The end all around us: apocalyptic texts and popular culture / edited
by John Walliss and Kenneth G.C. Newport.
     p. cm.— (Millennialism and society)
 Includes bibliographical references and index.
 ISBN 978-1-84553-261-1 (hb)—ISBN 978-1-84553-262-8 (pb)
 1. Popular culture—Religious aspects. 2. End of the world. I. Walliss,
John, 1974- II. Newport, Kenneth G. C. BL65.C8E53 2009
202'.3—dc22

2008039137

Typeset by S.J.I.Services
Printed and bound in Great Britain by Lightning Source UK Ltd, Milton Keynes

Contents

List of contributors

The Editors

Dr John Walliss is senior lecturer in the Department of Theology and Religious Studies, and Director of the Centre for Millennialism Studies, Liverpool Hope University.

Revd. Professor Kenneth Newport is Assistant Vice Chancellor (Research and Academic Development) and Professor of Christian Thought in the Department of Theology and Religious Studies, Liverpool Hope University.

Contact Details for Contributors

Dr John Walliss is senior lecturer in the Department of Theology and Religious Studies, and Director of the Centre for Millennialism Studies, Liverpool Hope University.

Christopher Partridge, Department of Religious Studies, Lancaster University, Lancaster LA1 4NY, UK. c.partridge@lancaster.ac.uk

Keith Kahn-Harris, Centre for Urban and Community Research, Goldsmiths College, London, SE146NW. kkahnharris@blueyonder.co.uk

Mick Broderick, MCC/Arts, Murdoch University, South Street, Murdoch, WA 6150, Australia. mick.broderick@murdoch.edu.au

Kenneth Newport, Dept of Theology and Religious Studies, Liverpool Hope University, Hope Park, Liverpool, L16 9JD. knewport@hope.ac.uk

Gary Baines, History Department, Rhodes University, PO Box 95, Grahamstown, 6140, South Africa. g.baines@ru.ac.za

Lee Quinby, Macaulay Honors College, 35 W. 67th St., NY, NY 10023, USA. leequinby@aol.com

Roslyn Weaver, PO Box 191, Moss Vale NSW 2577, Australia. roslynweaver@gmail.com

Jennie Chapman, Department of English and American Studies, School of Arts, Histories and Cultures, University of Manchester, Oxford Road M13 9PL.

BIC codes

HRBM21 (Books of the New Testament)
HRBM3 (Biblical Studies)
HRQM9 (Contemporary Apocalyptic Sects and Cults)
GTSC (Popular Culture)
GZ (Controversial Knowledge)

Introduction

John Walliss and Kenneth G. C. Newport

Of all the books of the Bible, few have had the enduring influence on western culture—and particularly on the arts—as has the Book of Revelation. From at least the fourth century CE down to the present day, its beguiling narrative and striking visual imagery have inspired a variety of artists and musicians (and more recently, film makers) from Albrecht Dürer, Hieronymus Bosch and William Blake through to Ingmar Bergman, Andrei Tarkovsky and Jake and Dinos Chapman. It has also, albeit in a secularized form, found expression in innumerable horror and science fiction comic books, as well as in an equally innumerable number of Hollywood movies dealing with planetary disaster and "the end of the world". Indeed, for reasons that are clear from even a cursory reading of the text (particularly in its King James Version), the Book of Revelation, perhaps more so than any other book, Biblical or otherwise, cries out for such artistic representation.

The nine essays in this volume focus on the influence of the Book of Revelation and the apocalypse more generally on various sites within popular culture, tracing the way in which its themes, language and motifs are manifested across film and music and in literary and online texts.[1] In his essay, Gary Baines examines the way in which apocalyptic themes are found in the work of Bob Dylan. Dylan's repertoire, Baines argues, is rich in symbolism and reflects not only his own concerns as an artist but also those of his audience. Baines examines the apocalyptic and dystopian threads within his work, tracing in particular Dylan's evocation of themes of destruction and renewal, and judgement and redemption from the 1960s to the present day. Whereas Dylan's early "protest" songs were concerned with notions of judgement and annihilation with little or no hope of redemption, Baines argues, the work Dylan produced following his "born again" conversion in the late 1970s, emphasized instead notions of redemption, albeit conceived within a Christian premillennial framework. Although Dylan no longer subscribes to this position, for Baines his work is still dystopian; it is shaped by pessimism and fatalism. As Dylan himself states in one of his subsequent songs; "the world could come to an end tonight, but that's alright" ("I and I", *Infidels*, 1983).

Dystopian themes are also explored by Keith Kahn-Harris in his chapter on a radically different musical genre from that of Dylan; extreme metal. Kahn-Harris traces the evolution of the genre out of punk movement and early heavy metal and thrash metal bands such as Iron Maiden, Judas Priest and Metallica into an identifiable musical genre in the early 1980s, highlighting the genre's exploration of the apocalyptic and dystopian. Bands like Deicide, Slayer, Impaled Nazarene and Marduk, Kahn-Harris shows, frequently make reference to broadly apocalyptic themes and images in their lyrics, imagery and musical arrangements (indeed, he argues, the genre's systematic breaking of musical rules—of speed, melody and harmony—is itself an apocalyptic prefiguring of a world in which rules and boundaries collapse into chaos). However, rather than necessarily reflecting the beliefs and values of their creators, these should, he argues, be seen instead as artistic expressions; the extreme metal scene providing a dedicated artistic space where the apocalypse can be contemplated, experienced vicariously and in some cases delighted in.

Moving again across musical genres, Christopher Partridge's chapter explores the articulation of apocalyptic themes within reggae. Partridge traces the emergence of Rastafarianism and reggae out of Jamaican culture and, specifically, a cultural background of slavery and oppression, focusing on the movement's evocation of themes around exile and redemption as metaphors for a return to an Ethiopian "Zion". In doing so Partridge focuses in particular on "Babylon" as a metaphor for an oppressive establishment that, it is expected, will shortly be destroyed in an apocalyptic conflagration. Linked to this, Partridge also discusses the concept of "chanting down Babylon", whereby, it seems, Rastafarian art and music may itself play a crucial role in resisting "Babylon", and may indeed contribute to its demise.

The second group of essays move the focus from music to film. John Walliss' chapter discusses a number of "end of the world" films released over the course of the last decade. From threats of alien invasion, through "super-viruses", to environmental/social meltdown, these films, he argues, reflect both the concerns of their audiences and also contemporary, post Cold-War geo-political realities. In doing so, Walliss argues, the language and imagery of the apocalypse has not only been co-opted by popular culture, it has also, crucially, been subverted. Whereas texts such as the Book of Revelation present apocalyptic scenarios as supernatural events, outside the scope of human agency, and as necessary events within sacred/human history, these films secularize and invert it so that the apocalyptic event becomes both natural or human-made in nature and avoidable through human agency. Indeed whereas apocalyptic texts are invariably critical of the status quo, according to Walliss within these films the apocalyptic hero is the saviour of the established order.

Developing some of the themes in Walliss' chapter, Lee Quinby focuses on how Judeo-Christian apocalypticism is increasingly being shaped by contemporary concerns to produce apocalyptic films characterized by what she terms "a romance of doom, death and deferral". Focusing on three recent films, *28 Days Later*, *Children of Men* and *Apocalypto*, she shows how in each, themes of lost fertility, for both humanity and the earth, the control of women's sexuality and reproduction, and the blurring of masculinity and femininity abound as prime ways of expressing destruction, chaos, doom—and sometimes hope. In doing so, Quinby highlights the ways in which issues of masculine chivalry and feminine purity are modified within the films, so that in each film not only are traditional splits between masculine and feminine traits rendered more fluid and ambiguous, but that is a representational shift away from the traditional dualism that equates purity with virginity towards an elevation of fertility and sexual experience. Indeed, she argues, the films place an emphasis on these shifting gender roles as one of the means by which apocalyptic destruction may be averted.

Moving from the West towards the Far East, Mick Broderick's chapter discusses several strains of eschatological discourse found within *anime*. Whereas many commentators on *anime*, he argues, have foregrounded the apocalyptic or destructive aspect of the genre, in his chapter he seeks to look "beyond the apocalypse" to forms of post-apocalyptic utopia envisioned in *anime*. Drawing on the classic *anime Akira*, as well as the recent examples of *Spriggan* and *Appleseed*, he discusses how these films present apocalyptic destruction as either the pathway to a new order, or as a way of returning balance in a corrupt and moribund world, often through transhumanist technological hybridity or psychic/supernatural human evolution.

Moving away from films to literary representations of the apocalypse, Jennie Chapman's chapter discusses the phenomenally successful *Left Behind* series of novels. Drawing on the work of the "Birmingham School" of cultural studies and Michael Kammen, she argues that the success of the novels challenge the analytical distinctions made by these commentators between subculture and mainstream and popular and mass culture. While the novels have achieved commercial success, they have not been incorporated into, and made safe by, the dominant order, but are instead still cast as a niche cultural product. In this way, she suggests, the novels are a cultural anomaly; occupying a position somewhere between popular culture, mainstream culture and even evangelical culture. Going further, she argues that a more useful way of framing the novels is as part of a long running trajectory of popularized interpretations of prophecy, that takes Biblical apocalyptic texts and filters them through layers of Darbyite dispensationalism, Hal Lindsey, disaster movies, action novels and political popularism.

Echoing John Walliss' and Lee Quinby's chapters earlier in the volume on the way in which contemporary apocalyptic films can reflect and possibly shape contemporary concerns, Roslyn Weaver's chapter discusses the ways in which literary science fiction provides a powerful framework for critiquing dominant and oppressive groups and practices within society by projecting contemporary dangers and concerns into often dark and dystopian futures. In this way, she argues, the science fiction genre creates a literary space in which writers may invent new worlds in order to interrogate and potentially inspire change in prevailing cultural constructions. While apocalypse can also be utilized for negative ends, Weaver suggests that this is a misuse of a genre that has been enormously influenced by biblical apocalypse, itself a literature of dissent from minority groups. Her chapter surveys some of the ways in which science fiction writers have used apocalypse for a range of political and ideological viewpoints.

Finally, in his chapter, Robert Glenn Howard shifts our attention towards the ways in which apocalyptic ideas are disseminated and actively negotiated by individuals within cyberspace. Connecting with each other through online participatory media, Howard argues that these individuals form a sort of ekklesia or "church" that emerges from everyday Internet discourse about the End Times. Because this "virtual" church is formed only through the expression of shared ideas online, it may be functioning to distance its members from the broader values and beliefs necessary for them to profitably engage their geographically local communities.

In an edited collection of this length, it is only really possible to scratch the surface of the ongoing influence of apocalyptic ideas and imagery on popular culture. Indeed, such is the extent and the constantly developing nature of popular culture that the academic critics of it can never really hope to keep pace. These essays do, however, contribute to the debate and, hopefully, do so in important and insightful ways. Certainly it is the editors' view that the essays presented here do at least give some indication of the sheer breadth of popular material in which apocalyptic ideas seem to resonate; music, films, literature and the internet all attest to the lasting allure of "The End" (however that is conceived). But in these essays too one begins to get a sense not just of breadth but of depth as the authors show just how fundamental and central apocalyptic ideas, and representations of those ideas, are in popular belief systems as they surface in some perhaps academically unexpected, but influential, places. Academics, including contemporary theologians and biblical scholars, may largely have lost their interest in determining the "signs of the [end] times" (cf. Matt 16:3). For many "out there" in the darkness beyond the academic camp-fire (as Paul Boyer has put it), however, interest in such matters is very much alive and well.

Note

1.   The chapters grew out of a colloquium organized by Liverpool Hope University and the University of Manchester and held at Ripon College Cuddesdon, Oxford in September 2005. The editors would like to acknowledge the unconditional financial support of The Panacea Society, Bedford for both organizing the colloquium and producing this volume.

Songs of fate, hope and oblivion: Bob Dylan's dystopianism and apocalyticism

Gary Baines

Introduction

In spite of the many twists and turns in his career, including reinventions of his public personae and many changes in his songwriting style, Bob Dylan still commands considerable influence as a cultural broker with the generation that has grown up with his music. He is undoubtedly one of the most influential recording artists of the last four decades. This influence is not confined to other artists but extends to fans, aficionados, music critics, scholars, as well as so-called "Dylanologists" who are fixated with everything he does. His albums sell well and there are thousands of internet sites devoted to his music and lyrics. Whatever he does is still treated as a high-profile media event. Indeed, Dylan's iconic status is second to none in popular culture.

Dylan's repertoire is rich in symbolism and his songs have a universal provenance that connects with audiences. Many of his songs reflect important concerns; one such is the expectation, or in some cases fear, that we are living in the "last days". It is not only the current generation of fundamentalist American Christians that believes that it is the last (Camp, 1997: 124, 189), but a broad cross-section of the general public does too. Many anticipate or await the apocalypse. They share Dylan's dystopian sensibility, or his sense of pessimism and powerlessness in the face of the world having reached a "point of no return". And Dylan's invocation of apocalyptic imagery seems to resonate with those who have nothing but contempt for society and the achievements of the modern world, who regard the current social order as wholly corrupt and evil, and who feel that because the present world is irredeemable, it will or must be destroyed. So Dylan is able to tap into the storehouse of apocalyptic symbols with which his audiences are familiar and for some of whom strike a chord. As Benjamin (1998: 25, 45) has remarked: "Apocalyptic symbols are so rich, or else so vacuous, that they lend themselves to endless reinterpretations and uses." This is as true of religious millenarian groups as it is of the products of contemporary popular culture.

Dylan has been called a "poet of pessimism" (Boucher, 2004: 4) although not all his songs are devoid of hope for change and transformation. Still, his body of work is suffused with images of disaster, destruction, judgement and the end of the world. Even a cursory examination of Dylan's songs reveals both explicit as well as implicit references to the apocalypse. Marqusee (2003: 238) remarks that: "Often the language used to evoke the apocalypse is biblical, but in Dylan's work … apocalypse is a social category; a response to the bomb; the imminence of social transformation, the impossibility of social transformation, the cataclysm of war." In other words, Dylan's apocalypse might make specific allusions to biblical eschatology, but it is as likely to be used generically. It is sometimes to be taken literally but other times metaphorically. It veers between the hope of redemption and renewal, mere survival, and the resignation of annihilation or obliteration. It is a constant but certainly not a consistent feature of Dylan's religious vision. In short, Dylan's vision is not singular; his is a differentiated apocalypse. In order to try make some sense of Dylan's vision of the world and its future, and explain why his audiences identify with it, we will first try to understand how the apocalyptic imagination functions in contemporary society. Then we will trace the contours of Dylan's dystopianism in the ebb and flow of his life. Finally, we will track the appearance of the apocalyptic idiom and narrative in Dylan's repertoire.

The Apocalyptic Imagination and Popular Culture

The apocalyptic imagination flourishes in times of severe stress or crisis. This may take the form of: massive human-made catastrophe or natural cataclysm, of technology that runs amok or approaches meltdown, or of escalating tensions between nuclear powers that threaten the very survival of the species. Whereas religious doomsayers see such "signs of the end times" as *confirmation* of God's foreordained plan, secular apocalypticists see such occurrences as *causes* of the end (Wojcik, 1997: 131). The preoccupation with

portents or causes of the end is characteristic of the apocalyptic imagination. In this worldview the end is both imminent and inevitable.
And the apocalyptic imagination is protean; it assumes many guises
in the contemporary world. It is a sense of foreboding as much as an
attitude, an orientation to ultimate concerns as much as a commitment to a specific end time narrative (Strozier, 1995: 250). The phrase
"apocalyptic imagination" was used as the title of Collins' (1984) seminal study of Jewish apocalyptic literature and its influence on Christian texts. But it has outgrown any narrow or specific application and
come to be used as a catchall term for any vision of the end of the
world. Armageddon and the mushroom cloud have become part of
a common fund of apocalyptic images. The ubiquity of such images
has caused Carey (1999: 270) to suggest that: "Apocalyptic terms of
reference are so deeply ingrained in Western culture that they assume an archetypal function". Indeed, the apocalypse might well be
embedded in our collective consciousness for it functions as myth,[1]
teleology and narrative device in our culture.

So apocalypticism has become pervasive in our ostensibly secular
society. It has taken hold of our imaginations and found expression in
non-religious discourse (Barkun, 1983: 257–80). Secular doomsday
visions are usually characterized by a sense of pessimism, absurdity
and nihilism (Wojcik, 1997: 97). Whilst religious discourse invariably holds out the hope of redemption following judgement and renewal, the secular apocalypse offers only the prospect of annihilation
and oblivion. But I believe that the dichotomy between the religious
and secular apocalypse has been overstated. Instead, I would argue
that religious and secular discourses have become well and truly
imbricated. Bendle (2005) reckons that a crucial shift within the apocalyptic tradition has occurred since the unparalleled horrors of the
Great War. He notes the loss of faith in progress towards a far more
pessimistic view of the human condition. In secular terms this
amounted to a shift from a utopian to a dystopian vision. In religious
terms this was reflected in the shift from post-millennialism to pre-
millennialism with predictions that a period of unprecedented
human suffering would precede the second coming of Jesus. He concludes that "it is this dark vision that now shapes the contemporary
apocalyptic imagination in both its religious and secular forms" (2).

In its religious form, the apocalyptic narrative is essentially the
story of the cosmic struggle between good and evil culminating in
divine intervention, judgement of the wicked, the salvation of a

select few and the creation of a new world order cleansed of evil. This story has its genesis in the religious traditions of the Middle East. Cohn (1995: 21–37) has traced its origins to the ancient Persian (Iranian) religion of Zoroastrianism. The apocalyptic texts of the Hebrew scripture, such as the books of Ezekiel and Daniel, owe their vision to the suffering of Jews caused by the desecration of the temple and exile from their land (Boyer, 1992: 22–31). Redemption from such trials and tribulations is only possible for the faithful, God's elect. This apocalyptic strand in the Judaic tradition was reified when the Book of Revelation was admitted into the canon of the Christian Bible. This version of the apocalypse features a fantastic cast of characters like the Beast, the whore of Babylon, etc. The third monotheistic faith to have emerged in the Middle East, Islam, also has an apocalyptic paradigm which manifests itself periodically in messianic and millennial movements (Arjomand, 2002: 125). This shared apocalyptic tradition in Judaism, Christianity and Islam shaped not only the eschatology of these religious communities, but also served as an imperative in major currents or trends in history and contemporary culture (Amanat, 2002: 1–2).

The apocalyptic imagination can be fuelled by any number of cataclysms and crises. The establishment of the state of Israel and the detonation of nuclear devices have been widely regarded as ushering in the end times. With the advent of the Cold War, the world has experienced periodic bouts of anxiety occasioned by events such as the Berlin airlift, Cuban missile crisis, etc. Such anxiety became particularly acute during periods of escalating tensions in the early 1960s and then, again, in the 1980s when Reagan upped the ante in the Cold War stakes. Apocalypticism has, however, outlived the Cold War and actually experienced something of a resurgence at the advent of the new millennium. It now finds expression in forms of "endism" such as "ecocatastrophism",[2] "technomillenialism",[3] and in the ideas of proponents of a range of political eschatologies.[4] And it is likely to grip the imagination and influence public discourse into the foreseeable future.

The fecundity of the apocalyptic imagination has stimulated an enormous creative endeavour. It has produced an array of literature from poems through novels to comic books; a number of genres of Hollywood films; and innumerable song lyrics. The study of these texts has to date been rather uneven. There has been a plethora of publications related to the apocalyptic imagination and cinema (see, for example, Shaheen, 1978; Broderick, 1996; Perrine, 1997; Evans, 1998; Newman, 2000; Dixon, 2002; Shapiro, 2002, as well as the chapters by Walliss, Quinby and Broderick in this volume), as well as some on the literature of the "last days" (see, for example, Anisfield, 1997; Wagar, 1982; Brians, n.d.). But there exists (as far as I know) no systematic study of the theme of the apocalypse in song lyrics.[5] All we have are occasional allusions to the influence of apocalypticism on specific subcultures and their music. For instance, Lipsitz (1994: 221) refers to the 1960s counterculture's "powerful apocalyptic strain". Hebdige (1979: 27) has observed that "the rhetoric of punk was drenched in apocalypse", and Greil (1989: 5) speaks of the "blank apocalypse of punk" in referring to its nihilist posturing. In a more extensive treatment of the topic, Wojcik (1997: 121, 130) insists that "apocalyptic ideas were not necessarily the defining characteristic of punk worldview" but was "an expression of style, a fashion statement, a way to shock, or a means of articulating a sense of nihilism or anger". Dawes (2002: 77; see also Partridge in this volume) has noted that the lyrics of reggae music such as those of Bob Marley reflected a Rastafarian eschatology with its sense of apocalyptic dread. But apart from some work on Dylan (see Crotty, 2003: 307–33; Marqusee, 2003: 61, 236–37; Gamble, 2004: 17–20; Gilmour, 2004: 71–90),[6] there are no studies of the influence of apocalypticism on specific artists. This literature provides a point of departure for my own treatment of Dylan's apocalypses.

The Contours of Dylan's Dystopianism

The most common approach by writers wishing to make sense of Dylan's body of work is the biographical one. This is typified by the work of Heylin (1992), Shelton (1997) and Sounes (2001). Each of these works has its merits, but mistakenly assumes that the minutiae of Dylan's personal life will be directly reflected in his lyrics. Whilst Dylan's life story obviously offers clues to personal references in his verse, he often projects his own experiences into the stories of historical, biblical, mythical and wholly invented figures. And the characters in Dylan songs are frequently composites constructed from many sources, including his imagination. So it is simplistic to suppose that biographical referents can provide a definitive interpretation of Dylan's often vague and cryptic lyrics. Indeed, Dylan is downright uncooperative with the media and has been known to deliberately

– even perversely – make misleading statements in interviews about his songs. Throughout his lengthy career, Dylan has remained a very private person. Even his autobiography (Dylan, 2004) does not provide any real secrets or revelations about his personal life story.

A second approach to understanding Dylan is in line with the tradition of literary criticism that emphasizes the value of studying texts freed from the constraints of historical context. This is exemplified by Gray's (2000) monumental lit-crit study, Ricks' (2003) thematic approach (2003), and Gilmour's (2004) synchronic treatment of Dylan's lyrics. None of these authors give much attention to when and where a given song was written, and assume that the songwriter's intention can be read from the text of Dylan's lyrical poems (Boucher, 2004: 146). Although these works contain some very illuminating commentary, they are pre-occupied with providing insightful interpretations and identifying influences in Dylan's work.

None of the above commentators dispute the influence of the Bible on Dylan's body of work. In fact, there are two studies entirely devoted to this topic (see Cartwright, 1992; Gilmour, 2004). It is well known that Dylan reads the Bible extensively and is especially familiar with the King James (Authorized) version. Despite his Jewish background, Dylan's knowledge of the Bible is not confined to the Hebrew Scriptures. However there is some difference of opinion as to the purpose to which Dylan uses the Bible. There is also some disagreement as to whether the Bible is more important in some periods of his life than others. Writing of the 1960s, Marqusee (2003: 237) holds that for Dylan's creative process "the Bible's resonant language [and] metaphorical power was greater than that of newspapers and magazines". As with many observers of current affairs, he used the rich imagery of the scriptures to construct narratives or landscapes in his songs. This has the advantage of being able to capture a scene with a great economy of expression or to relate a story in a few words. If biblical images serve as a heuristic device for Dylan (Gilmour, 2002: 10), the same can be said of the apocalyptic motifs that he employs.

Dylan is clearly familiar with a range of apocalyptic texts from the scriptures, including the Book of Revelation. Crotty (2003: 322) has shown that Dylan is acquainted with relatively obscure apocalyptic texts such as the Books of Baruch which are canonical only to Catholics. But we should not presume that Dylan's apocalypticism is wholly inspired by religious sources. For, as we have seen, the apocalypse is redolent in public discourse. And Dylan is like a sponge; he absorbs ideas and images from a vast array of sources. Mellers (1981: 143) holds that Dylan is a "folk artist" in the sense that his sources are absorbed at a more or less pre-conscious level. Yet, he is equally ready to acknowledge and affirm his debts to and respect – even reverence – for traditions of popular music and literature. In seeking to understand Dylan's predilection for referencing the apocalypse, I have no wish to revisit the debate on intertextuality. Suffice it to say, "Dylan is well aware of the significance of sources or influences in his work" (Gilmour, 2004: 18) and has readily admitted to having no qualms about being a "thief" of others' ideas.

Dylan, more so than other contemporary songwriters, has a particular gift for conjuring up images which are able to capture the public imagination. Even his so-called '"finger-pointing" songs of the early 1960s stimulated the imagination of listeners rather than proscribing a message. Dylan found himself at the forefront of folk revival movement and being proclaimed the "spokesman for his generation". But he renounced formal politics and debunked the power of music to transform society when in a 1965 *Newsweek* interview he declared that: "I've never written political songs. Songs can't save the world" (cited in Schwartz, 2000: 83). If his public statements are anything to go by, Dylan apparently came to believe that social justice was not attainable and so disavowed conventional political solutions to the problems that beset American society in the mid-1960s. Gamble (2004) suggests that this transition from optimism to pessimism was expressed in Dylan's musical output; that songs of redemption such as "Blowin' in the Wind" (1962) gave way to those of survival as in "Desolation Row" (1965). However, I will show that certain song lyrics during his "protest phase" evince an unremittingly bleak world without any prospect of renewal or salvation. These songs of oblivion were not necessarily recorded and/or released but were still part of his early output and, hence, should be regarded as expressing his dystopianism.

Dylan was not alone amongst the cultural elite who expressed alienation from society in the mid-1960s. Cold War tensions caused much public anxiety and created an atmosphere in which doomsayers flourished. The heightened anxiety spawned literary, cinematic and musical works which evoked the apocalypse. Dylan had a host of imitators, one of whom was Barry McGuire, who released a recording of P. F. Sloane's "The Eve of Destruction" in 1965 which went to the top of the Billboard charts. The song graphically catalogued social ills such as hatred, rampant violence and war. It included the lines:

> If the button is pushed, there's no running away,
> There'll be no-one to save with the world in a grave,

The stark, literal images lacked Dylan's subtlety (Boucher, 2004: 181). Notwithstanding the rather crass evocation of apocalyptic imagery and the hectoring tone of the song, it reflected disaffection with the establishment that would find fuller expression in the counterculture. The warning of the imminent end of the world obviously resonated with the growing concerns of many in American society that the world was set on the path of destruction.

Boucher (2004) makes a fairly compelling case for a correlation between Dylan's personal crises and his fitful spiritual journey. Following a motorcycle accident in 1966, he turned to the Bible for solace. This was followed by the death of his father in June 1968 and the reaffirmation of his Jewish identity and heritage. Dylan's divorce from Sarah Lowndes in 1977 took an emotional toll and his subsequent disavowal of his Jewishness suggested inner turmoil. During the Rolling Thunder Revue he was in constant contact with musicians who testified to having given up their dependency on drugs and other substances with the support of Jesus Christ, their saviour. Dylan's search for inner peace led to a religious experience that he later described as having been "born again". During this period he produced three albums: *Slow Train Coming* (1979), *Saved* (1980) and *Shot of Love* (1981) that gave expression to his new-found faith and marked a return to social criticism. Gamble (2004: 17) argues that what unites the Christian albums with his "protest" albums is that "Dylan was singing songs of redemption, proclaiming that America could be saved if it realized its errors and repented". In other words, Dylan's insistent dystopianism was checked by a renewed faith in some sort of panacea for society's ills that rested on divine intervention.

During this time, Dylan' was exposed to the post-millennial teachings of the Vineyard School of Discipleship predicated on large-scale revival preceding the establishment of the kingdom of God on earth. But he was also introduced to the pre-millennialism of Hal Lindsey's best-selling *The Late Great Planet Earth* (1970). Heylin (1992: 333) reckons that this became his "second bible and added an apocalyptic edge to his worldview". I would rather contend that Dylan's apocalypticism assumed a rigid dispensationalist form after he appropriated Lindsey's literalist interpretation of apocalyptic passages in the Bible. Dylan's eschatology emphasized the imminence of the 'rapture' (see Jenni Chapman's chapter in this volume for a discussion of the rapture). He became more convinced than ever that the political world was irredeemable. His reading of the Bible within a fundamentalist framework inspired some aw(e)ful and fearsome imagery that was not in keeping with his more figurative use of apocalyptic references during other periods of his career. Dylan took to using the platform provided by his stage performances to harangue his audiences with long, rambling monologues in which he warned that they were living in the end times. His intensity and self-righteous fervour alienated all but his most faithful fans. There is sufficient evidence from the content of these "apocalyptic stage raps" (Turner, 2001), let alone his song lyrics, to suggest that Dylan's new-found faith gave a fillip to his apocalyptic imaginings

Gamble (2004: 19) argues that Dylan's distancing himself from Christianity in the 1980s did not mean that his religious vision disappeared; rather it found a new emphasis. This is, he suggests, because "at the root the religious vision is only a more extreme vision to which Dylan has always subscribed". This is evident because Dylan never abandoned apocalyptic rhetoric altogether, it simply assumed a new form as he became more preoccupied with his own mortality than with the survival of humankind. Indeed, his own near-death experience after contracting pericarditis in 1997 occasioned a new kind of concern, that his own end might predate the extinction of life on earth. Dylan's dystopian sensibility remained true to form but it found expression in different representations of the apocalypse.

The Apocalyptic Idiom and Narrative in Dylan's Songs

In this section I am concerned to understand how the apocalyptic idiom and narrative functions to make meaning in Dylan's music. I will attempt a diachronic reading of selected songs in Dylan's repertoire. Accordingly, I will examine a particular song as a product of a specific time and place (in relation to the outline of Dylan's career provided in the previous section). Comparison can then be made with songs written at other times, making allowances for such things as the changed context, as well as Dylan's development as an artist, of the impact of life's experiences on his personal development, of the influence of books he was reading, music to which he was listening, and so on (Gilmour, 2004: 21 n. 6). This task is undertaken with two caveats: first, song lyrics are seldom created to be read as poetry but rather designed to be performed with musical accompaniment. Songs – even those of a lyrical poet like Dylan – constitute a package, a blend of text and texture (Boucher, 2004: 5). Second and conversely, Dylan seldom changes the lyrics of his compositions. He often experiments with the musical arrangement, style, tone and mode of delivery but the words remain intact. So I undertake this reading of Dylan's lyrics fully aware that their meaning may be difficult, if not impossible, to determine.

Some of Dylan's earliest material contains references to the wrath of a transcendant God and speak of the prospect of the obliteration of humankind. In 1962 Dylan penned "I'd Hate to Be You on that Dreadful Day". Its first verse consists of the lines:

Well, your clock is gonna stop
At St. Peter's gate
You gonna ask him what time it is
He's gonna say, 'It's too late'
I'd sure hate to be you on that dreadful day.

Here Dylan seems to reference Matthew 16: 18–19 and Revelation 20: 11–15. It suggests that Dylan believes that ultimately there will be a 'day of reckoning' when the wicked will be held to account for their deeds. This is not the promise of human retribution but of divine justice and otherwordly salvation.

In the same year, Dylan wrote "Let Me Die in My Footsteps" which was omitted from *The Freewheelin' Bob Dylan* album. Gray (2000: 461) calls this Dylan's "anti-nuclear panic song". The song was intended to deride the Kennedy administration's fall-out shelter programme that was supposed to enable Americans who took the necessary precautions and followed the prescribed drills to survive nuclear war. The second verse is as follows:

There's been rumors of war and wars that have been
The meaning of life has been lost in the wind
And some people thinkin' that the end is close by
'Stead of learning to live they are learning to die.
Let me die in my footsteps
Before I go under the ground.

The first line takes its cue from the words attributed to Jesus: "And when ye shall hear of wars and rumours of wars, be not troubled." These words taken from Matthew 24:6 and Luke 13:7 were reportedly uttered by Jesus while assuring his disciples that such signs heralded the kingdom of God. Dylan, however, indicates that he would prefer to die while living life to the full than carry on a subterranean existence in the shadow of nuclear holocaust. In the final verse he exhorts listeners to join him in condemning the military-industrial complex that promotes nuclear war. His sentiments fly in the face of those who believed that a post-apocalyptic wasteland could be survived and the earth renewed. He seems to reject the apocalyptic tradition that the consummation of history would usher in a world cleansed of evil and corruption.

Dylan employed rather more explicit apocalyptic imagery in "A Hard Rain's A-Gonna Fall" (1962). In spite of his denials that the song's natural imagery is a metaphor for nuclear fallout, many commentators have insisted that the song was a comment on the Cuban missile crisis of 1962 which, in the words of Henriksen (1997: 305), "made palpable America's proximity to Armageddon". Crotty (2003: 317) calls it "the pre-eminent cultural monument to the dread of nuclear holocaust which characterised the early 1960s". However, Marqusee (2003: 60) has pointed out that the song was being performed in Greenwich Village before Kennedy and Krushchev's confrontation came to a head. Marqusee adds that: "Dylan was able to write 'A Hard Rain' before the event not because he was a prophetic mystic, but because he was a political artist in a political milieu with an astute sense of prevailing anxieties." It is with good reason that this era, which was characterized by a growth in the Cold War tensions between the USA and USSR that pushed these countries to the brink of a nuclear showdown, has been dubbed the "age of anxiety". And Dylan articulated and audiences identified with such fears.

Aside from being the best-known and perhaps the most comprehensively imagined of Dylan's many apocalyptic songs (Crotty 2003: 317), "A Hard Rain" is a powerfully evocative work. Its power stems from its reworking of the traditional folk ballad's form and structure by marrying it with a long free-verse poem in the style of the French symbolists (Williamson, 2004: 257). The singer/narrator reels off a string of images which can be read as portents of a global crisis accompanying obliteration by nuclear war. But the images also can be seen as predictions of a cataclysmic event, like Noah's flood. Whether the crisis is a consequence of God's judgement rather than humankind's self-destructive impulse, the post-apocalyptic landscape is as harrowing as a Hieronymous Bosch canvas. The narrator encounters scenes of destruction and devastation described by lines such as:

> I've been out in front of a dozen dead oceans
> I've been ten thousand miles in the mouth of a graveyard

in the first stanza. And the third stanza suggests that the rain has a *tsunami*-like effect:

> I heard the roar of a wave that could drown the whole world

Many of the images of a post-apocalyptic world conjured up by Dylan are both striking and original. But, at the same time, certain images are oblique and obscure with no evident scriptural references. Like much great poetry, it is the overall mood of "A Hard Rain" that gives the song its sense of despair and desolation. Dylan's vision is panoptic and prescient, evoking literal as well as metaphorical disasters.

If "A Hard Rain's" plaintive tones voiced the fears of impending doom, "Talking World War III Blues" (1963) expresses the dread in comic terms. Dylan's black humour is not unlike that which Stanley Kubrick brought to bear on the subject of nuclear holocaust in his film *Dr Strangelove (Or How I Learned to Stop Worrying and Love the Bomb)*. Dylan reworked the blues song structure to suit his purpose of satirizing a war which would necessarily be the last waged by the human species. In "Talking World War III Blues", Dylan dreams that he has survived a nuclear war almost alone. He emerges from the sewers like a denizen of the deep to find a strangely surreal scene above ground. His plea for food is rebuffed by a shotgun-wielding survivor who has taken refuge in a fallout shelter. When he finds a woman and euphemistically suggests they "go and play Adam and Eve", the proposition is rejected on the grounds of "what happened last time they started". Procreation is considered futile on account of humankind's propensity for self-destruction. Needing somebody to talk to, Dylan's first-person narrator calls the "operator of time" but instead of a human voice he hears a recording that endlessly repeats that it is three o'clock. After an hour he hangs up. This image suggests that time has been stopped in its tracks, and is reminiscent of the timepieces found at ground zero in Hiroshima which marked the precise moment when the atomic bomb had exploded over the city. When the narrator consults a doctor to interpret his dream, he is informed that the doctor has the same dream. So it seems that all survivors have similar dreams. Then the narrator offers a Faustian bargain to the listener: "I'll let you in my dreams if I can be in yours". The dream is actually another version of Dylan's nightmare that imagines survival in a post-apocalyptic world to be pointless. The resignation implicit in the words of this verse suggests fatalism.

Another doom-laden song is "All Along the Watchtower" on *John Wesley Harding* (1968) which Dylan described as "the first Biblical-rock album". This tautly constructed, self-contained song is not in the narrative style of so much of Dylan's work. Rather, it represents his reworking of a situation ballad (Zak, 2005: 24–5). It references the Biblical verses Isaiah 21:5–9 in which the Old Testament prophet predicts the judgement and fall of Babylon for her sins against Israel:

> Prepare the table, watch in the watchtower, eat, drink, arise ye princes, and anoint the shield. For thus hath the Lord said unto me, Go, set a watchman, let him declare what he seeth … behold, here cometh a chariot of men, with a couple of horsemen

There is probably also an allusion to the prophet Ezekiel, who as God's watchman, was sent to Israel rather than

> to many people of a strange speech and of an hard language, whose words thou canst understand (3: 6).

Some writers have also noted a connection to the book of Revelation in the images of the approaching riders: a reference to the horsemen of the apocalypse in Chapter 6, to the thief in Chapter 3, and in the song's admonition that "the hour is getting late" (Zak, 2005: 24 n.97). In fact, the thief and the joker, who are harbingers of catastrophe, are archetypal characters in Dylan's stock of apocalyptic images. The wind that howls from Dylan's tortured harmonica towards the end of "All Along the Watchtower" is an eerie echo of the wind of change in "Blowin' in the Wind" (1963). It no longer promises change for the better but presents the haunting spectre of impending doom. Marqusee (2003: 238) reckons that it is the same storm of history that presages "universal and inescapable judgment … [of] history lived on the brink of destruction and revelation". The inexorability of history consumes all before it. This teleology conveys a sense of the end of the world as inevitable and pre-ordained. Crotty (2003: 328), however, remarks on the song's lack of closure: "We are not sure whether the event foreshadowed in the narrative will come to pass or not, or whether it will be cataclysmic or redemptive if it does." This comment captures the contradictions inherent in Dylan's apocalyptic vision that is characterized by a tension between judgement and redemption.

If there was any doubt about the apocalyptic tone of Dylan's "All Along the Watchtower", in the hands of Jimi Hendrix the song was transformed into a consummate musical example of the genre. Indeed, Hendrix made it sound like a grand, tragic foreboding of his generation as if the apocalyptic prophecies were being played out upon the landscape of late-1960s America (Riley, 1999: 182). Dylan subsequently not only adopted Hendrix's arrangement of his song but also emulated the mood of the cover version.

If Dylan had toned down his apocalypticism in the early 1970s, it made a reappearance towards the end of the decade. This is apparent on his album *Street Legal* (1978). For instance, on the track "Señor (Tales of Yankee Power)", the sense of the apocalypse is evident in the lines:

> Señor, Señor, do you know where we're headin'?
> Lincoln County Road or Armageddon?
> Seems like I been down this way before.

Although the song appears to be an indictment of American imperialism and its abuse of that country's self-proclaimed mission and destiny, it can equally be said to refer to life's journey in search of salvation. Dylan invariably conflates the problems of the individual with the American predicament. So when Gray (2000: 208) asserts that: "The quest for salvation might well be called the central theme of Bob Dylan's entire output", he means to imply that Dylan has more than himself in mind for his religious vision embraces the nation as well. Gray likens this quest for salvation to a train journey, a metaphor that Dylan borrowed from the blues but used to good effect on the first album of his Christian trilogy.

With regard to the title track of the album *Slow Train Coming*, Williamson (2004: 290) writes that: "The dramatic charge that comes from the energy of the apostate is striking, while the fire-and-brimstone prophecy of imminent apocalypse adds a potent spiritual terror." Notwithstanding its obvious alarmism and right-wing political rhetoric, it is a powerful song. The following track "Gonna Change My Way of Thinking" includes the lines:

> Jesus said be ready
> For you know not the hour I come.

The lines refer to statements attributed to Christ in which he warns his followers to prepare for his return because he comes like a thief in the night (Matthew 24:43, Luke 12: 39). This image is also invoked on "When He Returns", the final track on *Slow Train Coming*. It references the rapture and the millennium with the reference to 'His' (presumably Jesus Christ's) plans to "set up His throne". The "Second Coming" is a recurrent theme throughout the album.

The follow-up album *Saved* continues in this vein. References to Armageddon and the Last Judgement gleaned from Revelation 20: 11–15 are to be heard in the closing verse of "Are You Ready?" which echoes "I'd Hate to Be You on that Dreadful Day". Here Dylan appeals to listeners to ready themselves for the 'Second Coming':

> When destruction comes swiftly
> And there's no time to say fare thee well
> Have you decided whether you want to be
> In heaven or in hell?
>
> Are you ready? …
> Are you ready for Armageddon?

He also reprises the trope of the thief in the night heard in "Let Me Die in My Footsteps". The appropriation of fire and brimstone imagery and the calls for repentance evident in Dylan's "born-again" work only goes to confirm that Dylan's religious vision had become uncompromising and unforgiving during this short-lived period.

Apocalyptic imagery of doom and destruction continues to form an essential backdrop to Dylan's song lyrics beyond his Christian phase. But by the time of the release of *Infidels* (1983), Dylan appears to have become more comfortable with the prospect of the end. On the track "I and I" he sings somewhat laconically: "The world could come to an end tonight, but that's alright". But he remained convinced that he was living in the "last days". This is exemplified in "Shooting Star", the last track on *Oh Mercy* (1989), where Dylan intones:

> Listen to the engine, listen to the bell
> As the last fire track from hell

Goes rolling by, all good people are praying
It's the last temptation
The last account
The last time you might hear the Sermon on the Mount
The last radio is playing.

The repetition of "last" in these lines emphasizes the finality of Dylan's end-time vision constructed in this verse. But these were not Dylan's last words on the subject of the apocalypse.

The first Dylan composition following his hospitalization for pericarditis in 1997 was his contribution to the soundtrack of the film *Wonder Boys* called "Things Have Changed" (1999). The immediate crisis of having to face up to his own ageing and mortality might have been over, but the lyrics are still pre-occupied with impending doom:

I'm standing on the gallows with my head in a noose
Any minute now I'm expecting all hell to break loose.

This does not appear to be an instance of gallows humour. In fact, the lines are intoned in deadly earnest. While no longer a fundamentalist, Dylan's vision has not changed fundamentally. Later lines in the same song invoke the apocalypse:

I've been walking forty miles of road
If the bible is right the world will explode.

These lines would appear to be derived from 2 Peter 3: 10 which reads:

The heavens shall pass away with a great noise, and the elements shall melt with fervent heat, the earth also and the works therein shall be burned up.

As we have seen, such images of an approaching day of God's judgement recur throughout Dylan's work. Indeed, this examination of select songs illustrates that despite the variable content of Dylan's narratives, there is considerable consistency and underlying regularity in the apocalyptic idiom.

Conclusion

Dylan's religious vision reflects a constant but contradictory feature of the apocalyptic imagination, namely, a tension between the notions of end as destruction and renewal, of judgement and redemption. Dylan's early 1960s apocalyptic songs were primarily about judgement and annihilation with only a faint hope of redemption. His complete loss of faith in the potential of politics to transform the world in the mid-1960s meant that all hope of redemption was forsaken and that humankind would have to pin its hopes on surviving the inevitable apocalypse. Then during his 'born again' phase, Dylan's lyrics emphasized the need to prepare for the kingdom of God which was at hand. His songs promised redemption but only for a select few who were "saved" (in appropriate scare quotes) and so would be spared the wrath of God. Subsequently Dylan appears to have resigned himself to the inevitability of the end, both his own and all of humankind. His dystopianism shaped the persistent pessimism and fatalism evident in his lyrics. Dylan's songs of fate, hope and oblivion reflect the variable content of his apocalyptic imagination.

Acknowledgements

The author wishes to express his appreciation to the Rhodes University Joint Research Committee for making the funding available to present a version of this paper at the "Millennial Texts: Creation and Reception" Colloquium.

Notes

1.   The Oxford Dictionary of Current English defines myth as "a purely fictitious narrative usually involving supernatural persons, actions or events and embodying some popular idea concerning natural or historical phenomena – but often used vaguely to include any narrative having fictitious elements, etc. I employ the term, following Hynes (1990: ix), to mean "not … a falsification of reality, but an imaginative version of it, the story … that has evolved and has come to be accepted as true". My usage of the term also implies Liebman and Don-Yehiya's sense that myth is "a story that evokes strong sentiments and transmits and reinforces basic societal values" (1983: 7).

2.   "Ecocatastrophism" refers to "the expectation of an impending environmental calamity [which] incites political actions that slow global economic growth". See Marxsen (2003: 325).

3.   "Technomillenialism" refers to the meltdown of computer technology predicted by Y2K scaremongers.

4.   These include polemical literature and racist rantings of right-wing millenarian survivalists, as well as the academic writings of Fukuyama (1992) and Huntington (1996).

5.   A tentative start has been made by Hook (1991) and Boyer (1992: 8–10). Hook's contention that while rock groups do not "offer a complete and definitive doctrine of apocalypticism," they make frequent and blatant use of the apocalyptic idiom" is self-evident. However, his thesis that certain aspects of rock and roll (sub)culture are reminiscent of medieval apocalyptic and millenarian movements is unconvincing. And his comparison of youth counter-culture and the Free Spirits of the Middle Ages is contrived. Nor am I sure that the Free Spirit movement can be classified as apocalyptic.

6.   An exception is an early piece by Campbell (1975: 696–707). I did not find his typology of a black, red and green apocalypse particularly instructive. Campbell's argument that Dylan's conjuring up of a bucolic idyll which he terms the "pastoral apocalypse" is to me anything but apocalyptic. In fact, it amounts to a nostalgia for a mythicized past rather than a preoccupation with an imagined judgement and salvation.

References

Abbas Amanat, "Introduction: Apocalyptic Anxieties and Millennial Hopes in The Salvation Religions of the Middle East" in Abbas Amanat and Magnus T. Bernhardsson (eds), *Imagining the End: Visions of the Apocalypse from the Ancient Middle East to Modern America* (London: I. B. Tauris, 2002), pp. 1–19.

Nancy Anisfield, (ed.), *The Nightmare Considered: Critical Essays on Nuclear War Literature*, (Bowling Green, OH: Bowling Green State University Popular Press, 1991).

Said Amir, Arjomand "Messianism, Millennialism and Revolution in Early Islamic History" in Amanat and Bernhardsson, *Imagining the End: Visions of the Apocalypse from the Ancient Middle East to Modern America*, 2002, pp. 104–25.

Michael Barkun, "Divided Apocalypse: Thinking About the End in Contemporary America", *Soundings*, 66, 3 (Fall 1983): 257–80.

Mervyn F. Bendle, "The Apocalyptic Imagination and Popular Culture", *Journal of Religion and Popular Culture*, v. XI (Fall 2005), URL: http://www.usask.ca/relst/jrpc/art11-apocalypticimagination.html (accessed 23 November 2006)

Marina Benjamin, *Living at the End of the World*, (London: Picador, 1998).

David Boucher, *Dylan & Cohen: Poets of Rock and Roll*, (New York: Continuum, 2004).

David Boucher and Gary Browning (eds), *The Political Art of Bob Dylan*, (London: Palgrave Macmillan, 2004).

Paul Boyer, *When Time Shall Be No More: Prophecy Belief in Modern American Culture*, (Cambridge, MA: Harvard University Press, 1992).

Paul Brians, *Nuclear Holocausts: Atomic War in Fiction, 1985–1984* (n.p., n.d.): http://www.wsu.edu/~brians/nuclear/ (accessed 29 May 2005).

Mick Broderick (ed.), *Hibakusha Cinema: Hiroshima, Nagasaki, and the Nuclear Image in Japanese film,* (New York: Kegan Paul International, 1996).

Gregory S. Camp, *Selling Fear: Conspiracy Theories and End-Time Paranoia,* (Grand Rapids, MI: Baker Books, 1997).

Gregg M.Campbell, "Bob Dylan and the Pastoral Apocalypse", *Journal of Popular Culture,* 8, 4 (1975): 696–707.

Frances Carey, "The Apocalyptic Imagination: Between Tradition and Modernity" in Francis Carey (ed.), *The Apocalypse and the Shape of Things to Come,* (London: British Museum Press, 1999), pp. 270–319.

Bert, Cartwright *The Bible in the Lyrics of Bob Dylan,* (Bury, Lancashire: Wanted Man, 1992 [1985]).

Norman Cohn, "How Time Acquired a Consummation", in Malcom Bull (ed.), *Apocalypse Theory and the Ends of the World,* (Oxford: Blackwell, 1995) pp. 21–37.

John J. Collins, *The Apocalyptic Imagination: An Introduction to the Jewish Matrix of Christianity* (New York, Crossroad, 1984).

Mike Corcoran (ed.), *Do You, Mr Jones? Bob Dylan with the Poets and the Professors,* (London: Pimlico, 2003).

Patrick Crotty, "Dylan's Last Words" in Corcoran (ed.), *Do You, Mr Jones? Bob Dylan with the Poets and the Professors*, 2003, pp. 307–33.

Kwame Dawes, *Bob Marley: Lyrical Genius,* (London: Sanctuary, 2002).

Wheeler Winston Dixon, *Visions of the Apocalypse: Spectacles of Destruction in American Cinema,* (London: Wallflower, 2002).

Bob Dylan, *Chronicles: Volume 1,* (London: Simon & Schuster, 2004).

Joyce A. Evans, *Celluloid Mushroom Clouds: Hollywood and the Atomic Bomb,* (Boulder, CO: Westview Press, 1998).

Francis Fukuyama, *The End of History and the Last Man,* (Harmondsworth: Penguin, 1992).

Andrew Gamble, "The Drifter's Escape" in Boucher and Browning (eds), *The Political Art of Bob Dylan,* 2004, pp. 12–34.

Michael J. Gilmour, "They Refused Jesus Too: A Biblical Paradigm in the Writing of Bob Dylan", *Journal of Religion and Popular Culture*, 1 (Spring 2002), pp. 1–15.

Michael J. Gilmour, *Tangled Up in the Bible: Bob Dylan and Scripture,* (New York: Continuum, 2004).

Michael Gray, *Song and Dance Man III: The Art of Bob Dylan,* (London: Continuum, 2000).

Marcus Greil, *Lipstick Traces: A Secret History of the Twentieth Century,* (London: Secker & Warburg, 1989).

Dick Hebdige, *Subculture: The Meaning of Style,* (London: Methuen, 1979).

Margot A. Henriksen, *Dr Strangelove's America: Society and Culture in the Atomic Age,* (Berkeley, CA: University of California Press, 1997).

Clinton Heylin, *Dylan: Behind the Shades: The Biography,* (London: Penguin Books, 1992).

Nick Hook, "Lets Go to the Apocalypse: The Apocalyptic Idiom in Rock and Roll", Undergraduate research paper, (St Paul, MN: Macalester College, 1991).

Samuel Hynes, *A War Imagined: the First World War and English Culture,* (New York: Collier Books, 1990).

Samuel P. Huntington, *The Clash of Civilizations and the Remaking of the World Order,* (New York: Simon & Schuster, 1996).

Charles S. Liebman and Eliezer Don-Yehiya, *Civil Religion in Israel: Traditional Judaism and Political Culture in the Jewish State,* (Berkeley, CA: University of California Press, 1983).

Hal Lindsey with C. C. Carlson, *The Late Great Planet Earth,* (Grand Rapids, MI: Zondervan, 1970).

George Lipsitz, "Who'll Stop the Rain? Youth Culture, Rock 'n' Roll and Social Crisis" in David Farber (ed.), *The Sixties: From Memory to History,* (Chapel Hill, NC: University of North Carolina Press, 1994), pp. 206–34.

Mike Marqusee, *Chimes of Freedom: the Politics of Bob Dylan's Art,* (New York: New Press, 2003).

Craig S. Marxsen, "Prophecy de Novo: The Nearly Self-Fulfilling Doomsday Forecast", *The Independent Review,* VII, 3 (Winter 2003), pp. 325–42.

Wilfred Mellers, "God, Modality and Meaning in some Recent Songs of Bob Dylan", in Richard Middleton and David Horn (eds), *Popular Music 1: Folk or Popular? Distinctions, Influences, Continuities,* (Cambridge: Cambridge University Press, 1981), pp. 143–57.

Kim Newman, *Apocalypse Movies: End of the World Cinema,* (New York: St Martin's Griffin, 2000).

Toni A. Perrine, *Film and the Nuclear Age: Representing Cultural Anxiety,* (Abingdon: Taylor & Francis, 1997).

Tim Riley, *Hard Rain: A Dylan Commentary,* (New York: Da Capo Press, 1999).

Richard Schwartz, *Cold War Culture: Media and the Arts, 1945–1990,* (New York: Checkmark Books, 2000).

Jack Shaheen (ed.), *Nuclear War Films.* (Carbondale, IL: Southern Illinois University Press, 1978).

Jerome F. Shapiro, *Atomic Bomb Cinema,* (New York: Routledge, 2002).

Robert Shelton, *No Direction Home: The Life and Music of Bob Dylan,* (New York: Da Capo Press, 1997).

Howard Sounes, *Down the Highway: The life of Bob Dylan,* (New York: Grove Press, 2001).

Charles B. Strozier, *Apocalypse: On the Psychology of Fundamentalism,* (Boston: Beacon Press, 1995).

Steve Turner, "Watered-Down Love", *Christianity Today,* 21 May 2001, available at www.christianitytoday.com (accessed 14 June 2005).

W. Warren Wagar, *Terminal Visions: The Literature of Last Things,* (Bloomington, IN: Indiana University Press, 1982).

Paul Williams, *Bob Dylan: Watching the River Flow: Observations on his Art-in-Progress 1966-1995,* (London: Omnibus, 1996).

Nigel Williamson, *The Rough Guide to Bob Dylan,* (London: Rough Guides Ltd., 2004).

Daniel Wojcik, *The End of the World As We know It: Faith, Fatalism, and Apocalypse in America,* (New York: New York University Press, 1997).

Albin J. Zak, "Bob Dylan and Jimi Hendrix: Juxtaposition and Transformation 'All Along the Watchtower'", *Journal of the American Musicological Society*, 57, 3 (2005), pp. 599–644.

Discography

Bob Dylan, *The Freewheelin' Bob Dylan* (Columbia, 1963)

Bob Dylan, *John Wesley Harding* (Columbia, 1967)

Bob Dylan, *Street Legal* (Columbia, 1978)

Bob Dylan, *Slow Train Coming* (Columbia, 1979)

Bob Dylan, *Saved* (Columbia, 1980)

Bob Dylan, *Shot of Love* (Columbia, 1981)

Bob Dylan, *Infidels* (Columbia, 1983)

Bob Dylan, *Oh Mercy* (Columbia, 1989)

P.F. Sloan, *Eve of Destruction* (Dunhill, 1965)

Various, *Wonder Boys OST* (Columbia, 2000)

End of the World Music
Is Extreme Metal the Sound of the Apocalypse?

Keith Kahn-Harris

Introduction

Visions of the apocalypse have permeated human history. Although the ways in which the apocalypse has been envisaged vary enormously, a distinction can usefully be made between apocalypticism in pre-modern and modern times. In pre-modern times (and today in some non-western contexts), visions of the apocalypse stemmed from a lack of control over the human environment. In a seemingly capricious and uncontrollable universe, the end of the world was easy to imagine. Religion and magical rituals may attempt to assert control over the environment; however such attempts take place on the symbolic plain or are founded on a view of the natural world that sees it as epiphenomenal to spiritual realities. They are not founded on a naturalistic view that sees the world as knowable on its own terms.

In contrast, Western modernity is based on the principle that the world is founded on certain universal laws that can be discovered and that through their discovery the world can be fashioned to suit human desires. The world envisaged at the dawn of modernity by enlightenment thinkers was (potentially at least) predictable and controllable. Yet self-confident eighteenth- and nineteenth-century modernities have been followed by twentieth- and twenty-first century modernities that are ever less confident in human capabilities to transform our world in positive ways. World wars, genocides and environmental destruction are results of the modern project. Even such positive results of modernity as discoveries in medical science have been shown to have frightening unintended consequences, such as antibiotic resistance. It has become apparent that the ability of moderns to shape the world in humanity's favour is at least matched by their ability to cause unprecedented levels of suffering. Indeed, nuclear weapons, global warming and other modern developments have the power actually to destroy human life on earth. If pre-moderns would have seen the world as outside of human control (other than symbolically and religiously), in recent decades moderns have become aware that humans have the power to make human life on earth untenable or unbearable. This realization is perhaps even more frightening than pre-modern fears of human lack of control, as many of the risks with which humans are faced with are the result of unintended consequences of human action (Beck 1992).

We are therefore living in a world where the apocalypse has come to be a real possibility, something that can be brought about by humanity's intended or unintended actions. Our survival as a species has come to be predicated on our ability to deal with this threat. As Michel Foucault points out:

> what might be called society's "threshold of modernity" has been reached when the life of the species is wagered on its own political strategies. For millennia, man remained what he was for Aristotle: a living animal with the additional capacity for a political existence; modern man is an animal whose politics places his existence as a living being in question. (Foucault 1981: 143)

It is ironic therefore, that the first period in human history in which the end of the world has become a real possibility, is also the first period in which it has been possible to remove apocalyptic concerns from the political realm. To be sure, nuclear war and global warming have returned apocalyptic themes to the realm of political calculation, but the much stronger tendency has been to exclude the apocalypse as a practical possibility. As Bruno Latour (1993) has argued, modernity is founded on a denial of the mutually implicating relationship of nature and society. Such phenomena as global warming fit uneasily into modernist discourses that either treat nature as impossibly transcendent or as an easily controllable object that can be shaped to humanity's desire. We have seen how difficult it has been to generate political concern for the very real apocalyptic possibilities of global warming and the fulsome denials by some unreconstructed modernists that it is even occurring. The apocalypse has fit most readily into modernity in more discreet realms than the political, in particular in the realms of religion and art.[1]

The apocalypse raises difficult and troubling themes—life, death, destruction and our place in the world. Art has always provided a space in which to explore such themes. But in modernity the function of art in society changed in important ways. Whereas art was once inseparable from religion and other social rituals, in modernity art came to occupy its own semi-autonomous space (Bourdieu, 1993). In nineteenth-century Western musical discourse for example, the best music was seen to be that which was "transcendent", that signified only itself and that was an object for disinterested contemplation rather than part of vulgar everyday practice (Chanan, 1994). "Transgressive" artistic practices that explored dangerous themes such as sex and death were relegated to the margins, and vulgar "carnivalesque" practices were also suppressed (Stallybrass and White, 1986). On the other hand, art that was intended to respond to and shape the conditions of everyday life, such as socialist realist art, also shunned the exploration of more dangerous and transgressive concerns in favour of "uplifting" themes.

Of course, artistic practice has changed considerably as the twentieth century has progressed. Western popular music, modern art, television and film, have all contributed to the weakening of modernist ideas of the transcendence of art. Nevertheless, in modernity art's connection to practice is an issue that is up for negotiation, in contrast to pre-modern art's embeddedness in practice. The pre-modern apocalypse may have been dreaded or invited, but it was always generative of a whole host of practical responses. This is not always the case in modernity. Modern apocalyptic art has the potential to be highly ironic. In a world where the apocalypse has, for the first time, become truly possible, apocalypticism can be relegated to the realm of fantasy. In a world in which there are manifold possibilities to explore apocalypticism, its "real" implications can be ignored. Apocalyptic themes can be denuded of their wider significance and "enjoyed" for the *frisson* they generate.

This chapter explores a form of contemporary popular culture, extreme metal, which has exploited this ironic potential. Extreme metal has explored apocalyptic themes in gleeful detail, but the relationship of those themes to practice is complex, variable and contingent.

The Roots of Extreme Metal

At least since the Second World War, mass-mediated popular culture has been a fertile source for the apocalyptic imagination. The shadow of the holocaust, the threat of nuclear annihilation and rapid technological progress all contributed to a sense of unease. Sci-fi, horror, movies, comic books and pulp fiction all presented dystopian (and sometimes utopian) visions of the future. By the end of the 1960s there had emerged an increased fascination with the darker sides of human existence that has been called "apocalypse culture" (Parfrey, 1990). Apocalypse culture, whilst not always explicitly concerned with future apocalyptic conflagrations, is that which seeks to collapse the boundaries, limits and assumptions inherent in the modern vision of the world. It can involve a return to (often invented) pre-modern, non-western or pagan traditions. It can involve a desire to engage with dark or unpleasant desires. It can involve the challenging of categories of beauty in art. It can involve a challenge to the separation of art and everyday life. The apocalypse prefigured by apocalypse culture is primarily that which will engulf western modernity rather than the world as a whole.

Alongside this diverse apocalypse culture, the 1960s also saw the apocalypse feature as an occasional theme in mainstream popular music. Popular music was perhaps slower to develop visions of the apocalypse than other forms of art. It was folk rock that started most seriously to address "issues" through popular music. Barry McGuire's "Eve of Destruction" and Bob Dylan's "Masters of War" and "Talkin' World War III Blues" are examples of songs protesting against the threat that war presented to life on this planet in the modern age (see the chapter by Gary Baines in this volume). At the same time, rock music in the 1960s also had an air of optimism even to its protest, embodied in hippy hopes of a new "Age of Aquarius". It was only in the late 1960s that visions of the apocalypse in popular music came to take on a more nihilistic edge. The Doors' "The End" was a powerful, if incoherent, presentation of the end of all hope. Zager and Evans's "In The Year 2525" presented a doom-laden view of the ultimate destination of the human race.

The connections between the apocalypse culture and popular music grew stronger from the late 1960s onwards. Most famously, Charles Manson, who drifted at the edge of Californian popular music culture, drew on The Beatles' "Helter Skelter" in the creation of his vision of unleashing an apocalyptic war. But it was in the coalescence of heavy metal and of punk in the 1970s that embedded apocalypse culture in popular music culture. These two music scenes were and are centrally concerned with the darker sides of human existence, of which apocalyptic themes played a part. From the collision between these two scenes, extreme metal was born.

Punk Roots

The development of punk in the mid- to late 1970s provoked fears among its detractors (particularly in the UK) that it was a sign of the breakdown of civilized society. The "moral panic" (Cohen, 1987) that punk engendered was part of the process through which the punk scene coalesced into a self-aware entity (McRobbie and Thornton, 1995). As such, there was a kind of collusion between the fears provoked by punk and the vision of the punks themselves. Richard Hell's "Blank Generation" and the Sex Pistol's "No Future" were slogans that embodied a nihilistic vision of a world falling apart (Wojcik, 1997). Punk semiotics echoed this nihilism with clothing itself being torn apart and fixed together inappropriately, with styles chaotically torn from their original contexts (Hebdidge, 1979). Nihilism is not necessarily the same as apocalypticism, but the two are closely related. Punk's vision of a pointless, meaningless world is a vision of a world that has reached the end of its usefulness.

Apocalypticism in punk has frequently been a response to catastrophic or potentially catastrophic events. The holocaust was an obsession for the early American punk scene, many of whom were Jewish (Stratton 2005; Beeber 2006). However, the holocaust, like other early punk interests, was not responded to directly (The Sex Pistol's "Belsen Was A Gas" notwithstanding). Rather, it was a kind of "ghost at the feast", a cataclysmic event that informed the sensibilities of early punks.

As punk developed, it became more common to address directly "real world" issues. In the early 1980s there developed an actively political anarchist punk scene. A central concern of anarcho-punks such as Crass, Conflict and Discharge was nuclear war, a concern fuelled by the ratcheting up of cold war tensions following the Reagan and Thatcher accessions. Discharge in particular was obsessed with the threat of nuclear annihilation:

> Now in darkness world stops turning
> Mass death and destruction
> ('The End' from *Hear Nothing, See Nothing, Say Nothing*, 1982)[2]

Importantly for Discharge as for other anarcho-punk bands, their apocalyptic obsessions were tempered by faith in the possibilities of a political response. Discharge's "Protest and Survive" (again, from *Hear Nothing, See Nothing, Say Nothing*) warns that "the savage mutilation of the human race is set on course" but that "it is up to us to change that course".

Another focus for punk's apocalyptic imagination was environmental destruction, which became a more important theme following the end of the cold war. The "straight edge" scene has explored these environmental themes most assiduously. Straight edge (named after a song by the Washington DC band, Minor Threat) emphasizes strict personal control over the body, including following a vegan diet and in particular abstinence from alcohol and narcotics. This strict control is deemed necessary to avoid the temptations and degradations of a corrupt, immoral world. Straight edge has become more and more concerned with environmental destruction as it has developed. A straight edge lifestyle is seen both as a way of surviving a world that is being destroyed and as a way of preventing that destruction. As the American straight edge band Earth Crisis put it on the eponymous title track of *Gomorrah's Season Ends* (1996):

> An effective revolutionary through the clarity of mind that I've attained. I see it all for what it is as Gommorah's season ends in the grave. So many have become demoralized that now a change must be forced or all will perish in the lunacy once it befalls.

Straight edge bands have espoused religious principles and there are a number of Christian straight edge bands (despite their often biblical language, Earth Crisis are not one of them). As in religious visions of apocalypse, there is ambivalence in how the apocalypse is seen in straight edge. The apocalypse is at once just punishment for immoral behaviour but at the same time the threat of the apocalypse acts as a warning to change this behaviour.

Straight edge's apocalyptic ambivalence is revealing of a similar ambivalence in punk apocalypticism more generally. Punk apocalypticism runs along a continuum ranging from nihilism, through warnings about the threat of the apocalypse, to asserting one's "saved" status in the face of the apocalypse. The punk scene has developed in a number of different directions since the early 1980s. But what different punk scenes share is a groundedness in "reality", in social conditions, in an earthy materiality. This anchoring, sometimes weak sometimes strong, keeps punk's apocalyptic imagination within the limits of the possible. Whether it is warned of, nihilistically savoured or seen as something to rise above, the punk apocalypse is a fundamentally imaginable one. This is an important contrast to the heavy metal apocalypse.

Heavy Metal Roots

From its inception as an identifiably distinct musical genre at the tail end of the 1960s, heavy metal drew liberally on the darkest imaginings of western culture. A fascination with the occult and with Christian eschatology has led inexorably to an interest in the apocalypse. As in punk, "real world" events have frequently provided the stimulus for the heavy metal apocalyptic imagination. Further, heavy metal is often as moralistic as punk can be. Iron Maiden's "Two Minutes To Midnight" for example (from *Powerslave*, 1984) contains a strong, if fatalistic, critique of humanity's propensity to wage war. The title of the song refers to the Bulletin of Atomic Scientists' "Doomsday Clock":

> 2 minutes to midnight,
> The hands that treaten [sic.] doom.
> 2 minutes to midnight,
> To kill the unborn in the womb.

At the same time, Iron Maiden, like other heavy metal bands, are too fascinated by the imagery and mythology of war to respond to it in a purely critical way. Iron Maiden's work contains many songs about warriors and war that are neither celebratory nor condemnatory, but revel in myths and histories. The apocalyptic imagination in heavy metal is tied into much more fantastic, if often confused, mythologies than the punk apocalyptic imagination is. For example, Black Sabbath's "War Pigs" (from *Paranoid*, 1970) depicts a scenario in which those who make war receive their punishment at the hands of God or Satan (it is not clear who):

> Day of Judgment, God is calling
> On their knees the war pigs crawling
> Begging mercy for their sins
> Satan, laughing, spreads his wings

Heavy metal's apocalyptic scenarios often bear a strong resemblance to Christian ones. Judas Priest's "Exciter" (from *Stained Class*, 1978) envisages a figure for whom "salvation is his task", who has "come to make you snap out of the state that you are in" and to whom one must "fall to your knees and repent if you please". The eponymous title track to *Painkiller* (1990) tells of a similarly unearthly figure that comes to save mankind from the apocalypse:

Planet's devastated
Mankind's on its knees
A saviour comes from out the skies
In answer to their pleas

In the sense that such lyrics take as their starting point the evils of the world, they share with punk apocalypticism a diagnosis of doomed world. However, they use this diagnosis as a point of departure for fantastic imaginings.

Apocalyptic Themes in Extreme Metal

Extreme metal emerged in the early 1980s out of the collision between heavy metal and punk.[3] Thrash metal, developed by bands such as Venom, Metallica and Slayer added punk's speed and simplicity to the metal blueprint. The relationship between metal and punk has been constantly renegotiated within extreme metal. Some extreme metal genres such as thrash and grindcore are closely connected to punk, whereas others such as black (Satanic) metal and doom metal are more musically distinct. Extreme metal represents a musical radicalization ("fundamentalism" as Deena Weinstein (2000) has called it) of both punk and metal. As thrash developed into death metal in the 1980s, the music progressively abandoned elements such as melody and harmony that tied metal into other genres. This radicalization in turn affected punk, which developed a proliferation of musically radical "hardcore" sub-genres.

Extreme metal's most striking feature is its sound. Although there are many different kinds of extreme metal, they share a fascination with "transgressive" sounds—speed, lack of melody, harsh vocals, etc. It could perhaps be argued that this systematic breaking of musical rules is apocalyptic in and of itself, in that it prefigures a world in which rules and boundaries collapse into chaos. However, it is also the case that extreme metal is far from musically chaotic, but is a complex, tightly structured form of music (see for example Berger, 1999). Further, the scene within which it is produced and consumed is similarly well ordered. Extreme metal is founded on an ambivalence about order and boundaries; a strong desire to collapse everything into formless "abjection" (Kristeva, 1982; Reynolds and Press,

1995) that coexists with a similarly strong desire for structure and discipline. Yet the act of continually pushing musical boundaries, even if this pushing stops before the point of collapse, certainly makes apocalyptic lyrics more likely. A form of music as harsh and bleak as extreme metal needs lyrics that complement it.

Extreme metal's concern with the loss of order and boundaries starts with the body and fascination with its destruction. The body is frequently the locus for apocalyptic themes, particularly in death metal. One example of this is Obituary's *The End Complete* (1992). The cover of the album features a barren, post-apocalyptic waste-land, yet the songs on the album focus not only on large scale destruction but on personal suffering: "I'm in Pain", "Sickness", "Rotting Ways", etc. Death metal's interest in death and the destruction of the body often has a gleeful element to it. Contrast for example the sober treatment of suicide in Ozzy Osbourne's "Suicide Solution" (from *Blizzard Of Ozz*, 1980) which, as Robert Walser (Walser, 1993: 148–50) argues, is a complex meditation on depression and self-destruction; with celebrations of suicide in extreme metal such as "Sacrificial Suicide" by US death metal band Deicide (from *Deicide*, 1990):

> Suicide, end my life
> I must die—Satan

Or S.O.D's "Kill Yourself" (from *Speak English Or Die*, 1985):

> Kill yourself, kill yourself
> Why don't you kill yourself?

The destruction of bodies is a frequent preoccupation of extreme metal's apocalyptic imagination. The apocalypse is often signified by mass slaughter, piles of dead, mutilated bodies and rivers of blood. Consider "Raining Blood" from Slayer's *Reign In Blood* (1986) which revels in blood-soaked conquest:

> Raining blood
> From a lacerated sky
> Bleeding its horror
> Creating my structure
> Now I shall reign in blood!

Interest in mass slaughter in extreme metal is a continuation and extension of heavy metal's interest in war. Although, as we saw in the case of Iron Maiden, war is frequently criticized in heavy metal, "old-fashioned" military traditions that glorify honour and nobility in war are also celebrated. War is an even more prevalent theme in extreme metal than in heavy metal and there are bands who concentrate in little else. Indeed, there is an entire sub-genre of "war metal". In extreme metal, war is treated as ultra-destructive, sometimes pointless, but also as something to be celebrated nihilistically. Finland's Impaled Nazarene are one band obsessed with war as a process of glorious destruction. Many of the songs on their album *Suomi Finland Perkele* (1994) are barely coherent celebrations of apocalyptic mass murder. On "Genocide" for example:

> Scum being raped, scum being killed
> Scum is dying, I keep on laughing

For Impaled Nazarene, war is an evil, Satanic process, but a Satanic process to be celebrated, as on "Ghettoblaster":

> Firestorm—genocide
> Kill them all before they kill you
> Radiation—overkill
> Apocalyptic truth of the year one (666)

"Total War—Winter War" celebrates the Finnish winter war with Russia of 1940–41, referring implicitly to Goebbel's famous speech calling for "total war" (which actually occurred in 1943) in its chorus:

> Do you want total war? Yes we want total war!
> Do you want fucking war? Yes we want fucking war!

The Second World War has been a feature of extreme metal lyrics. Other bands have come close to glorifying the Nazis in World War Two. The Swedish black metal band Marduk's album *Panzer Division Marduk* (1999) glorifies the death and destruction brought by the tank battles on the Russian front in the Second World War. The Nazi cause in World War Two is the ultimate apocalyptic symbol, in part because the Nazi regime ultimately destroyed itself with an irrational self-destructiveness. However, open support for Nazism in extreme metal is almost exclusively confined to the separate Nazi black metal scene. In extreme metal there is a desire to flirt with and explore dangerous symbolism, but little desire to support political causes. Glorification of war in extreme metal is generally a glorification of destruction that war causes rather than glorification of cause itself.

Nuclear war was also a very popular theme in extreme metal in the 1980s as can be seen in band names from that period such as Nuclear Assault and Megadeth. As in other kinds of warfare, the actual identities of the protagonists in a nuclear conflict are rarely referred to. Rather, the details of nuclear apocalypse are recorded as in Carnivore's "World Wars III & IV" (from *Carnivore*, 1985):

> Silence and darkness the species of man is extinct
> The boiling oceans into which the continents sink
> Gravity gone the moon collides with a dead earth
> Flaming world out of orbit flying into deep space

Extreme metal lyrics in the 1980s frequently treated the nuclear apocalypse as a just reward for humanity's failings, as in the concluding lines in Metallica's "Blackened" (from ... *And Justice For All*, 1988):

> Fire
> Is the outcome of hypocrisy
> Darkest potency
> In the exit of humanity
> Colour our world blackened

Lyrics about nuclear destruction have become much rarer since the early 1990s. Another man-made apocalypse that has been discussed in extreme metal lyrics is that which is brought about by ecological devastation. In the 1980s, the American thrash metal band Nuclear Assault specialized in lyrics about both nuclear and environmental destruction. Their 1989 album *Handle With Care* featured a number of lyrics about ecological devastation, as on "Inherited Hell":

> A time in the future, not too far away
> The death of our world, we are told
> Destroyed by neglect, now breeding despair
> The home of mankind is despoiled

Ecological catastrophe is treated as an index of humanity's corrupt nature. At times the tone is that of the biblical prophecy, but without holding out the hope of repentance and return to God. Nevermore's "Final Product" (from *This Godless Endeavour*, 2005) warns:

> Look at the world, look at the hell, look at the hate that we've made
> Look at the final product, a world in slow decay
> ...

There are those that believe the world is ending again
That impending Armageddon is inevitable and waiting

"Sentient 6" from the same album, is sung from the perspective of some kind of robot or cyborg that will ultimately destroy humanity:

Sequence activate, trip the hammer to eradicate, I must eliminate
I will spread swift justice on their land
Termination imminent, cleanse the parasite insects, the heathens

This song also contains a backwards message saying "I am the bringer of the end, fear me, I am the beast that is technology". Similar themes of robot or cyborg technology providing a terrifying end to humanity can be found in other extreme metal recordings, such as Fear Factory's *Demanufacture* (1995). This is in contrast to Judas Priest's "Exciter" and "Painkiller" in which a non-human *deus ex machina* rescues humanity from itself. Extreme metal lyrics tend to treat the man-made apocalypse as unavoidable and salvation as impossible. Unlike punk where (as we saw with Earth Crisis) there is at least some hope for change, extreme metal generally offers no hope. Yet this hopelessness has not prevented extreme metal bands from drawing extensively on Christian imagery. In a kind of dark parody of the Christian possibility of redemption, extreme metal revels in mankind's "fallenness". The darker side of Christian mythology is celebrated as in 'The Four Horseman', one of Metallica's earliest songs (from *Kill 'Em All*, 1983):

Killing scores with demon swords
Now is the death of doers of wrong

One of the striking features of the Christian redemptive apocalypse is that, for it to take place, an horrific amount of suffering must take place. In that Christian apocalypticism has at times focused on the horrific aspects of the apocalypse, it can sometimes be hard to tell whether extreme metal's interest in the apocalypse affirms or undermines Christianity. It is unclear whether Slayer's "South of Heaven" (the title track of their 1988 album) for example, is a dramatization of the triumph of God, the triumph of the devil, or the fate of those "left behind" on judgement day:

An unforeseen future nestled somewhere in time.
Unsuspecting victims no warnings, no signs.
Judgment day the second coming arrives.
Before you see the light you must die.

As extreme metal developed in the 1980s and 1990s, interest in the more lurid elements of Christian mythology developed into forms of openly Satanic extreme metal. What Satanism actually means varies enormously. For some it is a fully-fledged religion in which the devil is worshipped, for others an extreme form of anarchism, for others a burlesque form of transgressive play (Baddeley, 1999). What different Satanisms share is a delight in the inversion of Christian symbolism and mythology. In this "world turned upside down" (Bakhtin, 1984; Stallybrass and White, 1986) the apocalypse can be inverted into the triumph of Satan and of evil. Black metal, the openly Satanic form of extreme metal that arose in the late 1980s and early 1990s, was from its inception interested in this inversion. The seminal Norwegian black metal band Mayhem entitled their 1986 demo *Pure Fucking Armageddon* and its title track provided a barely coherent celebration of the end of time:

> Anarchy, Violent torture,
> Antichrist, Lucifer, Son of Satan
> Pure Fucking Armageddon

Black metal has developed complex and sometimes impenetrable mythologies based on a heady cocktail of Satanism, Paganism and other ideologies. The Book of Revelation is often drawn on, sometimes implicitly and sometimes explicitly—as on "The Dawn of the New Age" off Satyricon's *Nemesis Divina* (1996) which is an edited extract from the book itself.[4] Christian eschatology, particularly that offered by The Book of Revelation is confusing and open to multiple interpretation and black metal bands exploit these ambiguities to the full. Dense eschatological scenarios are woven that reference and even satirise their Christian origins, as on songs such as Cradle Of Filth's "From The Cradle To Enslave", the title track of their 1999 EP:

> Tablatures of gravel law
> Shall see Gehennah paved
> When empires fall and nightmares crawl
> From the cradle to enslave. …

> This is the end of everything

The black metal attitude to the apocalypse is variously celebratory and despairing—sometimes both at once. Again, in this black metal mirrors Christian eschatology which both fears and welcomes the apocalypse. There is also a strain within black metal that sees the apocalypse as a "cleansing" and a paving the way for the rule of the "elite". Christianity is treated as a weak-minded perversion of man's [sic.] lustful and animal nature. The apocalypse paves the way for a return to a pre-Christian, Pagan order in which only the strongest (to include, presumably, black metallers) will survive. In this form of black metal ideology inverted Christianity, Paganism and social Darwinism intermingle. This is also where fantastic mythology meets the realism found in other forms of extreme metal and punk. There is a short step from weaving fantasies of an inverted Christian apocalypse, to a fascistic avocation of the slaughter of the weak. Although most openly Nazi black metal is confined to the self-contained Nazi black metal scene (Burghart, 1999), fascist and racist sentiments are expressed within the black metal scene (most famously, Varg Vikernes of Burzum, now in prison for the murder of fellow Norwegian black metaller Euronymous of Mayhem, is now an out-and-out Nazi). But even some black metal scene members have crossed the line into outright fascism and racism. For example, the Swedish black metal "supergroup" War[5] included a song entitled "I Am Elite" on their 1997 album *Total War*, which contained the following lines:

Mightier than any god
I'm greater than any man
I am elite

...

Jews and kikes stay away

The album's title track also proclaims that "Armageddon is fucking here". This close association between Nazi/Social Darwinist elitism and apocalypticism in black metal both affirms and undermines Nazism as a political ideology. Nazism was influenced by pagan ideology (Goodrick-Clarke, 1985). Part of Norse pagan mythology is the period of *Ragnarök* in which war between the Gods brings about the end of the world. This idea was adapted by Wagner as *Götterdämmerung* in the last part of the ring cycle. Wagner is a strong influence both on Nazism and black metal. Wagnerian references abound in black metal, as on Bathory's *The Twilight of the Gods* (1991). The end of the Nazi regime is frequently referred to as a Götterdämmerung, in that Hitler and his most fanatical acolytes deliberately tried to destroy Germany through refusing to order tactical retreats and through obliterating infrastructure. At the same time, Nazism was also a political ideology like any other in attempting to create a permanent transformation of the world and contemporary neo-Nazis tend to cleave to this vision of Nazism rather than its more apocalyptic strains. In cleaving to the more apocalyptic, occultist forms of Nazism, Nazi black metal tends to be isolated both from the rest of the black metal scene and from contemporary far-right politics.

Fantasy and Reality

The relationship between fantasy and reality in extreme metal is a complex matter. Whilst "real world" issues are explored, there is for the most part no political engagement with real world problems. As I have argued elsewhere (2004; 2006) members of the extreme metal scene tend to hold politics at arm's length at the same time as they enjoy exploring dark and dangerous themes. Further there is a notable disjunction between extreme lyrics and the non-extreme everyday lives of most extreme metal scene members. Many bands emphasize their down to earth "normality" in interviews and in their interactions within the extreme metal scene. The extreme metal scene is a complex infrastructure bound together by a strong, self-conscious community with moral norms of interaction. It is true that there have been some dramatic attempts to disrupt the comfortable mundanity of the extreme metal scene, as in the church burnings and murders that have at times accompanied Scandinavian black metal (Moynihan and Søderlind, 1998). However, such disruptions are relatively uncommon, albeit celebrated, and many of the most disruptive elements of the black metal scene now live comfortable secure lives. If the violence of the early 1990s Norwegian black metal scene heralded *Ragnarök* (as a chapter in Moynihan and Søderlind's book puts it (301–32), then *Ragnarök* appears to have stalled.

It is also easy to find examples of bands that appear actively to undermine the seriousness of their lyrical themes. Nuclear Assault, for example, who were apparently so concerned about the possibilities for human extinction, included many joke tracks on their albums. Dani, vocalist and lyricist with Cradle Of Filth, whose "From The Cradle To Enslave" is one of the most sophisticated explorations of apocalyptic imagery in extreme metal, and who once claimed that "if I was in control of the world, I would wipe out half of it instantly and without remorse" (see Kahn-Harris, 2006: 40), continually cracks self-deprecating jokes on stage and in interviews. It is also not hard to find jokey references to the apocalypse in metal culture. Finland's Lordi won the 2006 Eurovision song contest with the song, "Hard Rock Hallelujah" that proclaimed the "arockolypse" and announced that the "day of rockoning" was at hand. Contrary to its often po-faced public image, metal culture, including extreme metal culture, is thick with irony, humour, satire and self-deprecation.[6]

Compare this frequent bathetic undermining of apocalyptic themes in extreme metal with the deep and often politically-oriented seriousness of punk. Of course, punk has its share of bands and sub-genres that are more playful. However, the punk scene also celebrates and idealizes a much closer relation between musical and everyday practice. Punk icons such as Sid Vicious lived lives that were as self-consciously alienated and alienating as were their music. Anarcho-punk has always been tied in closely with ways of life that reject the comforts of modernity in favour of (variously) begging, living rough, living in communes, etc. Straight edge culture attempts to develop a seamless fit between music and everyday life. In contrast, one might be forgiven for dismissing much of extreme metal for simply playing at apocalypse culture. Are apocalyptic themes a genuine source of interest or concern for extreme metal scene members or are they simply signifiers to be played with?

Extreme metal is certainly playful in the manifold creativity with which it explores transgressive themes. Yet it cannot be dismissed as play-acting, as a pretence. The often stark difference between transgressive art and mundane everyday life can be seen as in fact protecting the potency of art. The frequent refusal to draw conclusions for everyday practice from the apocalyptic themes explored in extreme metal does not undermine and in fact probably increases the forcefulness of its apocalyptic fantasies. Enshrined in a dedicated artistic space, there is no distraction from the awesomeness of the contemplation of the end of the world. The apocalypse can be experienced vicariously and even delighted in. The gleefulness with which extreme metal records and celebrates human suffering can only work if it takes place in a space removed from everyday practice. When it "escapes" (as in the early 1990s Norwegian black metal scene) equilibrium is soon restored.

Is Extreme Metal the Sound of the Apocalypse?

One of the problems of tracing particular conceptual themes in a musical genre is that there is always the risk of overstating the importance of lyrics and ignoring the sound of the music. As I have argued, extreme metal lyrics that deal with the apocalypse are accompanied by music that pushes the boundaries of what is sonically possible in western music. This pushing of the boundaries always threatens the possibility of collapse. In this, there is a "fit" between music and lyrics. But we should not forget that the "naturalness" that is attached to the meaning of a particular sound is constructed rather than given. Extreme metal music's signification of the apocalypse does not arise from a naturally apocalyptic sound but from a set of constructed associations that emerge in a particular time and space. If extreme metal is the sound of the apocalypse, then it is today's sound of the apocalypse. In all apocalyptic art there is a delicious irony in that the end of time can only be expressed through signifiers that make sense at a particular time. The repeated failures of predictions of the apocalypse does not seem to stop people making them, in extreme metal as everywhere else (Terry, 1998).

In examining extreme metal apocalypticism, there is also the risk of overestimating how seamlessly music and lyrics are integrated. As my research has shown, a constant theme in extreme metal discourse is the primacy of music. Scene members constantly stress the centrality of "music" in their lives rather than (in particular) "politics". I put "music" in inverted commas because it is often not clear what music means. The meaning of the discursive trope "music" ranges from "the sounds themselves" through to a broad range of lyrical and para-musical associations and activities. The process through which music, lyrics and other signifying materials come to be associated with each other is far from straightforward. There are indeed those, particularly in black metal, who make a concerted attempt to produce an apocalyptically-themed *Gesamtwerk* in which lyrical themes, musical sounds, dress, ideology and everyday life are drawn together in a seamless whole. But it is also clear that for others, the creative process starts from producing musical sounds to which apocalyptic lyrical themes are added later—perhaps with little real commitment— as they somehow sound "fitting". Furthermore, because extreme metal lyrics are generally screamed or growled over a dense musical backing, they are frequently inaudible without a lyric sheet. This potential disengageability of music and lyrics leads to difficult herme-neutic problems (Kahn-Harris, 2002). It is possible to listen to ex-treme metal in such a way that lyrics are totally unimportant and even to be unaware of their content. Apocalyptic lyrics may at times be utterly trivial and marginal parts of extreme metal culture. Apoca-lyptic themes seem even more marginal when bands do not discuss the outside their music in interviews or refer to them in other forms of scenic discourse. Again, it is usually only black metal bands that attempt to extend their lyrical concerns outside the confines of the musical texts.

At times extreme metal seems to capture and distil the terror and excitement of eschatological contemplation. At times, one can ex-perience the *frisson* of the apocalypse through extreme metal in a way that few other artistic forms can match. But this extraordinary ability to condense and dramatize humanity's darkest fears and hopes is actualized variably, fleetingly and contingently. Doubtless, in a few centuries' time—assuming that the world does not end—extreme metal will be as dated (if nonetheless as interesting) a form of apoca-lyptic art as that of medieval painters. In any case, apocalyptic themes are only one set amongst a range of other themes explored in ex-treme metal, some of which are utterly banal. The apocalyptic possi-bilities in extreme metal are actualized under certain conditions, at certain times.

It is this slipperiness that marks out music as a form of artistic ex-pression. Non-verbal sounds can be intensely semiotically connected to particular verbalized themes, but they can also be abstract and hard to pin down. Extreme metal has exploited the slipperiness of music to the full, using it to variously engage and disengage from real world concerns. To return to my argument in the introduction, we are living in a world in which the apocalypse is at the same time a real consequence of human action and also a theme to be explored in art with few implications. Extreme metal's treatment of the apoca-lypse moves continuously between a consequence-free fantastic abstraction and a consequence-heavy seriousness that begs a politi-cal response. In the course of this playful movement, extreme metal's end of the world music fears, celebrates, negates and trivializes the apocalypse.

Acknowledgements

My thanks to Dr Nick Terry for his help in developing the early drafts of this chapter.

Notes

1.   It is also true that the rise of religious fundamentalism in recent decades has led those with strong religious beliefs in the apocalypse further to the centre of the political arena.

2.   All lyrics quoted in this chapter can be found in full at darklyrics.com

3.   For more on the characteristics of extreme metal, see my *Extreme Metal: Music and Culture on the Edge* (2006).

4.   This is not the first reference to the Book of Revelation in Heavy Metal—Iron Maiden semi-paraphrased from it in the introduction to the title track of 'The Number of the Beast' (1982).

5.   War are known as Total War in the US.

6.   See for example the Metal Humour website—http://metalhumor. blogspot.com/ (accessed 20 June 2007).

References

G. Baddeley, *Lucifer Rising: Sin, Devil Worship and Rock 'n' Roll* (London: Plexus,1999).

M. Bakhtin, *Rabelais and his World* (Bloomington, IN: Indiana University Press, 1984).

U. Beck, *Risk Society* (London: Sage Publications, 1992).

S. L. Beeber, *The Heebie-Jeebies at CBGBs: A Secret History of Jewish Punk* (Chicago, IL: Chicago Review Press, 2006).

H. M. Berger, *Metal, Rock and Jazz: Perception and the Phenomenology of Musical Experience* (Hanover, NH: Wesleyan University Press, 1999).

P. Bourdieu, *The Field of Cultural Production* (Oxford: Polity Press, 1993).

D. Burghart, *Soundtracks to the White Revolution: White Supremacist Assaults on Youth Music Subcultures* (Chicago, IL: Center for the New Community, 1999).

M. Chanan, *Musica Practica: The Social Practice of Western Music from Gregorian Chant to Postmodernism* (London: Verso, 1994).

S. Cohen, *Folk Devils and Moral Panics: The Creation of Mods and Rockers* (Oxford: Basil Blackwell, 1987).

M. Foucault, *The History of Sexuality: Volume One* (London: Pelican Books, 1981).

N. Goodrick-Clarke, *The Occult Roots of Nazism: The Ariosophists of Austria and Germany 1890–1935* (Wellingborough, Northamptonshire: The Aquarian Press, 1985).

D. Hebdidge, *Subculture: The Meaning of Style* (London: Methuen, 1979).

K. Kahn-Harris, "Death Metal and the Limits of Musical Expression", in M. Cloonan and R. Garofalo (eds) *Policing Popular Music.* (Philadelphia, PA: Temple University Press, 2002), pp. 81–99.

K. Kahn-Harris, "The 'Failure' of Youth Culture: Reflexivity, Music and Politics in the Black Metal Scene", *European Journal of Cultural Studies* 7 (2004), pp. 95–111.

K. Kahn-Harris, *Extreme Metal: Music and Culture on the Edge* (Oxford: Berg, 2006).

J. Kristeva, *The Powers of Horror: An Essay on Abjection* (New York: Columbia University Press, 1982).

B. Latour, *We Have Never Been Modern* (Cambridge, MA.: Harvard University Press, 1993).

A. McRobbie and S. Thornton, "Rethinking 'Moral Panic' for Multi-Mediated Social Worlds", *British Journal of Sociology* 46 (1995), pp. 559–74.

M. Moynihan and D. Søderlind, *Lords of Chaos: The Bloody Rise of the Satanic Metal Underground* (Venice, CA: Feral House, 1998).

A. Parfrey (Ed.) *Apocalypse Culture* (Venice, CA: Feral House, 1990).

S. Reynolds and J. Press, *The Sex Revolts: Gender, Rebellion and Rock n Roll* (London: Serpent's Tail, 1995).

P. Stallybrass and A. White, *The Politics and Poetics of Transgression* (London: Methuen, 1986).

J. Stratton, "Jews, Punks and the Holocaust: From the Velvet Underground to the Ramones—the Jewish-American Story" *Popular Music* 24 (2005), pp. 79–106.

N. Terry, "It's The End of the World As We Know It (And I Feel Fine)" *Terrorizer* 61 (1998), pp. 58–61.

R. Walser, *Running With The Devil: Power, Gender and Madness in Heavy Metal Music* (Hanover, NH: Wesleyan University Press, 1993).

D. Weinstein, *Heavy Metal: The Music and its Culture* (New York: Da Capo Press, 2000).

D. Wojcik, *The End of the World as We Know It: Faith, Fatalism, and Apocalypse in America* (New York: New York University Press, 1997)

Discography

Black Sabbath, *Paranoid* (Vertigo, 1970)
Carnivore, *Carnivore* (Roadrunner, 1985)
Cradle Of Filth, *From The Cradle To Enslave* (LABEL, 1999)
Deicide, *Deicide* (LABEL, 1990)

Discharge, *Hear Nothing, See Nothing, Say Nothing* (Music for Nations, 1982).
Earth Crisis, *Gomorrah's Season Ends* (Victory Records, 1996).
Fear Factory, *Demanufacture* (Roadrunner, 1995).
Impaled Nazarene, *Suomi Finland Perkele* (Osmose Productions, 1994)
Iron Maiden, *Powerslave* (EMI, 1984)
Judas Priest, *Stained Class* (CBS, 1978)
Judas Priest, *Painkiller* (Columbia Records, 1990)
Marduk, *Panzer Division Marduk* (Osmose Productions, 1999)
Mayhem, *Pure Fucking Armageddon* (demo, 1986)
Metallica, *Kill 'Em All* (Megaforce, 1983)
Metallica, *... And Justice for All* (Elektra, 1988)
Nevermore, *This Godless Endeavor* (Century Media, 2005)
Nuclear Assault, *Handle with Care* (In-Effect, 1989)
Obituary, *The End Complete* (Roadrunner, 1992).
Ozzy Osbourne, *Blizzard of Ozz* (Jet/Epic Records, 1980)
Satyricon, *Nemesis Divina* (Moonfrog Productions, 1996)
Slayer, *Reign In Blood* (Def Jam, 1986)
Slayer, *South of Heaven* (Def Jam, 1988)
S.O.D, *Speak English Or Die* (Megaforce, 1985)
War, *Total War* (Necropolis, 1997)

Babylon's Burning
Reggae, Rastafari and Millenarianism

Christopher Partridge

Introduction

With a keen focus on societal reform at all levels, Rastafarianism has a conspicuous millenarian orientation. Certainly, during the period within which classic reggae evolved out of ska and rocksteady in the late-1960s up until the early 1980s, most Rastas expressed a strident millenarian liberation theology. Nathaniel Murrell notes the principal beliefs of that period:

> belief in the beauty of black people's African heritage; belief that Ras Tafari Haile Selassie I, emperor of Ethiopia, is the living God and black Messiah; belief in repatriation to Ethiopia, qua Africa, the true home and redemption of black people, as "having been foretold and … soon to occur"; the view that "the ways of the white men are evil, especially for the black" race; belief in "the apocalyptic fall of Jamaica as Babylon, the corrupt world of the white man", and that "once the white man's world crumbles, the current master/slave pattern [of existence] will be reversed". Jah Ras Tafari will overthrow or destroy the present order, and Rastafarians and other Blacks will be the benefactors of that destruction; they will reign with Jah in the new kingdom. (1998: 5)

It is hardly surprising, therefore, that reggae, which is fundamentally related to Rastafari, articulates millenarian themes. The aim of this study is to provide an introduction to this discourse within reggae. That said, without some understanding of the roots and history of Rastafarianism, it will be difficult to make sense of such ideas. Hence, with references to reggae throughout, the chapter begins with an overview of the origins and ideology of Rastafari. While there is some discussion of key eschatological themes throughout the chapter, the final section, which turns specifically to reggae, focuses on the dominant millenarian theme, around which all others are oriented, namely "Babylon".

Do you remember the days of slavery?

It has been argued that democracy and liberation are far closer to the Jamaican than they are to many a white Western heart, in that they are viewed and cherished against a background of slavery and oppression. Leonard Barrett's seminal study of Rastafarianism even argues that the very psyche of Jamaican people is a product of their history:

> Jamaicans are by nature some of the most fun loving, hardworking, and gregarious people in the Caribbean. Treated with kindness and respect, they are likely to remain the most confident and dependable friends on earth. But if treated with impunity and disrespect, all the rage of a deep psychic revenge may surface with unpredictable consequences. This calm-and-storm personality of contemporary Jamaicans is a direct inheritance of that group of Africans who suffered the most frustrating and oppressive slavery ever experienced in a British colony. (1997: 29)

This is evident in reggae. Indeed, numerous indigenous Jamaican folk songs are, in effect, liberation theologies, which recall the days of slavery.[1] There is a sense in which the spirit of George Santayana's famous dictum permeates the religio-cultural milieu of reggae: "those who do not remember the past are condemned to repeat it".[2] Never again will Afro-Caribbeans submit to the yoke of the oppressor; there is a duty to remember their persecution by a dominant white society and to resist any attempts to repeat it; they must protect their freedom; they must recover and celebrate their roots and culture. The call to "remember the days of slavery" is a consistent theme of particularly "roots reggae"—reggae which focuses on the religion and culture of Rastafari. Typical is Misty in Roots' evocative "Slavery Days"—from their album *Wise and Foolish* (1981)—which includes the refrain "Let them remember the days of slavery". More famously, the musician Burning Spear (Winston Rodney)—who has dedicated his work to the memory and the message of the Jamaican social activist Marcus Garvey—also wrote a song entitled the "Slavery Days" (*Marcus Garvey*, 1975). Indeed, there are few, if any, roots reggae artists who have not reflected upon the days of slavery and articulated liberationist ideologies to some extent.

Fundamentally related to these narratives is an exilic discourse. Like the Israelites, with whom they strongly identify, Africans have been forcibly transported from the Promised Land to Babylon. They are living in exile. This, in turn, is often articulated as part of an apocalyptic discourse that looks forward to the end of the current exilic period. The time of mental and physical slavery will be terminated and a happier existence for black people will dawn. Indeed, as is evident in numerous reggae songs, we will see that believers consciously set their face towards "Zion", focus on deliverance and, very often, the apocalyptic destruction of oppressive bureaucracies and societies—"Babylon".

Afro-Christianity

The culture of resistance to colonialism and slavery that emerged in Jamaica, and which subsequently shaped the political discourse in reggae, has always had religion as a key component. And central to much religious discourse has been a form of millenarianism that can be traced back to their adoption of Christianity in Jamaica.

By 1838 the majority of Jamaican slaves had become at least nominally Christian. However, it is important to understand that this was largely due to the proselytizing efforts of black Baptist preachers such as George Liele, who travelled to Jamaica in 1783 following the American Revolution, rather than the activities of their white counterparts who, as Richard Burton has demonstrated, "began serious missionary work on the colony only in the 1820s, almost forty years after the first wave of slave converts had been made by black missionaries" (1997: 97). In fact, white Christianity only began to shape African Jamaican religion following emancipation in 1838. The point is that, what had emerged as a result of the 50 or so years of black proselytism was a confluence of West African indigenous religion and Christian traditions—what some have referred to as "Afro-Christianity" (Burton, 1997: 97; Edmonds, 2003: 32). Indeed, "even when Africans converted to Christianity, the elements of Christianity to which they showed the greatest affinity were those that reinforced their Afrocentric worldview, informed their struggle for liberation, and promised them eventual freedom from and redress of the evil perpetrated against them by the colonial system" (Edmonds, 2003: 33; see also Burton, 1997: 99–101). In short, slave religion increasingly tended to focus on the eschatological horizon, on the day of deliverance, on that day when their suffering would cease, when they would be released from their chains, when the oppressor would be overthrown, and when they would return to the Promised Land.

It is not surprising, therefore, that in the years immediately prior to the emergence of Rastafarian thought in Jamaica such Afro-Christian ideas merged with apocalyptic beliefs common within conservative forms of popular Christianity. A particularly conspicuous and interesting example of this is Alexander Bedward (ca. 1859–1930) who, as Burton comments, brought "the radical energies of Jamaican Afro-Christianity to their peak, whereafter it was superseded as the main challenge to the colonial order by the newly emergent millennialist cult of Rastafarianism" (1997: 116). Interestingly, while Bedward was vigorously anti-colonial, he accepted a Christian, colonialist theological premise that God was white and, also that, "during the post-apocalyptic millennial period of the new heaven and new earth, blacks would become white" (Chevannes, 1994: 28, 109). That said, as far as Bedward was concerned, while the white, Christian God was the African's eschatological hope, the white people of the world were destined for destruction. Moreover, there is evidence that, in 1920, Bedward himself declared that, not only was he the harbinger of their end, but he would be the instrument of their destruction. Indeed, he seems to have declared that he was actually the returned Christ. As such, he would, like Elijah, ascend to heaven in a flaming chariot (on Friday 31 December 1920) and, after three days, return for his flock, take them to glory, and then begin the events of the apocalypse and the destruction of the white race. Perhaps needless to say, at the appointed time and date, in front of thousands of followers, no flaming chariot appeared. Following three subsequent predictions, each with the same earthbound result, the cognitive dissonance of his remaining followers was assuaged a little when he declared that God had commanded him to remain on the earth to preach. However, in 1921, following his alleged claim to be Christ and incendiary declarations suggesting the overthrow of the colonial authorities, he was arrested and interned in Kingston Lunatic Asylum, where he died in November 1930—a few weeks after the coronation of Emperor Haile Selassie I in Ethiopia.

While we will be looking at such ideas in more detail below, it is worth simply noting here that, interestingly, not only have such Afro-Christian figures and doctrines had an influence on contemporary Rastafarian spirituality (see Lewis 1998: 154), but references to Bedward's millenarian preaching has surfaced in reggae. Perhaps the most notable example is "Bedward the Flying Preacher", a thoughtful reflection on him by the Jamaican singer Prince Far I, which recalls his millenarian claims and his demise (released on the Singers and Players' 1983 album *Staggering Heights*). Then, over a decade later, in 1996, "Bedward", a popular remix of the song, was released by the British dub collective Zion Train on Dub Syndicate's *Research and Development*. More generally, African Head Charge's *Songs of Praise* (1981) has frequent references to the Christian tradition. Again, Bim Sherman's 1982 song "Sit and Wonder" (Singers and Players featuring Bim Sherman, *War of Words*) references "When the Roll is Called Up Yonder" (1893), the popular nineteenth-century eschatological hymn by James Black.

From Babylon to Zion

In classic Judaic thought, statehood is understood in terms of the fulfilment of God's promises to the Patriarchs, the progenitors of the people. Hence, in the period of exile (135–1948), the longing to return to the homeland occupied a central place in Jewish religio-political discourse. Exile and redemption (i.e. the return to the land) were dominant theological themes. Influenced by these ideas, a similar form of Zionism—indeed, one which focuses on a messianic figure, as in traditional Jewish Zionism—evolved within Rastafarianism. However, for exiled Rastafarians, the land, Zion, was not Israel, but Africa. As Patrick Taylor puts it, "a past African Golden Age becomes a future millennial Zion" (1991: 102–03). This is clearly evident in "Africa" by The Mighty Diamonds (on *Right Time*), in which the continent is implicitly linked to the eschatological new Jerusalem. With reference to Africa being a place of "no more crying", "victimization", and "starvation", the song reflects the vision described in Revelation 21: "I saw a new heaven and a new earth ... God ... will wipe every tear from their eyes, and death shall be no more, neither shall there be mourning, or crying, or pain any more, for the former things have passed away."

The emergence of the Back-to-Africa movement in Jamaica followed a pattern that can be observed within other histories of the oppressed. Bearing in mind the colonial context, which came to be viewed through the lens of the Hebrew Bible, it is unsurprising that the African diaspora understood itself as an exiled people living in a hostile land/Babylon. As indicated above, this in turn led to a Zionist understanding of their homeland as pure and sacred (see Barrett, 1997: 115–17). Hence, while there is much that is Christian in

Afro-Caribbean religion, it is suffused with specifically Jewish theo-logical ideas that contribute to an interesting millenarian perspec-tive. Indeed, reinterpreting the story of the Israelites' journey from Egypt to the Promised Land, as detailed in the Pentateuch, not only did Afro-Christians and then Rastafarians think of Africa in terms of Zion, but they understood the Atlantic Ocean in terms of the River Jordan which needed to be crossed. This is evident in numerous reggae songs, such as, most notably, "Crossing the River Jordan" by Count Ossie and the Rasta Family (on *Man From Higher Heights*), "How Fe Cross the River Jordan" by Peter Yellow (on *Hot*), "Jordan River" by Burning Spear (on *Marcus Garvey*), "Promised Land" by Dennis Brown (on *The Promised Land*) and "Moving on to the Prom-ised Land" by Barry Brown (on *Cool Pon Your Corner*). In other words, as we will see, biblical material is detraditionalized in Rastafari and reggae.

As to the emergence of an identifiable Back-to-Africa movement—and Ethiopianism more generally—the key early influence was Ed-ward Wilmot Blyden (1832–1912), now considered the pioneer of Pan-Africanism (Lynch, 1967). In particular, he argued a thesis that is now at the heart of Rastafarian thought, namely that Ethiopia repre-sents the pinnacle of civilization and learning. Indeed, drawing on biblical references to the country, Ethiopia and the celebration of its supremacy became identified with Africa *per se*. Passages such as Psalm 68 are often cited: "Let God arise, let his enemies be scat-tered ... Let Ethiopia hasten to stretch out her hands to God." Hence, for many within the African diaspora, Ethiopia became a synonym for the entire African continent; it was the heart of Africa; it was a powerful symbol of a free, sovereign, and sacred Africa; it was, there-fore, as Neil Savishinsky has argued, "a potent source of inspiration for African nationalist leaders, many of whom chose the 'pan-African' colours of the Ethiopian flag as a symbol for their emerging political parties and newly independent states" (1998: 135). In short, Ethiopianism "espoused a vision of African liberation and a future Ethiopian empire" (Edmonds, 2003: 34). Again, Ethiopianism can be understood in terms of African Zionism.

It should be noted, however, that, in developing Ethiopianism—and thereby laying the intellectual foundations for back-to-Africa political and religious thought—Blyden was actually developing an idea, the embryo of which was already present in African American culture and, indeed, in Afro-Christianity. For example, the slave preacher George Liele had himself adopted the idea and in 1784 founded in Jamaica, what he initially called, the Ethiopian Baptist Church. As Barrett comments, "by the time of the emergence of the Black churches, Africa (as a geographical entity) was just about oblit-erated from their minds. Their only vision of a homeland was the biblical Ethiopia. It was the vision of a golden past—and the promise that Ethiopia should once more stretch forth its hands to God—that revitalized the hope of an oppressed people. Ethiopia to the Blacks in America was like Zion or Jerusalem to the Jews" (1997: 75). Again, for many Ethiopia became a focal point on the eschatological hori-zon, the Zion to which they were being called to return. It was this emergent Ethiopianism that Blyden developed from a Pan-Africanist perspective.[3] Drawing on classical sources, he argued that, rather than being the barbaric, dark continent described by white Chris-tians, such as, perhaps most eloquently and influentially, Joseph Conrad in his 1902 novel, *Heart of Darkness*, Africa was actually the cradle of civilization.

Ethiopianism, however, didn't develop into the culture of resis-tance in America that Blyden and many others hoped it would. Nev-ertheless, he looked forward to the day when a "black Moses" would lead the dispersed peoples of African origin back to their homeland and out of the land of oppression. Such ideas are, of course, still central to the thought of most Rastafarians. Indeed, the title track of one of the most important reggae albums of the 1970s (and, accord-ing to *Time*, the best album of the twentieth century), Bob Marley's significantly entitled *Exodus*, explicitly articulates this thesis. As well as the refrain "movement of Jah people" and references to "leaving Babylon" for "our father's land", there is also the petition to Jah to "send us another brother Moses", "come to break downpression", "wipe away transgression", and "set the captives free". The refer-ence to "Moses" is particularly significant, in that, drawing on imag-ery from the Hebrew Bible, Blydon prophesied the following: "The Negro leader of the Exodus who will succeed will be a Negro of Negroes, like Moses was a Hebrew of the Hebrews—even if brought up in Pharaoh's palace [i.e. at the heart of the land of oppression] he will be found. No half Hebrew and half Egyptian will do the work ... for this work heart, soul and faith are needed" (quoted in Lynch, 1967: 121). If, in Blydon's day, there was little sign of his vision being realized in North America, this was not the case in Jamaica. Largely because of its more militant history, the embers of radical political

Ethiopianism were smouldering and simply needed someone to fan them. That person was Marcus Garvey—who has since become central to Rastafari. Garvey would be Moses for the African diaspora, he would be the "Negro of the Negroes". As Barrett argues, "the movement that was to embody the Ethiopian ideology par excellence was the Back-to-Africa Movement of Marcus Garvey. It was in Garvey—the prophet of African redemption—that the spirit of Ethiopianism came into full blossom" (1997: 76).

Marcus Mosiah Garvey (1887–1940)—the significance of whose middle name is not lost on Rastas—was born in St Ann's Bay, Jamaica, and was to become the leader of the first genuine large-scale black movement. Indeed, with reference to Blyden's "prophecy", he was popularly referred to during his lifetime as "Black Moses". Like Blyden before him, central to his teaching and that of the Universal Negro Improvement Association (UNIA)—which he founded on 20 July 1914 in Kingston—was the return of Africans to Africa, the only place, he believed, where black people would truly be at home and be respected as a race. Very quickly the UNIA, and Garveyism in general, became influential and international, being the movement for African repatriation and self-government that many oppressed and depressed Africans had, since Blyden, been longing for. As Peter Clarke points out, "The Garvey movement, like the Rastafarian movement, was born perhaps as much from despair of ending injustice and discrimination in America as it was from a vision of Africa as a 'Land without Evil'" (1994: 37). Indeed, it's worth noting that the idea of Africa as Zion was encouraged by Garvey, who also spoke in these terms (see Davidson, 2006). Arguably the largest project of the UNIA was the founding of the Black Star Steamership Line. Owned solely by blacks, and thus a source of great pride, it was a project which was intended to encourage trade between black communities around the Atlantic and also, arguably, to provide the means for Africans to return to Africa.[4] However, as far as we are concerned, the point is that, again, like Blyden, Garvey is significant for insisting that Africans in exile should be proud of their blackness, consider returning to their homeland, lay the foundations for a new superior African civilization, correct the prejudiced white histories of Africa, recognize African civilization as the world's first and greatest, and worship a black God "through the spectacles of Ethiopia":

> We, as Negroes, have found a new ideal. Whilst our God has no colour, yet it is human to see everything through one's own spectacles, and since the white people have seen their God through white spectacles, we have only now started out (late though it be) to see our God through our own spectacles. The God of Isaac and the God of Jacob let him exist for the race that believe in the God of Isaac and the God of Jacob. We Negroes believe in the God of Ethiopia, the everlasting God—God the Son, God the Holy Ghost, the one God of all ages. That is the God in whom we believe, but we shall worship him through the spectacles of Ethiopia. (Garvey, 1986: 34)

Having said that, it is rather surprising that Garvey himself never visited Africa. Indeed, his vision of Africa was based less on actual knowledge of the continent and more on a particular reading of the Bible and was, therefore, largely romantic—in the sense that aspects of his thought are utopian and even reminiscent of the "noble savage" imagined by Jean-Jacques Rousseau. Nevertheless, while his dream of physical repatriation was not realized, he did succeed in focusing the minds of Africans on issues which were to become central to the millenarian thought of Rastafari. And, as will be discussed below, for many Rastas this very focusing of the mind came to be understood in terms of a return to Africa and thus as Garvey's fulfilment of his Mosaic calling. in other words, it came to be understood as an exodus from Babylon, a liberation from oppression and a journey to Zion. Psychologically, emotionally, culturally and spiritually Garvey had led his people back to the Promised Land. He had raised the African consciousness and ensured that Ethiopia would be the focal point for many African minds. In this sense, reggae is a superb example of what Garvey achieved, in that it articulates the significance of Ethiopia, not only to Africans, but to peoples of many races and cultures.

Of particular significance to Rastafarian Zionism are Garvey's comments concerning an African redeemer. For example, he interpreted Psalm 68:31 as follows: "We go from the white man to the yellow man, and see the same unenviable characteristics in the Japanese. Therefore, we must believe that the Psalmist had great hopes of the race of ours when he prophesied 'Princes shall come out of Egypt and Ethiopia shall stretch forth his [sic] hands to God'" (Garvey, 1986: 61). Indeed, while there is little evidence for the claim, many Jamaicans also believe him to have prophesied the following: "Look to Africa for the crowning of a Black King; he shall be the Redeemer"

(Barrett, 1997: 81) or "Look to Africa when a black king shall be crowned for the day of deliverance is near" (Clarke, 1994: 36).[5] Who would this messianic redeemer be? The answer, for Garvey and for many Jamaican Garveyites, came in 1930 with the enthronement of Haile Selassie I. Several days after the coronation, on 8 November, 1930, Garvey published an article in his Jamaican newspaper *The Blackman*, which referred back to his earlier comments:

> The Psalmist prophesied that Princes would come out of Egypt and Ethiopia would stretch forth her hands unto God. We have no doubt that the time has now come. Ethiopia is now really stretching forth her hands. This great kingdom of the East has been hidden for many centuries, but gradually she is rising to take a leading place in the world and it is for us of the Negro race to assist in every way to hold up the hand of the Emperor Ras Tafari. (the full text of the article can be found in Lewis, 1998: 145–46)

The Rise of Rastafari

On 2 November, 1930, Ras (meaning "Prince") Tafari Makonnen (1892–1975), the great grandson of King Saheka Selassie of Shoa, was crowned Negus of Ethiopia. Declaring himself to be in the line of King Solomon and taking the name Haile Selassie I (Might of the Trinity), as well as "King of Kings" and "Lion of the Tribe of Judah"— which are important biblical references—it is not surprising that when he was crowned in St George's Cathedral in Addis Ababa in front of representatives from many nations, those who had been inspired by Garvey's teaching saw more than the accession of another Ethiopian ruler. In Haile Selassie I/Ras Tafari many saw the Messiah, the fulfilment of biblical prophesy, even God incarnate. Indeed, this led to, as Robert Hill comments, "the full flowering of Ethiopianism as a broad-based popular movement", which "came to a head with the emergence of the Rastafari movement in 1933–34, and the mass-mobilization around the crisis of the Italo-Ethiopian War of 1935–36" (1983: 26–28). Also significant was a series of influential articles by L. F. C. Mantle published in *Plain Talk* between July and November 1935, entitled "In Defense of Abyssinia and its History". Part of Mantle's argument rested on an interpretation of the events in Ethiopia in terms of biblical prophecy, along with an articulation of the divinity of Haile Selassie. For example, on 2 November 1935, he stated the following:

> I beg to inform you hypocrites [i.e. clergy] that what you have taught
> us about Jesus, is fulfilling in the land of Ethiopia right now: with the
> said same Romans or so-called Italian or Fascist. These are the said
> people who crucified Jesus 2,000 years ago, and, as we read after
> 2,000 years, Satan's kingdom or organization shall fall; and righteous-
> ness shall prevail in all the earth, as the waters cover the sea … we are
> now in the time that the 2,000 years have expired. (quoted in Hill,
> 1983: 27)

The point is that this type of millenarian speculation, which focused on the divine significance of Selassie and the imminent destruction of Babylon, evil and Satan, was enormously influential (see
Owens, 1976: 188–94). For example, Annie Harvey, who, with her
husband David, founded "The Israelites" sect in 1930, seemed to
have taught the significance of Selassie/Ras Tafari in terms of a strident millenarianism:

> The Lord … raiseth up the poor out of the dust and lifteth up the
> beggar from the dunghill; to set them among princes and to make
> them inherit the throne of Glory … Stain your doorposts sons and
> daughters of Ethiopia. Prepare your kids with unleaven bread and wait
> for the command. The sound of chariots is near. The chariots from the
> East are now awaiting the sound of the bugles from the West. Horses
> are harnessed, front legs lifted high; ears are pricked. Only the shake
> of the bridle and the world war shall begin. Ethiopian children lift up
> your heads. ("Lift Up Your Heads", reproduced in Hill, 1983: 28)

It was into this climate of millenarian speculation that one of the
principal architects of Rastafarian religio-political thought began
preaching (Campbell, 1997: 71, 144; Cashmore, 1983: 22;
Chevannes, 1994: 121; Hill, 1983: 28; Smith *et al.*, 1960: 6; Spencer, 1998b: 361). Having lived in North America for some years,
Leonard Percival Howell had returned to Jamaica in November 1932.
He very quickly became the "catalytic agent in igniting the radical
millenarian consciousness that based itself on the doctrine of divine
kingship of Ethiopia's Ras Tafari" (Hill, 1983: 28). Again, this sacralized
view of the significance of Haile Selassie is evident within much
roots reggae and is often explicitly depicted on album covers. Indeed, it is believed that Rastas are, as Murrell and Williams comment, "divinely endowed, authentic interpreters of the Revelation
to John because their God, Messiah and King, Selassie, the Lion of
the tribe of Judah, was the only one found worthy in heaven and on
earth to open the book and break the seven seals of the apocalypse"

(1998: 340; see also Owens, 1976: 91). In other words, they identify the figure in Revelation 5:5 with Selassie: "the Lion of the tribe
of Judah, the Root of David". Hence, the place that Christ would
normally occupy in Christian millenarianism, is filled by Haile Selassie.
The Rastafarian writer John Moodie expresses his significance as follows: "Haile Selassie I, being of the line of Judah, root of David and
on the throne of David, crowned King of kings, Lord of lords, conquering Lion of the tribe of Judah, Elect of God, Light of the World,
King of Zion, fulfils many prophecies of the scriptures" (quoted in
Murrell and Williams, 1998: 341). Again, this is explicitly articulated
in many reggae songs and much reggae artwork. A good example is
Lee Perry's *Rastafari Liveth Itinually*, the cover of which is typically
millenarian, depicting Selassie in royal garb travelling in a chariot
pulled by a lion (which, of course, symbolizes his own status as the
Lion of the Tribe of Judah). The background is one of dark clouds and
volcanic fire and the songs on the album include "Ethiopian Land"
and "Judgment Day". In short, the overall message of the record
relates the significance of Selassie as the divine deliverer who will,
in the last days, come to judge the living and the dead (see Acts 10:
41–43; 2 Tim. 4:1; 1 Pet. 4:5). As Chris Morrow argues in his overview of reggae album cover art, "Haile Selassie is shown on album
covers mainly as a powerful deity or … king. On illustrated sleeves
like *African Museum All Star* and *Rockers Almighty Dub*, he assumes
supernatural powers, showering the earth with lightning and using
his dreadlocks to destroy the structures of Babylon" (1999: 24).

By the 1960s, the Rastafari movement, which Howell had done
so much to promote, was waxing, while his own influence was wan-
ing. Other Rastafarians, such as the musician Count Ossie, were
emerging as important interpreters of Rastafari. That said, it is beyond dispute that if, as Cashmore argues, "every element the
Rastafarian belief system could be found in Garvey's philosophy"
(1983: 24), Howell was the principal Rastafarian interpreter of those
elements. He laid solid foundations on which the new millenarian
movement could now build.

Emerging out of a history of slavery and oppression, Rastafari's
apocalyptic critique of the current world order and its accompanying semiotic promiscuity was fundamentally allied to a distrust of
those in governmental and ecclesiastical authority, but particularly
those in law enforcement (see Garrison, 1979: 24–25). Quite simply, Rastas were living in Babylon and the forces of Babylon could

not be trusted. The stark theological dualism they had learned from Afro-Christianity taught them to view Africa as Zion, their eschatological Promised Land, and all that lay beyond its borders as Babylon, the fate of which is terrible and secured. Hence, the police and the law enforcement agencies in general became "a special object of hatred as members began to be jailed in increasing numbers for ganga (marijuana) offences and, in particular, members of the Nyabinghi section of the movement, for resorting to violence as a means of resolving poverty and discrimination" (Clarke, 1994: 49). Having said that, violence actually ran counter to mainstream Rastafarian millenarianism, which emphasized change as a result of divine intervention, rather than violent revolution. Indeed, while followers of Howell did engage in violent resistance to attempts by the authorities to control their activities, as the movement evolved and as Howell's influence began to recede, this distinction tended to separate mainstream Rastafarian belief from that of the Garveyites. That is to say, the latter, like the Jewish Zionists who followed Theodor Herzl, were less inclined to wait for a supernatural solution to racial discrimination and suffering. Nevertheless, while this is true, one cannot of course generalize about Rastafarianism. As it is not a hierarchical institution with systematically worked out orthodoxies and orthopraxies, there are many versions of belief and practice. Hence, generally speaking, while Rastas do not seek the violent overthrow of Babylon, others have sought to stimulate the process of change by engagement in a politics of direct action. Therefore, while Joseph Owens is right to note that the Rastafarians' attitude towards the future is mainly one of passive endurance, since they believe that the dramatic apocalypse will occur with inexorable inevitability and that "man can do little to hasten or retard the preordained course of events" (1976: 189), as the movement expanded and evolved, particularly during the 1960s, it did attract the attention of Babylon. This, however, was less the result of violent direct action and more a response to its strident critiques of established religion, the government, the professional classes, and indeed any form of authority which maintained the status quo and thus effectively supported the "Babylon System" (Bob Marley, *Survival*). In short, the violence of their rhetoric led to a common perception that it was angry and dangerous. Indeed, to some extent, this perception is supported by numerous songs, not to mention album covers that explicitly articulate ideas of violent revolution and armed resistance to the forces of Babylon.

However, as I will argue below, such signifiers need to be understood in terms of "chanting down Babylon". Put simply, they are metaphors informed by a particular doctrine of the power of Rastafarian communication, particularly through the arts. Truth is a weapon which will, in the final days, defeat Babylon and Satan, the father of lies.

As the 1960s progressed the complexity of the movement increased with its appeal broadening. Gradually more privileged social groups, including particularly students, joined the movement. This broadening of appeal led to a development of thinking within the movement. The students and the more privileged who, while committed to notions of black power and Pan-Africanism, were also relatively comfortable and thus not particularly concerned to return to Africa. Hence, there was a strengthening of theories of *symbolic* repatriation. As in much Pan-Africanism and Rastafarianism today, although some (including a *white* Rasta I have spoken to) maintained the hope that they would one day relocate to Africa, many began to think in terms simply of a return to an African consciousness. In other words, the rhetoric shifted towards a focus on "mental decolonization, a process of deconversion, of turning away from the ethos, mores, and values of colonial society and a reconversion to the African view and way of life" (Clarke, 1994: 51). In short, it was argued that the mind of Babylon needed to be replaced by the mind of Ethiopia/Zion. This, in many ways, was an important theological and ideological shift, that has had significant practical implications. Rastas were not now thinking in eschatological terms of leaving their corrupt, oppressive societies for a better life in the Promised Land—often identified as Shashamane,[6] a theme which is interestingly articulated on African Head Charge's *In Pursuit of Shashamane Land*, particularly the first track of the album, "Heading to Glory". If they were going to stay where they were, the life here and now needed to be improved. Hence, along with the nurturing of an African consciousness, the oppressed were politicized. Increasingly, the true Rasta felt it a duty to challenge the social, spiritual and intellectual structures of Babylon from within. That said, although there were intellectuals—such as particularly the Guyanese historian Walter Rodney (see Rodney, 1969; Campbell, 1997: 128–33)—who were challenging the colonial government in Jamaica, it was quickly becoming apparent to many Rastas that it would be the artists and musicians who would be central to mobilizing the forces of good and most effective in "chanting down Babylon" (Marley). Hence, "roots reggae" was understood, not only as spiritual music, but also as a political, liberationist, anti-establishment, countercultural force.

Chanting Down Babylon

The concepts of Babylon and Zion are ubiquitous within roots reggae. Indeed, so embedded in the genre is the millenarian interpretation of these terms that it is often retained in music produced by non-Rastafarian musicians (as is particularly the case in dub reggae). Concerning the latter, it is interesting that in the late 1970s and early 1980s, Rastafarian millenarian terminology, especially "Babylon", became significant in punk and post-punk culture. For example, when, in 1979, The Ruts achieved chart success with "Babylon's Burning", some may have been bemused by the reference. For many, who had, like The Ruts—Paul Fox, Malcolm Owen, Dave Ruffy and John Jennings—become fascinated with reggae and the dub sound, the reference was obvious: Babylon was the oppressive, principally white, establishment which was due to experience, as many Rastas believed, an apocalyptic conflagration. Within two years, as if to confirm the stark message of "Babylon's Burning", The Ruts released another Rasta-influenced single to coincide with London's Southall race riots of July 1981, namely "Jah War" (both songs can be found on *The Crack*). If not an urban apocalypse, the inner cities of Babylon were certainly burning (see Gilroy, 2002; Leech, 1988: 61–74, 98–117). The point is that, as Ernest Cashmore comments, "the riots of 1980 and 1981 gave some indication of the growing currency of Babylon as a way of interpreting the world" (Cashmore, 1983: vi). Hence, while there is more than a little truth to Hebdige's thesis (1979) that British punk culture itself was a yearning for a "white ethnicity" similar to Rastafarianism, the point here is that its millenarian discourse became an important contribution to much countercultural thought, whether black or white. Indeed, the use of the term "Babylon" by Jamaicans to refer primarily to the police (Garrison, 1979: 24–25; Pollard, 1982: 29; Breiner, 1985–86: 33) quickly became the dominant subcultural understanding in Britain in the 1970s and 1980s—as indicated by the police sirens which introduce "Babylon's Burning" and the policemen standing on each side of Linton Kwesi Johnson on the cover of *Dread Beat An' Blood* (see also Johnson's poem "Sonny's Lettah (Anti-sus Poem)"—2002: 27–29; 1991: 25–27;

listen particularly to the reggae version on his seminal *Forces of Victory*). Again, Franco Rosso's film *Babylon* (1980),[7] Wolfgang Büld's *Reggae in a Babylon* (1978) and Don Letts' *Punk Rock Movie* (1978) are excellent documents of the desperate plight of youths in London during the late-1970s. Whether black or white (but especially black), poverty, police brutality, and racism shaped the lives of those who sojourned in Babylon (see Centre for Contemporary Cultural Studies, 1982; Gilroy, 2002). As one young Rasta poet commented at the time:

> Babylon is patrolling the street,
> always spitting at a nigger's feet.
> You try to fight back,
> but you're outnumbered,
> 'cause they bring the fleet.
> The day will come when we'll be strong
> to fight the Babylon back.
> Rise up you niggers and face the facts,
> you'll always be harassed because you're black …
> (Janet Morris, "Babylon", in Garrison, 1979: 25).

Regardless of its influence and reception beyond Rastafarianism, within the Rasta community the concept of 'Babylon' is of supreme doctrinal and ideological importance:

> Any interpretation of the significance of Rastafari must begin with the understanding that it is a conscious attempt by the African soul to free itself from the alienating fetters of colonialism and its contemporary legacies. To accomplish this freedom, Rastas have unleashed an ideological assault on the culture and institutions that have dominated the African diaspora since the seventeenth century. In Rastafarian terms, this consists of "beating down Babylon". They have also embarked on an ambitious endeavour of "steppin' outa [out of] Babylon" to create an alternative culture that reflects a sense of their African heritage. (Edmonds, 1998: 23)

The problems related to living in Babylon are not only addressed in numerous songs, but, again, also vividly depicted on a range of album covers. For example, the cover of *Babylon Street* by Gladiators reminds one of Jesus' comments concerning the broad and the narrow ways and, more particularly, of the nineteenth century evangelistic poster, "The Narrow and the Wide Gates". The band is placed in the foreground and Babylon Street, in the background, is a scene of vice and chaos. The righteous and the unrighteous are contrasted—the sheep and the goats (Mt. 25:32–34). Some albums, on the other hand, have vividly apocalyptic covers: Junior Byles, *Beat Down Babylon*; The Memory of Justice Band, *Mash Down Babylon*; U Roy, *Babylon Burning*; The Overnight Players, *Babylon Destruction*; Junior Ross, *Babylon Fall*; Yabby U, *Chant Down Babylon Kingdom*. Moreover, such references to the destruction of Babylon are often explicitly informed by the Book of Revelation. Indeed, so central is the final book of the Bible to the discourse of Rastafari, that it is itself not infrequently referenced: Jah Shaka, "Revelation 18" on *Revelation Songs*; Mike Brooks, *Book of Revelation*; Revelation, *Book of Revelation*; Max Romeo, *Revelation Time*. As Caroline Cooper has demonstrated with reference to Bob Marley's work, the central ideological concern in his lyrics is "radical social change. The existing social order, metaphorically expressed in Rastafarian iconography as Babylon, the whore, the fallen woman of St John's *Revelation*, must be chanted down" (1987: 4). In a way not dissimilar to Martin Luther's understanding of "the Babylonian captivity of the Church", we have seen that Rastas think of themselves, their religion, and their culture in terms of captivity within an unrighteous system. Again, this is expressed in numerous album titles, such as U Roy's *Dread in a Babylon*, Martha Velez's *Escape from Babylon*, and Merger's *Exiles in Babylon*. This, of course, is in keeping with Judeo-Christian apocalyptic discourse. Babylon functions as a symbol for all that is evil, brutal, oppressive, and Satanic[8] in a world to which the redeemed do not belong and which is destined to be terminated. Hence, as in Christian eschatology, so also in Rastafarianism, the fall of Babylon is the central eschatological motif signifying the termination of evil. Most Rastas will know by heart passages such as Revelation 14:8: "Fallen! Fallen is Babylon the Great, which made all the nations drink the maddening wine of her adulteries." Again, with particular reference to Revelation, there are songs warning of the coming judgement and the consequences of living an "unrighteous life" in Babylon: Trinity's "Judgment Day" (on Ranking Trevor and Trinity, *Three Piece Chicken and Chips*); Knowledge's "Judgment" (on *Straight Outta Trenchtown*); Don Carlos's "Judgment Day" (on *Plantation*); Greyhound's "Judgment Rock" (on *Black and White*); Mystic Eyes' "Judgment Time" (on *Burning Sampler*); Earl Zero's "None Shall Escape the Judgment" (on *Visions of Love*). Typical of the rhetoric of such songs is Bob Marley's "Ride Natty Ride" (on *Survival*), which speaks of the judgement of Jah and the unquenchable fires reserved for the wicked and those deceived by Babylon. Indeed, interesting in this respect is the cover of Marley's posthumous *Confrontation*, painted by the Rasta artist Neville Garrick. Marley, while depicted as a traditional Ethiopian horseman, is also ostensibly depicted as St George riding a white charger and slaying a dragon. Needless to say, rather than the unlikely merger of Marley and St George—a conspicuous symbol of English colonial and crusading power—the reference is more likely to be that of good finally conquering evil. More specifically, I suggest that it needs to be understood in terms of the defeat of Babylon and the slaying of Satan as described in Revelation 12: 7–9: "And there was war in heaven. Michael and his angels fought against the dragon, and the dragon and his angels fought back. But he was not strong enough, and they lost their place in heaven. The great dragon was hurled down—that ancient serpent called the devil, or Satan, who leads the whole world astray. He was hurled to the earth, and his angels with him."

Like much Christian premillenarian discourse, reggae, especially during the 1970s and 1980s, focused on biblical signs of the end, and more specifically on the prevalence of wars and rumours of wars, paying particular attention to nuclear holocaust and Armageddon. Although, bearing in mind the cold war context, this wasn't unusual within the popular music of the period, what is distinctive in reggae discourse is the explicit association of the superpowers with Babylon and of nuclear war with judgement, all of which is understood in biblical terms. A good example is Bunny Wailer's "Armagiddeon" (on *Black Heart Man*), which links "wars and rumours of war" (see Mt. 24:6) and nuclear apocalypse to "the gates of doom and hell", to spiritual battles between light and darkness, to human unrighteousness, and to Satan. It then continues with rhetoric concerning redemption and post-apocalyptic life when "night is passed and day is come". Similarly, many album covers of the period were especially apocalyptic in their depiction of imminent nuclear destruction and, often, in their articulation of Babylon's culpability. For example, the cover of Ranking Ann's *Something Fishy Going On* has, amidst a scene of nuclear Armageddon, Ronald Reagan and Margaret Thatcher in a nuclear submarine. Other typical examples are Peter Tosh's *No Nuclear War*, Mikey Dread's *World War III*, the Mighty Maytones' *Madness*, Michael Prophet's *Righteous are the Conqueror*, Mutabaruka's *Outcry*, Ranking Joe's *Armageddon*, and Steel Pulse's *Earth Crisis*. To take the last of these, the title song from the album is typical in that it references violence, corruption, environmental catastrophe and the possibility of nuclear holocaust in Babylon's "last days", repeating, in the chorus, references to "doctrines of the fallen angels" and the "eternal flames of hell". Also, as we have seen, not untypical of such narratives is its concluding premillenarian declaration of hope: "Jah kingdom rising".

Fundamentally related to the above is the belief that there are dark forces working against the "people of Jah", systems that psychologically and culturally propagate values and beliefs antithetical to the good life. That is to say, spiritual and political demonologies become conflated. Political organizations, social structures, multinational companies and world systems are understood to be inherently evil—concrete manifestations of Babylon and demonic activity. For example, a reggae musician and member of the Twelve Tribes of Israel sect once expressed to me that he would not use credit cards and that he was very reluctant to use the Internet, principally because of a broad conspiracy theory he subscribed to relating to the Antichrist. With reference to Hal Lindsey's *Late Great Planet Earth* and quoting Revelation 13: 16–18, he told me that he wanted to distance himself from electronic media in order to avoid becoming embroiled in the activities of the Antichrist—"the beast". The following passage from *Late Great Planet Earth* is perhaps worth quoting:

> Do you believe it will be possible for people to be controlled eco-nomically? In our computerized society, where we are all "num-bered" from birth to death, it seems completely plausible that some day in the near future the numbers racket will consolidate and we will have just one number for all out business, money, and credit transactions. Leading members of the business community are now planning that all money matters will be handled electronically. (1971: 113)

Following Lindsey and numerous others, and demonstrating a familiarity with Western conspiracy occulture, this artist was convinced that, through a secret society known as the Illuminati, the Antichrist would ensure that all transactions and people would bear his numerical mark. It was now apparent, he argued, that this would be done by means of microchips. It wouldn't be long, he reasoned, before the population would be required to have chips implanted in their hands or foreheads. Such ideas, of course, have an easy continuity within a premillenarian eschatology focused on Babylon and Revelation. Indeed, he is not the only reggae musician and member of the Twelve Tribes of Israel to have been persuaded by Lindsey's work. In an interview close to the end of his life, Bob Marley responded to a question about what books he reads as follows: "I'll tell ya one kind book that I love, the first book is the Bible. Next book that I ever read that I love is *Late Great Planet Earth*. 'Cause all dem prophesy is true" (Marley and Davis, 1983: 91).

In order to fully understand the concept of "chanting down Babylon" and the significance of reggae, something needs to be said about the Rastafarian understanding of the power of the spoken word. Rastas can explicitly contribute to the demise of Babylon through music and the arts in general, in that there is an emphasis on the supernatural efficacy of the word and, more broadly, Rastafarian communication—understood to be a manifestation of divine presence, with the power to create and destroy. That is to say, Rastas can literally "chant down Babylon". As Ziggy Marley has put it, "Babylon causes the system … It's a devil system … who cause so much problems on the face of the earth … And by 'chanting down' I mean by putting positive messages out there. That is the way we'll fight a negative with a positive … [The] thing is: action is under the words. It is how you live your life that is the important thing … So, as now you or me live a life according to the laws of life, which is the Father's law" (quoted in Spencer, 1998a: 266). This sacred mission to combat the negative with the positive in accordance with divine laws, gives reggae its eschatological role. More specifically, as Cooper comments it in her analysis of Bob Marley's lyrics, his "chant against Babylon is both medium and message. For Babylon, the oppressive State, the formal social and political institutions of Anglo/American imperialism, is bolstered by the authority of the written word, articulate in English. 'Head-decay-shun', the punning, *dread* inversion of the English word 'education', is antithetical to the cultural practices of Rastafarians, whose chant against Babylon has biblical resonances of the fall of Jericho" (1987: 5). Explicit in this respect is Marley's song "Chant Down Babylon", which argues that reggae music and "the voice of the Rastaman" are central to chanting down Babylon. Through such speech-acts, Rastas contribute to the destruction of Babylon, which will ultimately be effected by Jah Ras Tafari, Counquering Lion of the tribe of Judah, as foretold in Revelation. Consequently, understood in these terms, again, Rasta music becomes a powerful religio-political tool, which has eschatological import.

Part of this power is the ability to convert the mind of Babylon, undoing the "head-decay-shun". While Jamaicans have seen an end to colonialism, there has effectively, Rastas argue, been a colonization of the mind. Hence, there is a need for education and for a cultivation of a hermeneutic of suspicion about everything that has been learned in Babylon. As reggae musician Peter Tosh put it, "Babylon is where they tell you that everything that is wrong is right, and everything that is right is wrong. Everywhere is Babylon" (quoted in Steffens, 1998: 255). Hence, reggae musicians such as Tony Rebel, tend to have a sacralized understanding of their work: "I see myself as an instrument of the Most High and definitely it's not for me alone to chant down Babylon. I'm a link in a chain … We know that the music is very influential. The word is power. They chant around Jericho wall and it fell down. So, therefore, we can use music to chant down Babylon walls also. That is not a literal wall. Is like emancipating the people from those kind of mentality that is negative" (quoted in Spencer, 1998: 267). Again, the point is that reggae has a central role in Rastafarian eschatology. Hence, Marley's "Revolution" on *Natty Dread* emphasizes that truth (which reggae communicates) leads to "revolution", that this revolution is the solution which will lead to the post-apocalyptic world within which righteousness will "cover the earth … like the water cover the sea".

This notion of chanting down Babylon, challenging the negative with the positive and lies with truth, emerged following violent episodes with the police between the 1940s and 1960s, particularly as a result of militant Rasta activity associated with Howell's commune on Pinnacle Hill. Since those confrontations, which, as Spencer comments, "resulted in the Rasta elders' appeal for understanding and tolerance … Rastas have chosen the non-violent over the violent approach to bring down Babylon. The arts have become key 'weapons' in that strategy" (1998a). Hence, although Marley, who was particularly critical of the Roman Catholic Church, believing it to have a particularly corrupting role in the events of the last days, sung of his desire to bomb it in order to terminate lying preachers ("Talkin' Blues", on *Natty Dread*), overall it was clear that he was committed to chanting down Babylon, to a belief in the power of music to effect change.

Concerning Marley's understanding of the eschatological role of Roman Catholicism, it should be noted, of course, that it is not an entirely novel interpretation, it being very similar to some contemporary Protestant fundamentalist millenarian discourse (e.g. Hunt,

1994; Hislop, 2003), as well as some early Christian views of the city or empire of Rome (see Boxall, 2001: 57–59). However, while we have seen that Marley was certainly influenced by fundamentalist millenarianism, his thought concerning Rome was principally shaped by Rastafarian teaching concerning the Italian invasion of Ethiopia in the 1930s. As Roger Steffens writes, 'the Jamaican *Daily Gleaner* newspaper published photographs on its front pages of the Pope blessing Italian planes before they flew to Africa to murder innocent people with their cargo of guns and poison gas. This, to the Rasta in Jamaica, was inconceivable: How could an alleged man of God countenance such behaviour? The Pope, they reasoned, must therefore be the Antichrist, the leader of Babylon" (1998: 259). Marley explicitly concurred with this teaching in an interview with the music journalist Chris Boyle: "Babylon is a man-made power, evil, put together to rule the people by force. Keep them killing one another … So where did all the power come from? Rome. The Vatican. That's where they get white power. Pope is white power, represent the Devil. What he is defending is what he is" (quoted in Steffens, 1998: 259). Hence, again, in "Ride, Natty Ride" (on *Survival*), he interprets such Christian teaching in terms of "the Devil's illusion". Indeed, he reinterprets Psalm 118:22, which the New Testament understands to refer to Jesus (Mt. 21:42; Mk. 12:10; Lk 20:17; Acts 4:11; 1 Pet. 2:7)—"the stone the builders rejected has become the capstone"—in terms of Rastafari, which the church has lied about and rejected. Again, the dragon on the cover of *Confrontation*, discussed above, also almost certainly signifies the Vatican within the broader concept of Babylon. That is to say, in the spirit of non-violent resistance, the Rasta is defeating, "chanting down", this ecclesiastical manifestation of Babylon with truth.

Concluding Comments

"In Babylon, there is a theory of a world divided and a vision of how it will someday be totally transformed" (Cashmore, 1983: vi). This, we have seen, is explicitly articulated within reggae. With roots in slavery, colonial oppression, the experience of being in exile, an identification with the Israelites, and the eventual detraditionalization of key eschatological themes within the Bible, there was, within Rastafari, the development of a distinctive millenarian eschatology, central to which is an interpretation of the current circumstances of

Africans in terms of Babylonian captivity. This initially led to the articulation of Ethiopianism, a form of African Zionism, focused on Ethiopia and physical repatriation. However, as the possibility and appeal of repatriation declined, the interpretation of Zion and Babylon was internalized. Again, as periodic armed rebellion against Babylon in Jamaica proved too destructive and detrimental to the movement in the early years, gradually a more politically quietist millenarian perspective became dominant. While an Afro-Christian-influenced belief in an external Day of Judgement and the final destruction of Babylon remained in place, this internalization led to a more nuanced understanding of Babylon as a colonization of the mind. This, we have seen, is enormously significant for the understanding of reggae and the arts within Rastafarian millenarian discourse, in that the fall of Babylon came to be understood in terms of education. The chosen weapons in the fight against the Babylon system are now truth and a life lived righteously. Hence, not only reggae music and lyrics, but reggae cover art fulfilled a crucial missiological, not to say eschatological role in chanting down Babylon and encouraging people to board the "train to Zion" (Bob Marley, "Zion Train", on *Uprising*; U. Brown, *Train to Zion*; Linval Thompson, Wayne Jarrett, and Ranking Trevor, *Train To Zion Dub*).

Notes

1.   For example, the British black theologian, Robert Beckford, has argued that Bob Marley needs to be understood in terms of a liberation theologian (1998: 115–29).

2.   A few days after writing this, I was interested to hear it explicitly quoted by the Bristol (UK) reggae musician Armagideon on his "Grow More Dub" (*Through the Haze*, 1998).

3.   Pan-Africanism is complex, but at a fundamental level, is a political movement dedicated to the unification of all Africans to a single African state to which those in the African diaspora can return. More broadly and amorphously, Pan-Africanism seeks culturally to unite Africans in Africa and in the diaspora through literary and artistic projects.

4.   Some Garveyites dispute the claim that Garvey intended the company to provide transportation to Africa. It was simply there "to link the colored peoples of the world in commercial and industrial discourse" (Davis, 1994: 5).

5.   While the Garvey scholar Robert Hill argues that "no evidence has so far been found or cited to show that Garvey ever made this assertion", he does draw attention to a comment made in September, 1924 by James Morris Webb, a black clergyman concerning the advent of a "universal black

king" as the fulfilment of biblical prophecy (Hill, 1983: 25). Others have argued a similar thesis to Edmonds, namely that, although no documentation has been found, "it is likely that Garvey made some oral declaration ... and that it was kept alive in the memory of people steeped in oral tradition" (Edmonds, 2003: 147 n. 34).

6.   A small area of land in the South of Ethiopia given to Rastafarians by Haile Selassie. It is the particular focus of the Twelve Tribes of Israel sect, who, unlike some Rastas, encourage ideas of self-repatriation, rather than waiting for the supernatural intervention of Jah.

7.   The screenplay by Martin Stellman and Franco Rosso was also developed into a successful novel with same title by Mike Russell (1980).

8.   The concern with Satan, for example, is particularly explicit in Max Romeo's "Chase the Devil" (on *War ina Babylon*) and "Satan's Kingdom" by The Ethiopians and the Tribe (on *No Baptism*).

Bibliography

L. E. Barrett, *The Rastafarians* (Boston, MA: Beacon Press, 1997 [1988]).

R. Beckford, *Jesus is Dread: Black Theology and Black Culture in Britain* (London: Darton, Longman & Todd, 1998).

I. Boxall, "The Many Faces of Babylon the Great: *Wirkungsgeschichte* and the Interpretation of Revelation 17", in Moyise (ed.), *Studies in the Book of Revelation*, 2001, pp. 51–68.

L. A. Breiner, 'The English Bible in Jamaican Rastafarianism', *Journal of Religious Thought* 42.2 (1985-86), pp. 30-43.

R. D. E. Burton, *Afro-Creole: Power, Opposition, and Play in the Caribbean* (Ithaca, NY: Cornell University Press, 1997).

H. Campbell, *Rasta and Resistance: From Marcus Garvey to Walter Rodney* (St John's, Antigua: Hansib Caribbean, 1997 [1985]).

E. Cashmore, *Rastaman: The Rastafarian Movement in England* (London: Unwin Paperbacks, 1983).

Centre for Contemporary Cultural Studies, *The Empire Strikes Back* (London: Hutchinson, 1982).

B. Chevannes, *The Social Origins of Rastafari* (Kingston: Institute of Social and Economic Research, University of the West Indies, , 1979).

_____ *Rastafari: Roots and Ideology* (Syracuse, NY: Syracuse University Press, 1994).

B. Chevannes (ed.), *Rastafari and Other African-Caribbean Worldviews* (New Brunswick, NJ, Rutgers University Press, 1995).

P. B. Clarke, *Black Paradise: The Rastafarian Movement*, Black Political Studies No.5 (San Bernardino, CA: Borgo Press, 1994 [1986]).

J. Conrad, *Heart of Darkness* (Harmondsworth: Penguin, 1994).

C. Cooper, "Chanting Down Babylon: Bob Marley's Song as Literary Text", *Jamaica Journal* 19.4 (1987), pp. 2–8.

S. V. Davidson, "Babylon in Rastafarian Discourse: Garvey, Rastafari, and Marley", *Society for Biblical Literature Forum* (2006): <http://www.sbl-site.org/Article.aspx?ArticleId=496> (Accessed: 24 March, 2006).

S. Davis, *Bob Marley: Conquering Lion of Reggae* (London: Plexus, 1994).

S. Davis and P. Simon (eds), *Reggae International* (London: Thames & Hudson, 1983).

E. B. Edmonds, "Dread 'I' In-a-Babylon: Ideological Resistance and Cultural Revitalization", in Murrell, Spencer and McFarlane, *Chanting Down Babylon*, 1998, pp. 23–35.

_____ *Rastafari: From Outcasts to Culture Bearers* (New York: Oxford University Press, 2003).

L. Garrison, *Black Youth, Rastafarianism, and the Identity Crisis in Britain* (London: Afro-Caribbean Education Resource Project, 1979).

M. Garvey, *The Philosophy and Opinions of Marcus Garvey*, (A. J. Garvey, ed. (Dover: Majority Press, 1986).

P. Gilroy, *There Ain't No Black in the Union Jack* (London: Routledge, 2002 [1987]).

D. Hebdige, *Subculture: The Meaning of Style* (London: Methuen, 1979).

_____ *Cut 'N' Mix: Culture, Identity, and Caribbean Music* (London: Routledge, 1987).

R. Hill, "Leonard P. Howell and the Millenarian Visions in Early Rastafari", *Jamaica Journal* 16:1 (1983), pp. 24–39.

A. Hislop, *The Two Babylons: Romanism and Its Origins* (Edinburgh: B. McCall Barbour, 1998 [1953]).

D. Hunt, *A Woman Rides the Beast: The Roman Catholic Church and the Last Days* (Wheaton, IL: Harvest House, 1994).

L. K. Johnson, *Mi Revalueshanary Fren: Selected Poems* (London: Penguin, 2002).

_____ *Tings an Times* (Newcastle-upon-Tyne: Bloodaxe Books, 1991).

D. Katz, *People Funny Boy: The Genius of Lee "Scratch" Perry* (Edinburgh: Payback Press, 2000).

K. Leech, *Struggle in Babylon: Racism in the Cities and Churches of Britain* (London: Sheldon Press, 1988).

R. Lewis, "Marcus Garvey and the Early Rastafarians: Continuity and Discontinuity", in Murrell, Spencer and McFarlane (eds), *Chanting Down Babylon*, 1998, pp. 145–58.

H. Lindsey, *The Late Great Planet Earth* (London: Marshall Pickering, 1971 [1970]).

H. Lynch, *Edward Wilmott Blyden: Pan Negro Patriot 1832–1912* (Oxford: Oxford University Press, 1967).

R. N. Marley and S. Davis, "Bob Marley—A Final Interview", in Davis and Stephen, *Reggae International*, 1983, pp. 88–91.

C. Morrow, *Stir It Up: Reggae Album Cover Art* (San Francisco, CA: Chronicle Books, 1999).

S. Moyise, S. (ed.), *Studies in the Book of Revelation* (Edinburgh: T & T Clark, 2001).

N. S. Murrell, "Introduction: The Rastafari Phenomenon", in Murrell, Spencer and McFarlane (eds), *Chanting Down Babylon*, 1998, pp. 1–19.

N. S. Murrell and L. Williams, "The Black Biblical Hermeneutics of Rastafari", in Murrell, Spencer and McFarlane (eds), *Chanting Down Babylon*, 1998, pp. 326-48.

N. S. Murrell, W. D. Spencer and A. A. McFarlane (eds), *Chanting Down Babylon: The Rastafari Reader* (Philadelpia, PA: Temple University Press, 1998).

Y. S. Nagashima, *Rastafarian Music in Contemporary Jamaica: A Study of Socioreligious Music of the Rastafarian Movement in Jamaica* (Tokyo: Institute for the Study of Languages and Cultures of Asia and Africa, 1984).

J. Owens, *Dread: The Rastafarians of Jamaica* (London: Heinemann, 1976).

V. Pollard, "The Social History of Dread Talk", *Caribbean Quarterly* 28:2 (1982) pp. 17–40.

C. Potash (ed.), *Reggae, Rasta, Revolution: Jamaican Music from Ska to Dub* (London: Books With Attitude, 1997).

W. Rodney, *The Groundings with My Brothers* (London: Bogle-L'Overture Publications, 1969).

M. Russell, *Babylon* (London: New English Library, 1980).

N. J. Savishinsky, "African Dimensions of the Jamaican Rastafarian Movement", in Murrell, Spencer and McFarlane (eds), *Chanting Down Babylon*, 1998, pp. 125–44.

M. G. Smith, R. Augier and R. Nettleford, *The Rastafari Movement in Kingston, Jamaica* (Mona: Institute for Social and Economic Research, University College of the West Indies, 1960).

W. D. Spencer, "Chanting Change Around the World Through Rasta Ridim and Art", in Murrell, Spencer and McFarlane, *Chanting Down Babylon*, 1998a, pp. 267–83.

_____ "The First Chant: Leonard Howell's *The Promised Key*", in Murrell, Spencer and McFarlane, *Chanting Down Babylon*, 1998b, pp. 361–89.

R. Steffens, "Bob Marley: Rasta Warrior", in Murrell, Spencer and McFarlane (eds), *Chanting Down Babylon*, 1998, pp. 253–65.

P. Taylor, "Perspectives on History in Rastafari Thought", *Studies in Religion* 19 (1990), 191–205.

_____ "Rastafari, the Other, and Exodus Politics: EATUP", *Journal of Religious Thought* 17:1–2 (1991), pp. 95–107.

Discography

African Head Charge, *Songs of Praise* (On-U Sound, 1990).

African Head Charge, *In Pursuit Of Shashamane Land* (On-U Sound, 1993)

Armagideon, *Through the Haze* (Dubhead, 1998).
Mike Brooks, *Book of Revelation* (I Sound, n.d.).
Barry Brown, *Cool Pon Your Corner* (Trojan, 1979).
Dennis Brown, *The Promised, Land* (Blood & Fire, 2002).
Burning Spear, *Marcus Garvey* (Island, 1975).
Junior Byles, *Beat Down Babylon* (Trojan, 1972).
Don Carlos, *Plantation* (CSA, 1984).
Count Ossie and the Rasta Family, *Man From Higher Heights* (Vista, 1983).
Mikey Dread, *World War III* (Dread at the Controls, 1980).
Dub Syndicate, *Stoned Immaculate* (On-U Sound, 1992).
Dub Syndicate, *Echomania* (On-U Sound, 1993).
Dub Syndicate, *Research and Development: A Selection of Dub Syndicate
     Remixes* (On-U Sound, 1996).
Dub Syndicate and Lee Perry, *Time Boon X De Devil Dead* (EMI, 1987).
The Ethiopians and the Tribe, *No Baptism* (Crystal, 1991).
Gladiators, *Babylon Street* (Jam Rock, 1977).
Greyhound, *Black and White* (Trojan, 1971).
Jah Shaka, *Revelation Songs* (Jah Shaka Music, 1983).
Linton Kwesi Johnson, *Dread Beat An' Blood* (Virgin, 1978; Heartbeat, 1989)
Linton Kwesi Johnson, *Forces of Victory* (Island, 1979).
Knowledge, *Straight Outta Trenchtown* (Makasound, 2002).
Bob Marley and the Wailers, *Natty Dread* (Island, 1974).
Bob Marley and the Wailers, *Exodus* (Island, 1976).
Bob Marley and the Wailers, *Survival* (Island, 1979).
Bob Marley and the Wailers, *Uprising* (Island, 1980).
Bob Marley and the Wailers, *Confrontation* (Island, 1983).
The Memory of Justice Band, *Mash Down Babylon* (Platinum Press, 1983).
Merger, *Exiles in Babylon* (Ultra, 1977).
Merger, *Armageddon Time* (Merger, 1980).
Ras Michael and the Sons of Negus, *Nyabinghi* (Trojan, 1974).
Mighty Diamonds, *Right Time* (Well Charge, 1976).
Mighty Maytones, *Madness* (Burning Sounds, 1976).
Misty in Roots, *Wise and Foolish* (People Unite, 1982).
Mutabaruka, *Outcry* (Shanachie, 1984).
Michael Prophet, *Righteous are the Conqueror* (Greensleeves, 1980).
Ranking Trevor and Trinity, *Three Piece Chicken and Chips* (Cha Cha, 1978).
Max Romeo, *War ina Babylon* (Island, 1976).
Max Romeo, *Revelation Time* (Different Records, 1978).
Junior Ross, *Babylon Fall* (Stars, 1976).
The Overnight Players, *Babylon Destruction* (Cha Cha, 1981).
Lee Perry, *Rastafari Liveth Itinually* (Justice League, 1996)
Ranking Ann's *Something Fishy Going On* (Ariwa, 1984).
Ranking Joe, *Armageddon* (Kingdom, 1982).

Revelation, *Book of Revelation* (Burning Sounds, 1979).
The Ruts, *The Crack* (Virgin, 1979).
Singers and Players, *Staggering Heights* (On-U Sound, 1983)
Singers and Players featuring Bim Sherman, *War of Words* (On-U Sound, 1982)
Steel Pulse, *Earth Crisis* (Elektra, 1984).
Linval Thompson, Wayne Jarrett and Ranking Trevor, *Train To Zion Dub* (Tuff Gong, 1981).
Peter Tosh, *No Nuclear War* (CBS, 1987).
U Brown, *Train to Zion* (Blood & Fire, 1997).
U Roy, *Babylon Burning* (Burning Bush, 2002).
U Roy, *Dread in a Babylon* (TR International, 1975).
Various Artists, *Burning Sampler* (Burning Vibrations, 2001).
Martha Velez, *Escape from Babylon* (Sire, 1976).
Bunny Wailer, *Black Heart Man* (Island, 1976).
Yabby U, *Chant Down Babylon Kingdom* (Nationwide, 1976).
Peter Yellow, *Hot* (Black Music, 1982)
Earl Zero, *Visions of Love* (Epiphany, 1979).

Filmography

Babylon (1980)—director: Franco Rosso.
Countryman (1982)—director: Dickie Jobson
The Harder They Come (1972)—director: Perry Henzell.
Punk Rock Movie (1978)—director: Don Letts
Reggae in a Babylon (1978)—director: Wolfgang Büld

Apocalypse at the Millennium

John Walliss

Introduction

The closing decade of the twentieth centure witnessed an outpouring of millennial fears and expectations quite unprecedented in the modern world. In an era in which Francis Fukuyama (1993) was celebrating the post-Cold War "end of history" and arch-postmodernist Jean Bauldrillard (1995) was declaring ironically that the year 2000 would not happen—time's arrow having gone into reverse at some point in the 1980s—many, even if they did not embrace a Christian eschatology, still looked towards the transition from 1999 to 2000 (or 2000 to 2001 depending on their position) with a sense of trepidation. This was not, of course, a free-floating anxiety. A number of events that took place, or issues that emerged, in the 1990s played on fears of an apocalyptic dénouement to the century whether by the effects of extreme weather conditions, the AIDS epidemic, ebola and other viruses, the Y2K "Millennium Bug", variant CJD (Creutzfeldt-Jakob disease), or the actions of some "apocalyptic cult" such as the Branch Davidians, Aum Shinrikyô or the Order of the Solar Temple (see for example, Dunant and Porter, 1996; Wojcik, 1997; Walliss, 2004). Indeed, to take just the latter example, such was the concern among law enforcement agencies that the shift from 1999/2000 would herald a literal explosion of violence by apocalyptically-minded groups that several, most notably the Federal Bureau of Investigation (2002, 28) and the Canadian Security Intelligence Service, produced reports for their agents on what the FBI report, *Project Megiddo*, referred to as "individuals or domestic extremist groups who profess an apocalyptic view of the millennium or attach special significance to the year 2000".

As would perhaps be expected, these apocalyptic fears were also reflected within popular culture, most notably within film. Simultaneously tapping into and feeding from the general sense of *fin de siècle* anxiety, Hollywood treated cinema audiences to a number of films dealing with apocalyptic "End of the World" scenarios such as alien invasions (*Independence Day*), giant meteors (*Deep Impact*, *Armageddon*) or super-viruses (*12 Monkeys*). Other films, most notably the Kevin Costner films *Waterworld* and *The Postman* had as their backdrop a world that had been ravaged by environmental and/ or geo-political collapse. Not to be outdone, Satan himself, in the form of Gabriel Byrne, attempted in *End of Days* to escape his eternal prison and bring about the end of the world by producing a child with a human woman between 11 p.m. and midnight on the eve of the millennium.

The shift into a new century and calendrical millennium has not witnessed a significant slowing down of film releases either drawing on the idea of the end of the world as a motif (for example *Donnie Darko*), or explicitly dealing with "end of the world" scenarios (e.g. *28 Days Later*, *The Day after Tomorrow* and *The Core*). Indeed, 2000 saw the release of *Left Behind: The Movie*; an adaptation of the first volume of the series of "rapture" novels of the same name written by Christian premillennialists Tim Lahaye and Jerry Jenkins. Drawing on the authors' interpretation of Biblical endtime events, *Left Behind* revolves around the pre-millennial "rapture" of the Elect up to Heaven and its aftermath for those literally "left behind" during the Tribulation. This has been followed by two more sequels, *Tribulation Force* and *World at War*, both of which focus on the post-Rapture world where the Antichrist runs the United Nations, enforcing a universal religion on the world, and where a small number of remnant Christians (the so-called "Tribulation Force") try and oppose him. More recently, *Right at the Door* has drawn on contemporary, post 9/11 fears about terrorist attacks to present an apocalyptic vision of the terrifying aftermath of a radiological "dirty bomb" attack on Los Angeles, while *Flood*, drawing on contemporary environmental fears, depicts a massive flood striking London after overcoming the Thames Barrier.[1]

In this article I intend to present an analysis both of the use and abuse of the notion of the apocalypse within contemporary cinema through a critical engagement with the recent work of Frances Flannery-Dailey (2000), Mervyn Bendle (2005) and Conrad Ostwalt (1998, 2000, 2003). In particular I will explore Ostwalt's and Flannery-Dailey's claim that contemporary apocalyptic films are characterized by what the former refers to as a "desacralisation of the apocalypse", wherein the traditional notion of the apocalypse is secularized and placed within the sphere of human agency. Thus, rather than presenting a traditional image of the apocalypse as a divine event largely outside of the sphere of human agency, films such as, for example, *Armageddon* or *12 Monkeys* not only locate the cause of the apocalyptic event within the natural world (e.g. a comet or a supervirus), but also show how it may be prevented through human agency. In doing so, I will critique Bendle's claim that, in contrast to films produced during the cold war that dealt with the possibility of nuclear holocaust, contemporary apocalyptic films are hallmarked by an attitude of scorn and ridicule towards the everyday. This, I will show, is invariably far from the case. Rather, I will argue that without exception contemporary apocalyptic films are characterized instead by a valorization of the everyday wherein, in an almost Durkheimian way, the contemporary social order (understood typically as male and north-American) is reaffirmed and celebrated.

Before doing so, however, I should like to spend a brief moment clarifying what I mean by "apocalyptic films", particularly as in much of the literature the term has typically gone undefined and remained implicit its use (see Stone, 2001; Broderick, 1993, 252). The term "apocalypse" has its root in the Greek word *apokalypsis* meaning "revelation" or "to unveil" (O'Leary, 1994). Within Biblical and religious studies it is typically used to refer to a genre of Jewish and Christian literature which relate visions of the end of time/the world and the emergence of a new and perfect social order. This genre would include texts such as the Book of Daniel and the Book of Revelation, as well as other non-Canonical texts such as The Apocalypses of Thomas and Adam or the Revelation of Esdras, all of which present prophecies "unveiling" the shape of the future. However, within popular usage the term is used much more broadly to refer to any form of immense cataclysm or destruction; typically involving the whole planet (i.e. "the End of the World"). Thus, for example, fears of an all-out nuclear war or planetary environmental disaster may be understood as being "apocalyptic" in nature, even where they are not linked to any Biblical eschatology or a sense of an unveiling of history (Wojcik, 1997). The reason for this being that such events involve—in a manner akin to those described in apocalyptic texts—the cataclysmic destruction of all human life and/or the planet.

Here, my use of the term "apocalypse" and "apocalypse films" will stay closest to this latter understanding of a cataclysmic destruction of humanity and/or the earth. This, after all, is the one that will be deployed by both the producers and the audiences of such films (its use is thus justified from an emic perspective).[2] However, I will show how many films typically draw on several if not all of these overlapping understandings of the term and how, for example, a film may deal with the "end of the world", present its plot as a form of cautionary tale of what could happen in the future (a potential "unveiling"), and quote, or make reference to, real or invented apocalyptic texts. In doing so, I will explore some of the possible tensions or problems that may arise. To this end, my chapter is structured in three sections. In the first, I briefly outline Ostwalt's thesis of the "desacralization of the apocalypse" within film. Following on from this, in the bulk of the article, I develop and explore this thesis in relation to several of the films outlined in the introduction. Finally, I discuss some ways in which contemporary apocalypse films invert both the central characters and the message of apocalyptic texts.

Ostwalt on the "Desacralization of the Apocalypse"

In several recent contributions to the study of religion and film, Conrad Ostwalt has drawn attention to what he has termed the "desacralization of the apocalypse" within contemporary film. Taking as his initial starting point the notion that contemporary culture has undergone some degree of secularization, Ostwalt (1998, 4) argues that this has led not to the decline of religion (the position of, for example, Steve Bruce, 2002), but rather to a blurring of the boundary between the sacred and the secular wherein, for example, "cultural forms perceived to be secular might very well address religious questions and tap the religious sensibilities outside of recognizable religious institutions".[3] Equally, religions may themselves may adopt popular cultural forms in order to communicate and make their message relevant to modern, secular audiences (see for example Ostwalt, 2003, 57–87; Forbes and Mahan, 2005, part 2). In particular, he argues that this blurring of the sacred/secular boundaries "has assisted in creating a new apocalyptic myth … more palatable to contemporary popular culture"; a myth characterized by a fundamental desacralization of the traditional understandings of the apocalypse (Ostwalt, 2000: 20). The process of secularization thus results, Ostwalt claims, in the co-opting of the apocalypse by popular culture, so that, for example, film makers may now raise the spectre of the end of time in much the same way as Fundamentalist preachers, albeit with different motives. Indeed, going further he argues that such films may actually function religiously in that by confronting audiences with the possibility of imminent world destruction, they thereby "help viewers come to grips with human contingency" (Ostwalt, 2000: 1). Apocalypse films may thus operate for contemporary audiences in much the same way as *La Danse Macabre* and *momento mori* tombs once did for medieval and Renaissance Europeans (see Clark, 1950; Binski, 1996).

Nevertheless, Ostwalt argues, this new apocalyptic myth differs in significant ways from its Biblical forerunner. First, as noted above, within apocalyptic films there is a toning-down of the fatalism that one finds in apocalyptic texts. Where for example, the Book of Revelation, presents an account of the apocalypse as both supernatural in origin (brought about by God and with supernatural agents as the central *dramatis personae*) and as essentially unavoidable for either the living, or, indeed, the dead, contemporary apocalypse films reject this and posit an end that is both natural and, crucially, *avoidable* through human agency. In other words, whereas the wrath of God cannot be averted by humans, the same is not true of asteroids, super-viruses or alien invasions. The contemporary apocalyptic myth thus represents an example of what Daniel Wojcik (1997: 211) refers to in his typology of apocalyptic orientations as *cataclysmic fore-warning*, "in which apocalypse is said to be imminent but avoidable through human effort" and where "predictions of potential disastrous scenarios … are presented with the hope of motivating people to act to avert possible catastrophes and save humanity from approaching, but not inevitable, doom".

This links with the second and third characteristics of the new myth highlighted by Ostwalt (2000, 3); that "the cinematic apocalypse depends on a human messiah … to rescue humanity from those elements that threaten annihilation", and that although such films remove "the divine element from the apocalyptic drama" they still maintain "religious symbolism, imagery [and] language". As I shall discuss in more detail below, just as apocalypse films have secularized the potential causes of apocalyptic destruction, so too have they found a saviour in a non-supernatural form. Indeed, not only do such films secularize the apocalyptic hero, but, I will argue, in doing so they typically invert the apocalyptic hero by presenting him (and it is typically a male) as both a defender of the existing social order and as fundamentally flawed. However, despite removing the divine presence from the apocalypse, many of the films I will discuss below do not shy away from drawing, both overtly and covertly, on the language, symbolism or ideas found within apocalyptic texts. In some cases apocalyptic texts themselves—or texts invented by scriptwriters which sound suitably "apocalyptic"—may also be quoted within the films and form plot devices (see Denzey, 2004).

Fourth, as an arguable reflection of the cultural hegemony enjoyed by science, not only do apocalypse films "allude to the idea that religion has trivialised the apocalyptic threat", but they also typically find a solution to this threat through science. Religion is, of course, invoked. However, the real solution to the apocalyptic threat facing humanity is invariably found within these films in some combination of science and technology, not in miracles or divine intervention. Finally, pulling all these points together, Otwalt argues that within contemporary western society, popular culture has become the most effective purveyor of "our culture's eschatological consciousness" and that this has resulted in the emergence of "secular eschatological imagination" that simultaneously feeds into and is influenced by forms of popular culture, such as films.

Discussion

There is much of merit within Ostwalt's analysis, although I would argue against his latter assertion that popular culture has become the most effective purveyor of apocalyptic ideas. The years since 9/11 have witnessed, particularly in America, a resurgence of apocalyptic ideas and rhetoric linked with the "War on Terror" and the Bush administration's religio-political agenda (see McLaren, 2002; Lifton, 2003; Urban, 2006). This is not to deny either the role of popular culture in influencing contemporary apocalyptic sentiments, or the emergence of a secular eschatological imagination, but rather to highlight that, in America at least, the religious eschatological imagination has not gone away, and that in many ways it currently enjoys a more hegemonic political (and possibly also cultural) position than its secular equivalent (see Gribben, 2006 on the 'mainstreaming of prophetic expectation' in the late twentieth century).

Equally, while I would accept the general thrust of Ostwalt's thesis regarding a postmodern blurring of the distinction between the secular and the sacred, I would argue that a more nuanced understanding of the process of secularization is needed to grasp the role of religious ideas within popular culture (it is also a matter of intense debate whether it is possible to argue that the USA is a secular society—certainly the statistics would point to a different conclusion!—see Baylor Institute for Studies of Religion, 2006). For this, two potential avenues of theorization offer themselves to us. First, we may return to Peter Berger's (1990 [1967]) classic distinction between, on the one hand, the secularization of society and, on the other, the secularization of consciousness, to argue that, irrespective of the status of religion in the wider society, the prevalence of religious ideas within popular culture may be seen as evidence for the continuing fascination—or at least curiosity—that religious/spiritual ideas still hold for individuals. Or, on a mundane level, it may equally be true—and I would argue that it certainly is—that, as Wright argues, the foundational nature of the Bible and Christianity within the West make them almost a taken-for-granted set of ideas hardwired into culture (Wright, 2007). Consequently, even if they do not accept a traditional Christian eschatology, for example, audiences will still understand and react almost instinctively to apocalyptic imagery and language. Indeed, it could be argued that, within a culture steeped in Christianity, it is impossible to talk about the destruction of the planet and/or mass destruction of humanity and *not* invoke on one level or another the spectre (and it is often only a spectre) of Christian apocalypticism. As Will Self (1998, xiv) observes in his introduction to the Canongate edition of the King James translation of the Book of Revelation:

> Our sense of the apocalypse is steeped in the language of *Revelation*. In this century the star called Wormwood *has* fallen, and the sea has become as black as sackcloth of hair, and the moon has become as blood. We have heard the silence—about the space of half an hour—that accompanied the opening of the seventh seal, yet we are still here.

Second, we may draw on the more recent work of Christopher Partridge (2004, 2005) on what he terms "occulture" and, more specifically, his notion of "eschatological re-enchantment". Echoing to some extent the sentiments of Ostwalt, Partridge (2005: 2) argues that western societies are currently witnessing "a confluence of secularisation and sacralisation", where old forms of religion are drying up and being replaced by new non-Christian spiritualities. These new spiritualities, he argues, are both resources of and resourced by popular culture, or, more specifically, a "reservoir of [hidden, re-jected, and oppositional] ideas, practices and methodologies" that he terms "Occulture". Occulture, then, is simultaneously "the spiritual *bricolour*'s Internet from which to download whatever appeals or inspires", as well as being "the well from which the serious occultist draws" and "the cluttered warehouse frequently plundered by producers of popular culture searching for ideas, images and symbols" (2004: 85). More specifically for our purposes here, Occulture may be seen as a source for the apocalyptic themes, motifs and texts that the producers of popular culture may dip into at will to create new cultural products (be they films, novels, or song lyrics); products which then, in turn, become part of both the language of popular culture and the reservoir of Occulture (see Partridge, 2005, chapter 7).

Having examined briefly some of the potential shortcomings of Ostwalt's thesis, I now turn my attention to expanding upon his notion of the "desacralisation of the apocalypse". First, I would concur with him that contemporary apocalypse films represent a secularization of the apocalypse through their focus on both natural—typically "man-made"—disasters as the agent of cataclysmic destruction and the way in which they show how these may be prevented through human agency. As noted in the introduction, within these films the supernatural element is almost completely removed so that the agent of destruction becomes, for example, superviruses (*12 Monkeys, 28 Days Later*), giant meteors (*Deep Impact, Armageddon*), geopolitical collapse (*The Postman*), or some form of environmental catastrophe (*The Core, The Day After Tomorrow, Waterworld*). Similarly, destruction is averted, or at least mitigated against through the actions of heroic individuals (typically heroic north Americans).

This is not to say that supernatural—or at least non-human—agents of destruction or salvation are not also presented, but they appear much less often—specifically only in two films; *Independence Day* and *End of Days*. Indeed, *End of Days* is noteworthy among its peers for its exclusive focus on the supernatural as both the agent of potential destruction and, indeed to some extent, salvation. In contrast to, for example, the heroes of the above films who avert catastrophe through their human efforts, the hero played by Arnold Schwarzenegger ultimately comes to rely on faith. Indeed, as Walsh (2002) notes, this is in many ways the central theme of the movie. When we are introduced to Schwarzenegger's character (Jericho

Cane) he is shown as someone who has lost what faith he has in God after his family are murdered during a burglary. Later in the film when he is offered assistance by a shadowy group of Catholic clergy who are attempting to subvert Satan's plans, he retorts in a classic Schwarzenegger action hero way by telling them that "between your faith and my Glock 9 mm, I take my Glock". However, at the end of the film, shortly before his final confrontation with Satan, Cane, who has fled to a church, is shown contemplating the church's religious images and statues before throwing his machine gun to the ground and praying "please God, help me. Give me strength." Finally, Cane draws strength from statues of Jesus and St Michael in order to overcome the possession of his body by Satan and throw himself on to the latter's sword, thereby forcing Satan back to Hell. The journey of Cane's character through the film is thus for Walsh (2002: 7), one from anger to faith, or from being "an action hero ... to a prayerful believer", albeit one who ultimately has to rely on violence in order to defeat his foe.

That said, however, it is only at the end of the film that we are shown Satan as a supernatural entity—as a dragon (arguably an allusion to Revelation 12–13). For most of the film he is shown in human form; albeit a form with some degree of supernatural abilities. Similarly, the audience is not shown divine entities saving the day, but rather have to rely on the—albeit heavy-handed—symbolism of Cane contemplating religious iconography accompanied with choral voices. Indeed, the only "good" spiritual beings presented in the film are Cane's own deceased wife and child who appear right at the end of the film after Satan is vanquished and Cane lies dying. In this way, for all its supernatural elements, the film ultimately conforms to the standard narrative of the apocalypse film genre whereby human agency—albeit with spiritual strength—is able to triumph over the forces that seek to wreck destruction on humanity.

Linked with this privileging of human agency, apocalypse films also place a strong emphasis on science and technology as the means whereby their respective apocalyptic catastrophes can be averted or, at least, mitigated against. Both are, however, nevertheless typically presented in an ambivalent light, not least because they themselves are more often than not the cause of the catastrophe. In this way, apocalypse films may be seen on one level at least, as one manifestation of contemporary cultural unease about science within the west (see for example The Wellcome Trust, 2000; National Science

Board, 2004). However, when examined more closely, the films do not appear to be critiquing science *per se*, but rather, as Susan Sontag (1967) noted four decades ago, the *misuse* of science or even the ways in which, in spite of their best intentions, the fruits of scientists' labour may backfire or bring with them unintended consequences.[4] So for example, in *28 Days Later*, the virus that drives those infected with it to become filled with insane rage was, the film's opening scene reveals, initially created by scientists attempting to create a suppressant for rage and violence. Its release, we are shown, and the subsequent breakdown of civilization is the result, not so much of the direct actions of scientists themselves, but rather a group of animal rights protesters who unwittingly free the infected animals from an experimentation facility.

This trend is, however, best illustrated in *12 Monkeys*, where scientists are presented as both the heroes and villains of the film, with one set of scientists in the future sending a convict, James Cole, back in time to the present day in an attempt to stop a supervirus being unleashed by, it turns out, a "rogue" scientist. However, here again, the villain is not so much the scientists themselves who developed the virus, but rather the rogue scientist who seeks to use it. As with *28 Days Later*, the message of the film is thus that it is the misuse of science, and not science itself that is potentially dangerous, if not cataclysmic. Indeed, it is noteworthy that although the central character in *12 Monkeys* is James Cole, the ultimate hero of the film is arguably the lead scientist from the future who, it would appear, (possibly) succeeds where Cole does not. Thus, in the film's penultimate scene, after Cole has been gunned down by security at the airport, the rogue scientist is shown taking his seat on the plane next to a female passenger; the lead scientist from 2035 who, possibly knowing that Cole would fail, has seemingly travelled back in time in order to thwart the release of the virus. The question of whether she is successful is not answered in the film and, indeed, the whole film offers itself for multiple interpretations, but the final lines of dialogue in the film, which are hers, would suggest that she is: "Jones is my name. I'm in insurance".

This ambivalence does not extend, however, to one particular manifestation of the (mis)use of science and technology: nuclear weapons. In contrast to innumerable films from the 1950s through to the late 1980s which presented nuclear weapons as a negative force (see, Evans-Kasastamatis, 1999; Winkler, 1999; Shapiro, 2002;

McCrillis, 2002), within many contemporary apocalypse films they are presented in a much more positive light. In particular, whereas in films ranging from *The Day the World Ended* (1956), *On the Beach* (1959), to *Threads* (1985) and *When the Wind Blows* (1987), nuclear weapons were presented as the actual cause of global apocalyptic destruction, the chief protagonists in films such as *Armageddon, Independence Day, The Core* and *Deep Impact* utilize them in order to *avert* the destruction of the earth and/or humanity.[5] In *The Core*, for example, several nuclear warheads are detonated at the earth's core in order to restart the earth's rotation and thereby avert environmental disaster, at the climax of *Independence Day*, the hostile alien craft are destroyed by nuclear strikes, while in *Armageddon* and *Deep Impact* a meteor is defected from earth's path by detonating warheads beneath its surface. Indeed, in the latter film the warheads take on almost a semi-divine status when the mission to detonate them on the meteor is named the "Messiah Mission".

Again, as was the case with science and technology more broadly, this shift in the way in which nuclear weapons are presented may be linked with a distinction drawn within the films' narrative between the technology itself and its (mis)use. Thus whereas earlier films presented nuclear weapons in negative terms by explicitly linking them with their military use (which was always framed as a misuse), within these latter films, a clear distinction is drawn between their use for positive ends (saving the world/humanity) and negative ones (destroying the world/humanity). So, for example, during the press conference accompanying the launch of the mission to destroy the meteor in *Armageddon*, the US President, after introducing himself "not as the President of the United States, not as the leader of a country, but as a citizen of humanity", waxes poignantly on how:

> for the first time in the history of the planet, a species has the technology to prevent its own extinction. All of your praying with us need to know that everything that can be done to prevent this disaster is being called into service. The human thirst for excellence and knowledge, every step up the ladder of science, every adventurous reach into space, all of our combined modern technologies and imaginations, *even the wars that we have fought have provided us the tools to wage this terrible battle.* (emphasis added)

This notion that nuclear weapons are simply "tools" that can be redeployed to more positive ends is also expressed in *Deep Impact* where a voiceover (provided by TV news coverage) accompanying the launch of the mission describes how "with the help of Russian engineers, a technology that was designed to propel weapons of mass destruction will power the ship that will intercept the greatest threat that our planet has ever faced". However, the film that arguably best exemplifies this distinction between positive/negative use is *The Core*, where it is revealed the earth's core has stopped revolving as a direct consequence of a clandestine military project for producing earthquakes known as Project DESTINI (Deep Earth Seismic Trigger INItiative). In this way the central theme of the film is the (positive) use of one form of destructive military technology to undo the (negative) actions of another.

As well as presenting nuclear weapons in a positive light (or at least a morally ambiguous one), contemporary apocalypse films are also characterized by extremely positive portrayals of religion. This is particularly the case in the Hollywood films where one finds a highly sentimentalized form of religion presented, typically at the moment of gravest crisis and then at the point where the disaster is averted. So, for example, in *Deep Impact* after announcing on a live television broadcast that the "Messiah Mission" has failed in its attempt to completely destroy the approaching meteor, the US President (accompanied by syrupy music) concludes by telling his viewers:

> I wish … no, wishing is wrong, it's the wrong word now. That's not what I mean. What I mean is; I believe in God, I know a lot of you don't, but I still want to offer a prayer for our survival, mine included, because I believe that God—whomever you hold that to be—hears all prayers, even if sometimes the answer is no. So may the Lord bless you, may the Lord keep you, may the Lord lift up His divine countenance upon you, and give you peace.

However, it is also found in the British film *28 Days Later*, albeit in a more subtle way. In the scene where the central character, Jim, returns home after discovering about the viral outbreak to find his parents dead after having taken their lives we hear a lone voice singing the hymn *Abide with Me* on the soundtrack. Later in the film in a similarly emotive scene *Ave Maria* is played. According to the film's director, Danny Boyle, the two pieces were used to signify to the audience "the history or the culture of the past in Britain what had gone".[6] In this way, religion becomes a signifier for a cultural memory of a happier and more secure (pre-apocalyptic) age.

In contrast, apocalyptic beliefs, where they are presented at all, are typically presented in a much less positive light and are invariably dismissed either implicitly or explicitly within the narrative of the film as outlandish or strange. In the director's cut of *Independence Day*, for example, after the alien spacecraft have obliterated a number of world cities, an apocalyptic "end of the world" preacher (complete with a crucifix painted on his forehead) is shown amid the rubble and carnage, Bible and a "the time has come REPENT while you can" sign in hand declaring (in suitably King James Version-sounding English) to those trying to escape that "the end hath come! He's spaken his word and the end hath come!". Similarly, in *Armageddon*, when Bruce Willis' character asks a NASA employee why the public has not been informed of the approaching meteor, he is told that "If news of this got out there'd be an overnight breakdown of basic social services worldwide; rioting, mass religious hysteria, total chaos, you can imagine; basically the worst parts of the Bible". Finally, in *End of Days*—arguably, as I noted above, the most "religious" of the recent apocalypse films—cultural fears of what might take place on the transition to the new millennium (here defined as from 1999/2000) are similarly dismissed in a radio call-in:

Caller: I'm trying to figure out what everyone is predicting here. Is the world going to come to an end at exactly 12:01 on New Years or …

Host: I tell you what, lady, I think you should play it safe: not quit your job yet. I'll tell you something else, in two days this place is going to see the wildest party ever. We're gonna be there with the first 100 callers, we're gonna make the most noise, and we're gonna be the craziest, and if the world comes to an end what the hell? We're all gonna be together, and if it doesn't, then we'll all have the best night …

The one film that breaks from this view, however, is *12 Monkeys* which presents a more nuanced image of apocalyptic prophecy by raising the question of whether such prophecies may be inspired by (fore)knowledge of events. This theme runs throughout the film through its treatment of time travel and madness, but is expressed most explicitly in a scene in which the heroine, the psychiatrist Dr Kathryn Railly (played by Madeleine Stowe), is shown giving a public lecture in 1996 entitled "Madness and Apocalyptic Visions". During the course of the lecture she quotes Revelation 15:7 ("One of the four beasts gave unto the seven angels seven golden vials, full of the wrath of God, who liveth forever and ever"), which she then links to several historical visionaries who predicted the humanity would be wiped out by a plague of some sort. One of these is a First World War soldier who, after being hospitalized with a shrapnel injury, claimed to have come from the future "looking for a pure germ that would ultimately wipe mankind of the face of the earth, starting in the year 1996". This is greeted with chuckles from the audience, who clearly believe such prophecies to be symptoms of madness. However, shortly before this, the audience (who of course are already aware of the aftermath of the virus' release) had seen James Cole transported back in time to the trenches where he had met the soldier shown in Railly's slide presentation. Indeed, the soldier, it is revealed, is one of Cole's accomplices; Jose. Later, after discovering from the police that Cole has a First World War bullet lodged in his leg, Railly realizes that the larger photograph from which her slide is cropped shows Cole reaching towards Jose; an image that the viewer would also recognize from the previous scene. Later in the film, after Railly has come to accept Cole's claims, they are shown walking past a "end of the world" street-preacher who is quoting Revelation 16:17 to his listeners ("Then the seventh angel poured out his vial into the air"). As Cole walks past him, the preacher stops and shouts at him "You! You! You're one of us!"; the implication being that he, like Cole and Jose has also been sent from the future to warn humanity of the virus. Finally, the viewer is able to link this passage and Revelation 15:7 with the vials containing the virus which are shown being released in the airport at the end of the film. In this way, as Flannery-Dailey (2000: 20) notes, the view that apocalyptic prophecies are strange or outlandish, if not manifestations of insanity, is reversed within the film narrative and "true sanity is equivalent to knowing the apocalyptic future". Indeed, going further, prophecy becomes not so much a revelation of the future, but rather a statement of what, from the perspective of one from the future who has travelled back in time, has already occurred (what Railly refers to in her lecture as "The Cassandra Complex"—"in which a person is condemned to know the future but to be disbelieved, hence, the agony of foreknowledge combined with the impotence to do anything about it").[7]

Contemporary "Apocalypse Films" and the Inversion of the Apocalypse

Contemporary apocalypse films, then, are characterized by a fundamental desacralization—if not inversion—of the apocalypse. In contrast to texts such as the Book of Revelation, which present apocalyptic scenarios as supernatural events, outside the scope of human agency, and, indeed, as necessary events within sacred/human history, the films I have described both secularize and invert it in their narratives so that the apocalyptic event becomes both natural or human-made in nature and avoidable through human agency. Indeed, as I noted above, in general these films are dismissive of apocalyptic beliefs, painting them as weird or outlandish; the province of "the end is nigh" preachers and other social misfits.

However, perhaps the most fundamental inversion of the apocalypse within these films concerns the latter's posture *vis-à-vis* the current social order. Whereas, apocalyptic texts are inherently critical of the contemporary social order and look towards a time in not-to-distant future where it will be replaced with a divine order ("a new heaven and a new earth" to quote Rev. 21:1), these films are in contrast characterized by a explicit valorization of the contemporary social order. As Walsh (2002, 13) notes in his discussion of *End of Days*:

> Revelation envisions the present evil age divinely interrupted and re-placed by a new divine age and kingdom. By contrast, *End of Days* envisions a demonic interruption, ruining an American present and ush-ering in a kingdom of evil. *End of Days* is comfortable with the American present and wishes to preserve it against a monstrous foe (a pattern reminiscent of Cold War horror and science-fiction movies). Jericho's death is not the apocalyptic-engendering death of the hero of Mark or of the martyr heroes (including the lamb) of Revelation. Jericho's death restores normal life.[8]

This theme of preserving the existing social order against apocalyptic threats—whether they be meteors, aliens, or superviruses—is, as we have seen, the central plot within the majority of the films that I have discussed above (Indeed, according to Sontag, it is one of the central features of the science fiction genre). This is seen perhaps most clearly in *Deep Impact* where, in addition to the plan to destroy the approaching meteor the US Government also initiate a plan, in the words of the President, "to ensure the continuation of our way of life". This is a network of caves underground in Missouri designed to hold a million people (including "200,000 scientists, doctors, engineers, teachers, soldiers and artists" as well as randomly selected individuals) "for two years until the air clears and the dust settles". These caves, he goes on, again drawing on Biblical imagery, are "more than a dormitory. It's our new Noah's Ark", and will also contain seeds, seedlings, plants and animals so that the survivors can start over again in the post-apocalyptic world.[9]

However, we also find this valorization even, if not more so, in films which are set after the cataclysmic destruction of the current social order. Here, though, in contrast to the heroes and heroines seeking to defend it, we find it valorized instead through its absence vis-à-vis the chaos of the post-apocalyptic present. This is particularly the case in films such as *Waterworld* and to some extent *28 Days Later* where the central plot of the film is the quest by the chief protagonists for something approximating the old order (understood as "the answer to infection" and the mythical "Dryland" respectively). However, the film that I would argue exemplifies this trend is *The Postman*. Based on the novel by David Brin, and set in a post-apocalyptic USA of 2013, *The Postman* stars Kevin Costner as a drifter who finds a United States Postal Service uniform and a sack of old letters while looking for shelter from a storm in an abandoned jeep. Initially using the uniform as a way to bluff his way into an armed township, the drifter/Postman tells those inside that he is a representative of the "Restored United States of America" (the motto of which is "stuff is getting better every day") and is greeted as an almost messianic figure. Realizing the hope that he brings, the Postman sets about recreating a makeshift postal service and, in doing so, battles and ultimately triumphs over a local warlord, General Bethlehem (who is painted as an anti-American, far-right, Feudal lord). The central narrative of the film is thus an explicit paean to American idealism and a sense of shared norms and values—or what Brin (1998, no pagination) refers to as "the gracious little things that connect us today". According to Brin (1998, no pagination):

> The Postman was written as an answer to all those post-apocalyptic books and films that seem to *revel* in the idea of civilization's fall. It's a story about how much we take for granted—and how desperately we would miss the little, gracious things that connect us today. It is a story about the last idealist in a fallen America. A man who cannot let go of a dream we all once shared. Who sparks restored faith that we can

recover, and perhaps even become better than we were ... watching Kevin Costner's three hour epic is a bit like having a great big Golden Retriever jump on your lap and lick your face, while waving a flag tied to its tail. It's big, floppy, uncoordinated, overeager, sometimes gorgeous—occasionally a bit goofy—and so big-hearted that something inside of you has to *give* ... that is, if you like that sort of thing.

For these reasons, I would disagree with Bendle's (2005: 30, 31) claim that in contrast to earlier Cold War films where "everyday life was represented as invaluable in its innocence and simplicity, something whose loss in a nuclear war would be irrevocably tragic ... [within more recent films] everyday life is scorned and even vilified". In particular, I find particularly questionable his claim that:

contemporary cinema offers extremely misanthropic representations of the apocalyptic near future and communicates a fear and hatred of everyday people. The masses are depicted as mindless, barely functional vermin, ready to tear each other apart in a desperate rage for survival. Accompanying this is a depiction of the heroes and survivors being readily transformed into effective killers, capable of butchering large numbers of people who, perhaps only hours before, may have been their friends, allies, or even family members. (Bendle, 2005: 41)

Rather, I would argue that through its defence against catastrophe or through characters seeking out its approximation in the post-apocalyptic world, contemporary apocalypse films not only valorize everyday life but also, in an almost Durkheimian way, reaffirm it (Durkheim, 1961). While all of the films focus, as would be expected, on the broad impact (potential or actual) of the apocalyptic disaster, through, for example, the destruction or cities, they also draw viewers attention to how these disasters are played out and experienced on the everyday level, through personal losses and triumphs, the difficult choices made and so on. These films are, in other words, as much about the tragic breakdown of the repetition and taken-for-grantedness of the everyday ("normal life") as they are about the actual or potential destruction of whole societies (see Lefebvre, 1971; Felski, 1999–2000). This, again, in many ways is to be expected—viewers after all will find it easier to identify and have an emotional connection with "everyday" characters like them making difficult decisions or responding to huge turmoil than they would with, say, the decisions made by a President. So, on one level at least, the focus on the everyday is one technique whereby film-makers may pull their audiences emotionally into the narrative of the film.[10]

However, on an other level, I would argue that the films may also be seen as a symbolic reaffirmation of the everyday; an everyday which is presented as being under threat from catastrophic events, but which ultimately survives in one form or another.

This valorization of the existing social order/everyday links with the final way in which contemporary apocalypse films invert the message of apocalyptic texts, such as the Book of Revelation. Although some commentators have pointed to the heroes of apocalypse films as examples of "Christ Figures" or "Messiahs" (in the sense that they are saviours or ones who sacrifice themselves for others) (see Flannery-Dailey, 2000),[11] if they are Messiahs or Christ Figures then they are fundamentally different to those found within apocalyptic literature in several crucial ways. Primarily, whereas the Lamb/Messiah of Revelation is a violent, countercultural character (one who actually destroys the existing social order), the hero of apocalypse films is, as we have seen, one defends or seeks for an approximation of the existing order. Moreover, whereas the Christ Figure might traditionally be understood within both apocalyptic literature and more widely as a perfect individual (or even superhuman—*Superman* or otherworldly—*The Day the Earth Stood Still*—Koslovic, 2002, Etherden, 2005), the hero within apocalypse films is typically presented as human, all too human or, indeed, flawed in some way (see Roos, 2007).[12] So, for example, in *Waterworld*, the Mariner is a mutant with webbed feet and functional gills who is almost killed at the first Atoll he visits because of this. James Cole in *12 Monkeys* is a criminal who is introduced to the scientists as having "a history … violence, anti-social six, repeated violations of the Permanent Emergency Code, insolence, defiance, disregard of authority—doing 25 to life". Similarly, although *Independence Day* is bristling with several leading males, arguably the real hero of the film is Russell Casse, a single-parent, Vietnam veteran who lives in a trailer, works as a crop duster and who believes, much to the bemusement of everyone else, that he has been abducted by aliens, and who ultimately sacrifices himself to destroy an alien spacecrafts at the climax of the film. Finally, as noted above, the character played by Arnold Schwarzenegger in *End of Days* is presented at the beginning of the film as a down-on-his-luck ex-police officer whose life has fallen apart and who is contemplating suicide. Hardly, the stuff that Hollywood heroes—or, for that matter, messiahs—are typically made of![13]

Conclusions

Films, as a form of cultural expression, have always mirrored the times and the cultures in which they were produced. From the Cold War paranoia of films such as *The Invasion of the Body Snatchers* and *The War of the Worlds*, through to the nuclear Mutually Assured Destruction of *Dr Strangelove*, *WarGames*, and *When the Wind Blows*, film makers have both reflected and given voice to the cultural issues, events and neuroses of their day (O'Leary, 2000). Indeed, in many ways films such as these *cannot* be understood without reference to the context in which they were produced.

The films that I have discussed in this chapter were all released in a period of approximately nine years (1995–2004); a period of time spanning both the build-up and transition to the new calendrical millennium as well as the attacks of 9/11 and the subsequent "war on terror". They cover a period of time characterized by heightened anxiety and tensions concerning global warming and other natural disasters, "super bugs" and pandemics, as well as fears of terrorist actions, possibly involving Weapons of Mass Destruction. More broadly, from a geopolitical point of view, they cover a period of time following the fall of the Berlin Wall and the apparent victory of liberal Western democracy and a shift from a focus on a distinct, bounded enemy (the "Red Communism" of earlier films) to a series of diffuse military/political threats (such as the infamous "axis of evil" or "Islamic Radicalism"). It has also witnessed—whether as a manifestation of a Lyotardian "postmodern condition" or not—a growing cultural ambivalence about the benefits of science and technology and of experts and expertise.

These themes were all played out in various ways in the films that I have examined in this chapter. Each of them revolves either around some form of threat to the existing social order which is countered or at least mitigated against through the use of science or technology (often the technology of nuclear weapons decried in earlier films) or around attempts to restore some (often idealized) portion of that order. These threats being on the whole either natural disasters or human-made in form, rather than the outcome of, for example, nuclear hostilities between nations. Each of them valorizes human agency and self-sufficiency, showing how everyday—even apparently flawed—human beings (albeit typically North Americans) may rise to challenges and overcome great adversity. In sum, each of them is permeated with both a highly sentimentalized attitude towards the status quo and a sense of optimism towards the future and human powers. Threats may come and go, they tell us, but humans will rise to them and the everyday world will continue as normal; the apocalypse is neither now or nigh, nor is it preordained. It is, instead, just another series of problems for human ingenuity coupled with science and technology to address.

Notes

1.   During the course of writing this chapter, the sequel to *28 Days Later* (*28 Weeks Later*) and *Sunshine*, also by Danny Boyle, have been released theatrically and on DVD.

2.   For an analysis utilizing a different reading of "apocalypse" see Stone *Op. Cit*.

3.   See, for example, the literature that has been generated by the *Matrix* trilogy of films, e.g. Flannery-Dailey and Wagner, 2001; Lawrence, 2004; Baker, 2006.

4.   This is, of course, a long-standing motif in both science fiction and horror, traceable back at least to Mary Shelley's *Frankenstein* (1818). Within the genre of science fiction, the idea that science and (particularly nuclear) technology can backfire and bring with it unintended and negative consequences is found in a range of classic films, such as *Them* (1954), where atomic testing produces a species of killer ants, *The Day the Earth Caught Fire* (1961), where simultaneous nuclear bomb tests by Russia and the USA knock the earth out of its orbit towards the sun. It is also a major theme in *Godzilla (Gojira)* and its sequels (see Noriega, 1887, Napier, 1993).

5.   This shift is perhaps expressed in no better example than in *12 Monkeys*, which is based on the 1962 Chris Marker film, *La Jetée*. In Marker's film, humanity is wiped out by nuclear weapons, while in *12 Monkeys*, as we have seen, the medium of destruction has shifted to a supervirus.

6.   Quoted on the Director and Writer's commentary on the *28 Days Later* DVD.

7.   Of course, this would then entail the belief that the events described in the prophecies were then prevented from occurring by agents from the future.

8.   This draws parallels with older, Cold War-era films, which according to Broderick, were often 'highly reactionary' in nature;

> While some films have explored (albeit fleetingly) post-holocaust life as a site for ideological contestation, the cinematic renderings of long-term post-nuclear survival appear highly reactionary, and seemingly advocate reinforcing the symbolic order of the status quo via the main-

tenance of conservative social regimes of patriarchal law (and lore). In so doing, they articulate a desire for (if not celebrate) the fantasy of nuclear Armageddon as the anticipated war which will annihilate the oppressive burdens of (post)modern life and usher in the nostalgically yearned-for less complex existence of agrarian toil and social harmony through ascetic spiritual endeavours (Broderick, 1993, no pagination).

9. This 'Noah's Ark' theme is also found in *The Day the Earth Caught Fire*, although in this film the 'Ark' (if not 'New Jerusalem') is situated on another planet (see Sontag *Op. Cit.*, p. 215, Torry, 1991).

10. To give an example from another genre of film, the narrative of the film *Titanic* is as much about the tragedy of Jack Dawson and Rose DeWitt Bukater, as it is about the loss of an ocean liner.

11. Several of the films I have discussed feature the motif of the hero or heroine sacrificing themselves for others and/or in order to avert the cataclysm. In *Deep Impact*, for example, the two lead characters sacrifice themselves for others; the Messiah crew crashing their spacecraft into a large chunk of the meteor to destroy it (the first batch of warheads having split it in two) and Jenny Lerner giving up her place in the "Noah's Ark" caves for a mother and her child. Like the Messiah's Crew, Bruce Willis' character in *Armageddon* (Harry Stamper) also sacrifices himself to stay behind to manually detonate the warhead while the rest of his crew escape the meteor. Jericho Cane also, as discussed above, throws himself on St Michael's sword in order to thwart Satan in *End of Days*. Finally, at the climax of *Independence Day* the character played by Randy Quaid (Russell Casse) pilots his plane into an alien's craft beam weapon generator in order to prevent it from being fired.

12. Indeed, to return to an earlier point, it is interesting to note that in two of the films in particular (*The Day After Tomorrow* and *The Core*), the hero(es) and heroines are scientists of some form or other.

13. Indeed, Schwarzenegger's character and Willis' in *12 Monkeys* are both noteworthy for being radically different, and significantly more vulnerable from the traditional action hero roles that both of them are typically associated with. As the writer of *End of Days*, Andrew Marlowe, has noted in respect to Schwarzenegger's character;

> We always see Arnold as the action hero, larger-than-life character. I wanted to take that and bring it down more to a human level, show him a little bit more down and out, and take him on more of a character journey in the middle of an action movie (Quoted on the 'Writer and Director's Commentary' DVD feature to *End of Days*).

This point is echoed by the film's director, Peter Hyams who observes that in this role Schwarzenegger "plays probably the most vulnerable character he's even played, and the most accessible and touchable character" (*ibid.*)

Similarly, Terry Gilliam has described how part of his decision to cast Bruce Willis in *12 Monkeys* was an attempt to put "him into situations and [ask] of him things I don't think he's ever done before or that people haven't seen him do". In particular, Gilliam was interested in attempting to tone down the image that Willis had been associated with through his *Die Hard* films, and create a much more vulnerable character than audiences would, until that point, associate with him. Indeed, the finale of *12 Monkeys* was the first time that an audience would have ever seen Willis die on screen (he would subsequently do so again in Armageddon three years later). (Quoted in Lafrance, nd. See also Fulton and Pepe, 1998).

References

Geoff Baker, "Portraying the Quest for Buddhist Wisdom?: A Comparative Study of *The Matrix* and *Crouching Tiger, Hidden Dragon*". *Journal of Religion and Film*, 10.1 (2006). http://www.unomaha.edu/jrf/vol10no1/BakerQuest.htm.

Jean Bauldrillard, *The Illusion of the End* (trans. Chris Turner) (Cambridge: Polity Press, 1995).

Baylor Institute for Studies of Religion. *American Piety in the 21st Century: New Insights to the Depth and Complexity of Religion in the US* (2006) http://www.baylor.edu/content/services/document.php/33304.pdf

Mervyn Bendle, "The Apocalyptic Imagination and Popular Culture." *Journal of Religion and Popular Culture*, XI (2005) http://www.usask.ca/relst/jrpc/art11-apocalypticimagination.html

Peter L. Berger, *The Sacred Canopy: Elements of a Sociological Theory of Religion.* (New York: Anchor Books, 1990).

Paul Binski, *Medieval Death: Ritual and Representation* (New York: Cornell University Press, 1996).

David Brin, "The Postman: The Movie. An Impression by the Author of the Original Novel" (1998). http://davidbrin.com/postmanmoviearticle.html

Mick Broderick, "Heroic Apocalypse: Mad Max, Mythology and the Millennium." In Christopher Sharrett (ed.) *Crisis Cinema: The Apocalyptic Idea in Postmodern Narrative Film* (Washington, DC: Maisonneuve Press, 1993) pp. 251–72.

_____ "Surviving Armageddon: Beyond the Imagination of Disaster. *Science Fiction Studies*, 20.3 (1993) http://www.depauw.edu/sfs/backissues/61/broderick61art.htm

Steve Bruce, *God is Dead: Secularization in the West* (Oxford: Blackwell Publishing, 2002).

James M. Clark, *The Dance of Death in the Middle Ages and the Renaissance* (Glasgow: Glasgow University Publications, 1950).

Nicola Denzey, "Biblical Allusions, Biblical Illusions: Hollywood Blockbusters and Scripture." *Journal of Religion and Film,* 8.1 (2004). http://www.unomaha.edu.jrf/2004Symposium/Denzey.htm

Sarah Dunant and Roy Porter (eds). *The Age of Anxiety* (London: Virago Books, 1996).

Emile Durkheim, *The Elementary Forms of the Religious Life* (New York: Collier Books, 1961).

Matthew Etherden, "'The Day The Earth Stood Still': 1950's Sci-Fi, Religion and the Alien Messiah. *Journal of Religion and Film,* vol. 9.2 (2005). http://www.unomaha.edu/jrf/Vol9No2/EtherdenEarthStill.htm

Joyce Evans-Kasastamatis, *Celluloid Mushroom Clouds: Hollywood and the Atomic Bomb* (Jackson, TN: Westview Press, 1999).

Federal Bureau of Investigation. "Project Megiddo", in Jeffrey Kaplan (ed.) *Millennial Violence: Past Present and Future* (London: Frank Cass, 2002 [1999]), pp. 27-52.

Rita Felski, "The Invention of Everyday Life." *New Formations,* 39 (1999-2000), pp. 15–31.

Frances Flannery-Dailey, "Bruce Willis as the Messiah: Human Effort, Salvation and Apocalypticism in *Twelve Monkeys." Journal of Religion and Film* 4.1 (2000). http://www.unomaha.edu/jrf/Messiah.htm

Frances Flannery-Dailey and Rachel Wagner, R. "Wake Up! Gnosticism and Buddhism in *The Matrix." Journal of Religion and Film,* 5.2 (2001). http://www.unomaha.edu/jrf/gnostic.htm

Bruce David Forbes and Jeffrey H. Mahan (eds), *Religion and Popular Culture in America,* (Berkley, CA: University of California Press, 2005).

Francis Fukuyama, *The End of History and the Last Man.* (Harmondsworth: Penguin Books Ltd., 1993).

Keith Fulton and Louis Pepe. *The Hamster Factor, and other tales about the making of the 12 Monkeys* (included as an extra on DVD release of *12 Monkeys*), (West Hollywood, CA: Atlas Entertainment, 1998).

Crawford Gribben, "After *Left Behind*—The Paradox of Evangelical Pessimism." In Kenneth G. C. Newport and Crawford Gribben (eds), *Expecting the End: Millennialism in Social and Historical Context,* (Baylor, TX: Baylor University Press, 2006), pp. 113–30.

Anton Karl Koslovic, "Superman as Christ Figure: The American Pop Culture Movie Messiah." *Journal of Religion and Film,* 6.1 (2002). http://www.unomaha.edu/jrf/superman.htm

J. D. Lafrance, "Twelve Monkeys: Dangerous Visions" (n.d.) http://www.smart.co.uk/dreams/monkvive.htm

Henri Lefebvre, *Everyday Life in the Modern World.* (London: Allen Lane, 1971).

Robert J. Lifton, "American Apocalypse." *The Nation* (22 December 2003). http://www.thenation.com/doc/20031222/lifton

Matt Lawrence, *Like a Splinter in your Mind: The Philosophy Behind the Matrix Trilogy*. (Oxford: Blackwell Publishing, 2004).

Paul McLaren, "George Bush, Apocalypse Sometime Soon, and the American Imperium." *Cultural Studies Critical Methodologies*, 2.3 (2002). 327–33.

Neal R. McCrillis, "Atomic Anxiety in Cold War Britain: Science, Sin and Uncertainty in Nuclear Monster Films." In George Aichele, and Richard Walsh, *Screening Scripture: Intertextual Connections Between Scripture and Film,* (Harrisburg, PA: Trinity Press International, 2002), pp. 42–57.

Susan J. Napier, "Panic Sites: The Japanese Imagination of Disaster from *Godzilla* to *Akira*." *Journal of Japanese Studies*, 19.2 (1993), pp. 327–51.

National Science Board. *Science and Engineering Indicators 2004*. Two volumes. (Arlington, VA: National Science Foundation, 2004).

Chon Noriega, "Godzilla and the Japanese Nightmare: When Them! Is US." *Cinema Journal*, 27.1 (1987), pp. 63–77.

Stephen D. O'Leary, *Arguing the Apocalypse: A Theory of Millennial Rhetoric*. (Oxford: Oxford University Press, 1994).

_____ "Apocalypticism in American Popular Culture: From the Dawn of the Nuclear Age to the End of the American Century." In Stephen J. Stein (ed.) *The Encyclopaedia of Apocalypticism, Volume 3: Apocalypticism in the Modern Period and Contemporary Age* (London: Continuum, 2000), pp. 392–426.

Conrad Ostwalt, "Visions of the End: Secular Apocalypse in Recent Hollywood Film." *Journal of Religion and Film* 2.1 (1998). http://avalon.unomaha.edu/jrf/OstwaltC.htm

_____ "Armageddon at the Millennial Dawn". *Journal of Religion and Film* 4.1 (2000) http://www.unomaha.edu/jrf/armagedd.htm

_____ *Secular Steeples: Popular Culture and the Religious Imagination* (London: Trinity Press International, 2003).

Christopher Partridge, *The Re-Enchantment of the West: Volume 1. Alternative Spiritualities, Sacralization, Popular Culture and Occulture* (London: T&T Clark, 2004).

_____ *The Re-Enchantment of the West: Volume II. Alternative Spiritualities, Sacralization, Popular Culture and Occulture* (London: T&T Clark, 2005).

Lena Roos, "Age before Beauty: A Comparative Study of Martyrs in American Disaster Movies and their Medieval Predecessors." *Journal of Religion and Film*, 11.1 (2007), http://www.unomaha.edu/jrf/vol11no1/RoosMartyrs.htm

Will Self, "Introduction." In *Revelation, Authorised King James Version* (Edinburgh: Canongate, 1998), pp. vii–xiv.

Jerome F. Shapiro, *Atomic Bomb Cinema: The Apocalyptic Imagination in Film* (London: Routledge, 2002).

Susan Sontag, "The Imagination of Disaster." In Susan Sontag, *Against Interpretation and Other Essays* (Eyre and Spottiswoode: London, 1967).

Jon R. Stone, "A Fire in the Sky: 'Apocalyptic' Themes on the Silver Screen." In Eric M. Mazur and Kate McCarthy, *God in the Details: American Religion in Popular Culture* (London: Routledge, 2001), pp. 65–82.

Robert Torry, "Apocalypse Then: Benefits of the Bomb in Fifties Science Fiction Films." *Cinema Journal*, 31.1 (1991), pp. 7–21.

Hugh B. Urban, "America, Left Behind: Bush, the Neoconservatives, and Evangelical Christian Fiction." *Journal of Religion and Society*, 8 (2006) http://moses.creighton.edu/JRS/pdf/2006-2.pdf.

John Walliss, *Apocalyptic Trajectories: Millenarianism and Violence in the Contemporary World* (Bern: Peter Lang, 2004).

Richard Walsh, "On Finding a Non-American Revelation: End of Days and the Book of Revelation." In George Aichele and Richard Walsh, *Screening Scripture: Intertextual Connections Between Scripture and Film* (Harrisburg, PA: Trinity Press International, 2002), pp. 1–23.

The Wellcome Trust. *Science and the Public: A Review of Science Communication and Public Attitudes to Science In Britain* (London: The Wellcome Trust, 2000).

Allan M. Winkler, *Life Under a Cloud: American Anxiety about the Bomb,* (Champaign, IL: University of Illinois Press, 1999).

Daniel Wojcik, *The End of the World as We Know It: Faith, Fatalism, and Apocalypse in America* (New York: New York University Press, 1997).

Melanie J. Wright, *Religion and Film: An Introduction* (London: IB Tauris, 2007).

Films Cited

12 Monkeys (dir. Terry Gilliam, 1995)
28 Days Later (dir. Danny Boyle, 2002)
28 Weeks Later (dir. Danny Boyle, 2007)
Armageddon (Michael Bay, 1998)
Deep Impact (Mimi Leder, 1998)
Donnie Darko (dir. Richard Kelly, 2001)
Dr. Strangelove (Or, How I Learned to Stop Worrying and Love the Bomb) (dir. Stanley Kubrick, 1964)
End of Days (dir. Peter Hyams, 1999)
Flood (dir. Tony Mitchell, 2007)
Godzilla (dir. Irhiro Honda, 1954)
Independence Day (Roland Emmerich, 1996)
Invasion of the Body Snatchers (dir. Don Siegel, 1956)
La Jetée (dir. Chris Marker, 1962)
Left Behind: The Movie (dir. Vic Sarin, 2000)
On the Beach (dir. Stanley Kramer, 1959)
Right at the Door (dir. Chris Gorak, 2006)

Sunshine (dir. Danny Boyle, 2007)
Superman (dir. Richard Donner, 1978)
The Core (dir. Jon Amiel, 2003)
The Day after Tomorrow (dir. Roland Emmerich, 2004)
The Day the Earth Caught Fire (dir. Val Guest, 1961)
The Day the Earth Stood Still (dir. Robert Wise, 1951)
The Day the World Ended (dir. Roger Corman, 1956)
Them! (dir. Gordon Douglas, 1954)
The Postman (dir. Kevin Costner, 1997)
The War of the Worlds (dir. Bryon Haskin, 1953)
Threads (dir. Mick Jackson, 1985)
Tribulation Force (dir. Bill Corcoran, 2002)
WarGames (dir. John Badham, 1983)
Waterworld (dir. Kevin Reynolds, 1995)
When the Wind Blows (dir. Jimmy T. Murakami, 1987)
World at War (dir. Craig R. Baxley, 2005)

"The Days are Numbered"
The Romance of Death, Doom, and Deferral in Contemporary Apocalypse Films

Lee Quinby

Introduction

The concept of an end time has been a source of narrative inspiration for millennia. Indeed, tracing the range of ways to tell stories about the beginning as well as the end of time across time and culture is one way to pay tribute to the grand sweep of human imagination. Typically, stories of temporal endings carry a sense of threat. Even when, as in the ancient Egyptian world, there was no concept of a final end, but rather recurrent cycles of destruction and regeneration, the ends of days, months and decades were regarded as particularly vulnerable to disruption by demons (Cohn, 1993: 25). For most of human history, various civilizations have envisioned plural and overlapping times rather than a singular and linear time. It is only in the past two millennia that the concept of a final end-time, the Apocalypse, has taken hold, and even then primarily within a specifically Judeo-Christian framework (Weber, 1999). In this version, the end is not only final, it is decidedly deadly, an ultimate destruction of the earth and most of its inhabitants.

Although certain themes remain constant despite this shift from recurrent ends to a final end—for example oppositions between forces of order and chaos and good and evil—in the Judeo-Christian Apocalypse emphasis is placed on a monotheistic God as the ultimate cause of the final destruction, an outcome of unadulterated good over pure evil, and an eternal reward granted to a predetermined chosen group. The patriarchal nature of this final end-time version is unambiguous: God's wrath is hypermasculine in its militaristic, blood-soaked thirst for revenge, and it is only men—the spirit-infatuated faithful, "undefiled" by women—who are explicitly rewarded with a heavenly Kingdom on earth (Rev 14:4; Quinby, 1994: xv–xxii).

In Western cultures, this has been the predominant mode over most of the past two millennia. In this chapter, I refer to this patriarchal dimension as the *perennial* feature of apocalyptic representation. I also want to argue, however, that over the past two decades the circumstances of an increasingly globalized world have had a notable impact on apocalyptic belief. The accelerated interaction between cultures with clashing religious and political beliefs, dramatic changes in the lives and perceived value of women, the rapid spread of virulent strains of new viruses, and the promises and problems of technological prowess have affected traditional western apocalypse as it is manifest through Anglo-American popular culture. I refer to these as the *particular* in order to stress their distinct influence in reshaping traditional apocalypse. As a major vehicle of current ideologies, contemporary apocalyptic films resonate with this combination of the perennial and the particular to shape a romance of death, doom, and deferral. In short, whereas death and doom are integral to the perennial, the emphasis on deferral emerges out of the particular.

In this essay, I will focus primarily on three twenty-first-century films from the USA and the UK in order to point out some of the reconfigurations within popular culture apocalypse that result from this fusion of the perennial and the particular: *Apocalypto*, which is set in the past, just prior to the Spanish conquest of the Mayan civilisation; *28 Days Later*, which takes place in the present in England; and *Children of Men*, which comes to pass, again in England, twenty years hence. In the United States, where apocalyptic belief took early and deep root, the perennial themes of apocalypse have been notably nationalistic, with Hollywood cinema typically reflecting stark gender and race divisions, militarism, and absolutistic morality. While contemporary popular culture retains many of these perennial themes, it also gives currency to contradictory views that not only challenge traditional apocalypse as a necessary destruction but also veer towards humanity rather than divinity as its cause. In the twenty-first-century apocalyptic films upon which I focus, these conflicting trends have been crystallized through such cultural particulars as the 9/11 attack, losses in credibility for the United States as a moral leader because of the war on Iraq and uses of torture, and growing doubts about technological control, especially regarding environmental and human health.

As to be expected, given the patriarchal nature of apocalyptic belief, many of the currents of thought in the three films to be explored here revolve around representations regarding gender, thus revealing prevalent and often inconsistent attitudes over changed and still changing roles and expectations for men and women. In these films, themes of lost fertility, for both humanity and the earth, the control of women's sexuality and reproduction, and the blurring of masculinity and femininity abound as prime ways of expressing destruction, chaos, doom—and sometimes hope.

I refer to this portrayal as romance in order to highlight the gender/genre means through which masculine chivalry and feminine purity are revamped in these films.[1] As a genre, the literary romance emerged in the vernacular, that is, the popular culture of the medieval period. Traditional romance follows the quest of a heroic knight who fights forces of evil embodied in quasi-supernatural form, as with a dragon, and culminates in the hero's rescue of a fair maiden. What I am suggesting here is a two-fold dynamic: apocalyptic themes inspired the romance and continue to do so, and the romance has increasingly informed the way popular culture depicts apocalypse. The way this works in the post-apocalyptic films of interest here involves a shift in traditional gender roles: the masculine warrior of traditional romance retains his heroic stature but is nonetheless reduced in power while traditional notions of feminine purity are partially displaced by a theme of female fertility understood as bravery. In other words, the *perennial* hierarchy of male dominance is undermined by a *particular* elevation of female agency. As I will demonstrate through individual readings of the three films, this refiguring of romance tends to lead to the deferral of a final end. That deferral, in turn, both demands and enables a new ethical vision to replace that which led to the destruction the survivors have managed to endure. Together these films suggest that a post-apocalyptic vision in which a more egalitarian form of romance heroism is activated may be one of the key ways to be simultaneously critical of, and hopeful in, our time—regardless of what end of the political spectrum the vision is on.

A Different Romance

Apocalypse, of course, has long been a feature of mainstream and independent film-making. At the level of entertainment alone, scenes

of larger-than-life destruction get our adrenalin going. Battles of cosmic proportion, figures of an anti-Christ versus a Messiah, and the
final overcoming of evil by good have underwritten genres ranging
from wars to westerns and from alien invasions to asteroid impacts
(Mertens, 2003). In short, apocalyptic drama enables cinematic spectacle. One of the issues from a feminist perspective, or any perspective attuned to issues of social justice, for that matter, is how often
this form of spectacle reproduces the rigidly hierarchical gender
oppositions integral to the Book of Revelation, the paradigmatic
narrative that continues to underwrite apocalyptic inspired cultural
production.

In its simplest form, and regardless of whether one reads it as the
literal word of God or in literary critical terms, the Book of Revelation, is a story of revenge and rescue. If made as a film, the Netflix
plot summary might go something like this:

> A man named John has an elaborate vision of the complete destruction
> of the world, which deserves to be crushed because Satan's evil has
> endured in it. In his prophetic vision, tribulations like plagues, boils,
> rivers of blood and famine abound. A number of evil figures appear,
> including the reviled Whore of Babylon and the anti-Christ who wears
> the mark of the beast, the number 666, and gains control of the earth.
> Anti-Christ and his forces must be destroyed. Rightful revenge is thus
> waged against them and the Virginal Woman Clothed with the Sun is
> rescued. She gives birth to the Messiah. The final battle of Armaged-
> don is fought and won by the Messianic Warrior who rides a white
> horse. A millennium of harmony follows. Then a resurrection of the
> dead and the final judgement occur, with the majority of people being
> sent to eternal agony. The final rescue is for the chosen, who are
> rewarded by being ushered into the "New Jerusalem", a heaven on
> earth, where death and illness are forever banished.

Actually, film versions that attempt to adhere faithfully to the mar-
vellous imagery and intricate twists and turns of the Book of Revelation do not fare well on the screen. Graphic portrayals of Antichrist
come off as cheesy and the text's plot incoherence and reliance on
metaphysics are far too confusing for cinematic rendering. But trans-
lating the book's basic premise of revenge and rescue and wildly
imaginative images of hybrid creatures into a traditional romance
genre in which a hero wrestles with strange creatures, defeats the
enemy, rescues the lady in distress, and achieves harmony has helped
keep audiences riveted over many centuries—and this is equally

true over the last century in the case of film. Indeed, the captivating drama inherent in the apocalyptic script is part of the reason that male dominance and female subordination have remained so perennial a problem. Even within this brief rendition, the masculine versus feminine divide becomes clear. With female sexuality and authority depicted as a threat to the social order and a spiritualized form of masculinity represented as the path to salvation, apocalyptic masculinity has been made compelling (Quinby, 1999: Ch. 5–6).

Yet apocalyptic urgency and imagery have also been deployed in the name of critique of precisely this mode of dominant and dominating masculinity. Within film history, during the last half of the twentieth century when Cold War themes were accentuated and with nuclear weapons cast as the likely means of apocalyptic destruction, films such as *On the Beach*, *Dr Strangelove*, and the *Planet of the Apes* series, provided cautionary tales in which the ultimate catastrophe is shown to be the cost of Superpower rivalry. The three contemporary films I have singled out for discussion may be seen within this legacy of critique. Yet, with the Cold War now declared over, even as the proliferation of nuclear weaponry continues apace, and with terrorism, global climate change, technological accident and viral pandemic constituting the most publicly expressed fears of the new century, these films register a fascinating blend of the traditional gender roles of romance and a critique of those roles. Whether the romance turns tragic or ironic or even comic seems largely to depend on how the film regards traditional gender relations and the changes they are undergoing. In other words, gender transformation is not necessarily cast as the key issue at hand, but functions, rather, as a vehicle for representing levels of chaos and order.

To extend further the argument about these films exhibiting a fusion between the perennial and the particular, it is noteworthy that all three of the films of concern here depict a post-apocalyptic world in which the main action occurs after an onslaught of destruction. This shift in focus goes against the grain of traditional apocalypse that follows the Book of Revelation. In an insightful chapter on "Post-Apocalyptic Dystopias," John W. Mertens (2003, 163, 191) analyses the tendency to see "the apocalypse as the result of human choice and technology, considered at its broadest level, and the result of human power and human nature run amok" as a turn to "No-God that has led us into a world of despair". While Mertens is right in connecting the post-apocalyptic trend in film to the absence of the divine as integral to the plot of such films, I do not see such films as leading irrevocably towards despair. Indeed, my contention is that this shift marks a greater acceptance of human-oriented ethical responsibility and that these films warn against the kind of apocalyptic masculinity that has used divine authority to justify aggressive and violent conquest.

From another angle of analysis of contemporary popular culture, Mervyn F. Bendle (2005: 2) argues that there has been a "shift back toward traditional ideals and beliefs about the special role and destiny of the US associated with the long-standing civil religion underpinning American civilization". Rather than a world of despair, Bendle sees the "dark vision" that has taken over American popular culture as stemming from a re-accentuation of pre-millennialism, citing the huge popularity of the *Left Behind* series as a prime example. He calls this a shift from a Promethean view to an Augustinian one, in which filmic and literary depictions move from belief in "human self-determination to an Augustinian conviction of human sinfulness and weakness" (*ibid.*, 15). Although there is no doubt a swelling of fervent pre-millennialism throughout the USA, as Bendle says, in my view his argument flattens out the more variegated landscape of popular culture. In fact, what I see with apocalyptic films that are cast in the romance mode—whether they are post-apocalyptic or pre-apocalyptic cautionary tales about a coming destruction—is an assertion of the value of human agency that is not consonant with the pre-millennialist insistence on predetermination.

Of the three apocalyptic films I have cited as representing this discernible shift, Mel Gibson's *Apocalypto* strikes me as the most internally conflicted in its fusion of the perennial and the particular. This is not an aesthetic judgement so much as a philosophical one. Indeed, as far as entertainment is concerned, I agree with Anthony Lane, who, writing for the *New Yorker*, states that Gibson has "learned how to tell a tale, and to raise a pulse in the telling" (Lane, 2006: 100). Part of what he has learned is how to draw on powerful themes and scenes from previous blockbuster films, especially ones that he himself starred in, such as the *Mad Max* series made between 1979 and 1985. As with those ground-breaking films which depict human beings destroying one another with no implication of demonic intervention, *Apocalypto* presents a world in which human tyranny reigns supreme.

Although set in a specific time and localized places—a jungle village and Mayan city just before the Spanish arrive—*Apocalypto* has
a mythic quality about it that accentuates its depictions of human
nature as a psychological dramatization of the cosmic struggle between good versus evil.[2] For the most part, according to the portrayal in the film, innate violence and cruelty win out. There is also,
however, a suggestion that the degree of brutality that human beings
are willing to inflict on one another largely depends on how large
and complex a given society is, the idea being that societal size matters to the extent that it alienates human beings from nature. Furthermore, cruelty can be overcome, as evidenced by the gentle and
kind ways of many of the female characters and some of the males.
Over the course of the film, the action moves quickly from light-
hearted antics among the men of a relatively harmonious tribal group
to the full-blown atrocities of the Mayan civilization. In the case of
the tribe, led by Flint Sky (Morris Birdyellowhead), the wise and noble
father of the heroic protagonist Jaguar Paw (Rudy Youngblood), violence is played out in the hunt and only playfully administered to
each other in taunts about sexual potency to one of the fellow tribesmen. In other words, this small group is able to live in relative accord
with each other and nature by limiting the instinct to kill to non-
human animals like the tapir whose entrapment and slaughter sets
the stage for the human ravaging that is to come.

This difference between small group tranquillity and large group
viciousness is reinforced when another tribal group passes through
the jungle, fleeing from the raiders who have ravaged their village.
The leaders of the two tribes exchange signs of acknowledgement of
each group's value as a group and keep antagonism at bay. Beware
of fear, Flint Sky warns his son, and they return to their village for the
night. It may be that Flint Sky is suggesting that fear is one of the
things that leads to unwarranted violence, making one more likely to
attack in advance and without sufficient cause. But it is primarily
seen as that which weakens one's nobility. In any case, the tribe
soon has cause enough to be fearful of the sadistic raiders led by
Zero Wolf (Raoul Trujillo) who descend upon them in the night,
massacring many and capturing the rest. It should be noted at
this point, that eventually Jaguar Paw overcomes his fear and is
thereby enabled to be reborn into a fearsome warrior who exacts
revenge on his enemy—but not before he is brought to the edge of
destruction.

Once the peacefulness of the tribal community is broken by the initial apocalyptic attack, the villagers enslaved, and Flint Sky's throat cut, the film narrative follows the path of Jaguar Paw becoming a hero. In keeping with the traditional romance genre, as hero he must not only defeat the enemy, he must also preserve the dignity and life of a lady in distress, which he does over the course of the film. Significantly this is precisely where tradition also waivers in favour of current concerns. Rather than the virginal woman who is the customary one to be rescued, here we have Jaguar Paw's near-term pregnant wife, Seven (Dalia Hernandez), who is also mother to their son Turtles Run. Her extended belly becomes a central icon in the film, the literally embodied promise of a "new beginning", a phrase used explicitly several times. While her name as a sacred number and her endangered pregnancy align her with the perennial apocalyptic image of the Woman Clothed With the Sun (Rev. 12: 1-2), the camera eye on her belly also focuses attention to several issues of our day, ranging from anti-abortion sentiment to environmentally endangered human fertility. In this instance, then, current particulars of family value concerns trump the perennial focus on virginal purity. This is a plausible shift in focus for a film that is not about the birth of a messiah anyway, and more about literal and symbolic rebirth over and against the threat of a civilization undermined from within by its own corruptions.

That writer/director Gibson is concerned with internal moral decay is made clear at the opening of the film with his use of a quote from Will Durant: "A great civilization is not conquered from without until it has destroyed itself from within." In interviews, he has commented on the way the film is meant to indicate the common tendencies of civilization in decline. In his words, "The precursors to a civilization that's going under are the same, time and time again." He has further indicated that the specific target of nation in decline in this case is the United States, with explicit mention of the war on Iraq as he pointedly went on to ask, "What's human sacrifice if not sending guys off to Iraq for no reason?" (Gibson, 2006).

In addition to the ruthless human sacrifices that the Mayan raiders are about to inflict on their captives, a number of powerful scenes in the film encapsulate the debauchery of their civilization. Foremost among these is a mesmerizing segment in which a small, diseased girl appears out of a field of lesion-afflicted corpses left to rot in the sun. As one of the raiders shoves her away with a stick, she solemnly delivers this haunting prophecy: "You fear me. So you should. All you who are vile. Would you like to know how you will die? The sacred time is here. Beware the blackness of the day. Beware the man who brings the jaguar. Behold him reborn from mud and earth. Or the one he takes you to will cancel the sky and scratch out the earth. Scratch you out and end your world. He is with you now." In time, her words indeed come to pass.

As the tribal slaves enter the city, sight upon sight reinforces the blend of the perennial and the particular in the unfolding of this post-apocalyptic romance. Eerie human bodies create a feeling of the supernatural, as their phantom-like whiteness fills the screen. These are the workers who produce plaster for the magnificent city, covered in white dust that recalls the ashes of survivors of 9/11 fleeing from the collapsing Twin Towers. The pall that this whiteness casts across the people and the landscape registers them and the city as devoid of life, removed from nature. Other figures emerge fleetingly to tell the story of corruption: a market place in which the women are to be sold; alongside them, jezebels and whores of Babylon display their sexuality while their fattened sons enjoy the bloody sacrifice under way in which hearts are cut out of living men and their heads cut off and thrown down the pyramid steps.

Sacrifice gone wrong—not the messianic gift of Christianity, but the false worship of a corrupt civilization—underwrites the revenge and rescue theme of the film. Intended to appease the Mayan god whose displeasure is addressed by the priest, this is a sacrifice, as Gibson points out about Iraq, where the reasons cited for it are clearly wrong from the audience's perspective. As the men about to die look on, the priest declares: "The land thirsts. A great plague infests the crops. The scourge of sickness afflicts us...They say this strife has made us weak. That we have become empty. They say that we rot. Great people of the banner of the sun, I say we are strong! We are a people of destiny. Destined to be the masters of time. Destined to be nearest to the gods." The irony, of course, is that the fulfilment of the girl's prophecy about their actual destiny to be conquered by those who will "scratch you out and end your world" hovers over the scene. In the words of one of the two tag lines for the film: "No one can outrun their destiny."

Jaguar Paw's moment of destiny is marked by the solar eclipse that occurs just as his heart is about to be torn from his chest. Taken as a sign that the god is satiated with blood, the priest declares the end of the sacrifices for that day and he and the other surviving tribesmen are led off to a gladiator-style set of games. Yet again, *his* destiny is to elude death at the hands of these enemies. In the process he kills his counter-part, the son of Zero Wolf. He narrowly escapes, only to be set upon by the aggrieved father who now seeks personal revenge. During this high-throttle action segment, Jaguar Paw survives a leap over a waterfall, and kills several of the raider enemies, including Zero Wolf. But the key symbolic scene occurs when he submerges into a deep pool of mud, finally to arise, eyes resolutely staring out, and body slickly blackened. Emergent from this primal slime, he has been reborn as the creature for which he is named and become a fearless fighter for the good.

In the meanwhile, the plight of his wife and son has reached crisis. Trapped in the deep well where Jaguar Paw had helped them hide, helpless to get out because their rope was cut by one of the enemy, they now face rising flood waters. Seven has managed, literally, to keep their heads above water as the well fills up. Standing with her son perched on her shoulders, she valiantly gives birth to the new child, with the camera catching the final push that expels him from her womb. Thus the scene of the father's symbolic rebirth is paralleled by the birth of his son and the promise of their lineage continuing. Seven's fertility and courage become synonymous with one another. She may still be a lady in distress but she also emerges a co-saviour.

That new generations might continue occurs only because Jaguar Paw is able to escape the last two surviving raiders as all three of them run out of the rain forest and onto the beach just as three Spanish ships arrive on the shore and Christian missionaries step out. The enemies are so mesmerised by the sight of the ships that Jaguar Paw is able to slip away, rescue his wife and sons, and lead the three of them back into the dense growth as he utters the final words of the film: "We should go to the forest to seek a new beginning".

I have called *Apocalypto* a romance, but at this point I would qualify my designation by calling it a tragic romance, in short, a genre at odds with itself. To put it another way, the film is both pre-apocalyptic and post-apocalyptic. This doubled effect of pre-and post-apocalyptic action is part of what gives the film its contradictory set of messages. From the perspective of Jaguar Paw's way of life having come to an end, the bulk of the film is post-apocalyptic, taking place after the destructive event of his tribe's obliteration. It is also, however, a pre-apocalyptic film in the sense that viewers are well aware that the Mayan civilization as a whole is about to be destroyed by Spanish invaders. As a post-apocalyptic messianic figure, his acts of bravery are redemptive, but only in terms of his own life and the safety of his family. Even though his survival is thus hailed, a sense of doom hovers over his future. The impending destruction of the Mayan way of life at the hands of the Spanish conquerors has been fore grounded in the prophecy of the girl. That this is a deserved apocalypse is part of the perennial logic of the film that tells the story from the perspective of the heroism of the raiders' oppressed victims.

But where do we, as viewers, go from here? Are the Spanish missionaries to be deemed of equal brutality, as history informs us? Or are they to be regarded as valiant saviours who will bring Christian truth to the Americas? The latter is in keeping with what is known about Mel Gibson's Catholicism; the Mayan destruction may, in his view, be justified by how internally corrupt the Mayan civilization already is. As his use of the Durant quote indicates, were they not so utterly destroyed from within, they would not be so readily conquered from without. Given that impending devastation, what kind of new beginning is really possible for Jaguar Paw and his family now that the rest of their tribe has been decimated? How much hope does their deferral of death offer in light of the plight of their descendants today? Their re-entry into the forest symbolizes a new Adam and Eve, but that also suggests the two sons as a potential Cain and Abel, hence starting the cycle of death and destruction all over again.

It seems that Gibson's deep pessimism about recurrent decline contradicts his deep admiration for individual courage and fortitude so powerful that it can overcome destiny. While his use of traditional apocalyptic images extends the dramatic reach of his story, his evocation of heroic action in the face of the apocalypse goes against the insistence on a predetermined fate consonant with traditional apocalyptic belief. The second tag line of the film seems to bespeak this confusion of themes: "When the end comes, not everyone is ready to go". There is, in this, a possibility that one can "outrun their destiny" after all. My sense is that, on one hand, Gibson presents us with a film meant to serve as doomsday prophecy, which aligns him with the girl who reveals that the end is irrevocable. On the other hand, however, he gives us a film that promises hope for a new beginning and a way of being in harmony with nature. The prophecy of fateful tragedy and the inspiration of heroic overcoming don't quite mesh.

This coupling of apocalyptic doom and the deferral of ultimate death occurs in the other two films as well. In my view, *28 Days Later* and *Children of Men* achieve this double movement more coherently than does *Apocalypto*, in large part because, despite their use of perennial themes of apocalypse, they relinquish pre-determination as a given. Their use of the romance genre to evoke emphasis on human agency, even against odds of survival due to particular contemporary perils, is thus less contradictory. It is also significant that, in both films, the shift away from the perennially prede-termined is marked by portrayals of fluid gender identity and inclusive race relations. In each case, the romantic male hero is white and initially ineffectual as a warrior whereas the heroine is a woman of colour who, as not conventionally feminine, is heroically stalwart and a model for his becoming so himself.

28 Days Later places its romance of death, doom and deferral in the present day and draws on science fiction and horror genres to provide the momentum for its plot of destruction and survival against odds. As the tag line of the film puts it, "the days are numbered", evoking a sense of dread that deftly encapsulates a prevalent fear about current threats to contemporary life. While anticipation of a divinely-caused imminent end is a perennial theme in apocalypse, in this case, the threat takes a particular and human-caused form: the rapid spread of a deadly virus inadvertently unleashed on the population of England. Reverberating with dread of current epidem-ics, including such headline blasters as Ebola virus, Mad Cow Disease and Avian Flu, and resonant with older episodes of the bubonic plague and influenza, this one provides a novel slant. It is a blood-borne virus that infects one with rage, turning a human being into a ferociously biting zombie who, then boiling with rage, ferally attacks anyone in the vicinity. The viral fury stops at no one, not even one's own child, lover, parent or friend.

The manner in which the rage virus is loosed also picks up on a particular anxiety of contemporary culture, namely, scientific experi-mentation gone awry. Opening shots of the film present a confronta-tion between animal rights activists and scientists who have infected chimpanzees with the rage virus as part of their research. The camera eye brings viewers into the Cambridge Primate Research Centre, filled with caged chimps looking plaintively out from glass and steel enclosures. Panning past a series of television screens show-ing human-on-human violence, we see a chimpanzee strapped to a cot, hooked up with various monitors to record his or her reactions to the scenes of atrocity. Several activists enter the lab, and despite frantic warnings by the technician on duty, they release the imprisoned chimpanzees. A frenzy of chimpanzee-on-human violence then ensues, with the infected chimp leaping on a female activist. In moments, her eyes reddened with rage, she begins to projectile vomit blood. The screen darkens and then opens again to announce that it is 28 days later.

The threat is hardly over, however, although it has run a devastating course throughout England. The film thus focuses on the time following the bulk of destruction to the nation's population, to show how life might be played out and played on beyond apocalypse. Viewers are brought into this realization through the perception of the protagonist, Jim (Cillian Murphy), a survivor of the deadly assaults only by chance. An injured bicycle courier, he has been in a coma for the duration of the viral apocalypse. Introduced to viewers through a close-up of his suddenly opened eye, bright and clear, an inverse shot of the rage-filled eyes of the woman who has unleashed the virus on the human population. Jim's naked body also parallels the chimp of the opening scene. In a Christ-like pose, his starkly white and enfeebled body is distended not on a crucifix, but rather a hospital bed, with arms outstretched and affixed to tubes connecting him to vital fluids and monitors that trace his life signs.

Unaware of the threat at large, still dazed, and finding himself alone in the deserted medical facility, he dons hospital garb and makes his way into a deserted London. There, newspaper headlines blare enigmatic messages about evacuation efforts, closed-off borders and military orders declaring "shoot to kill". Even to a formerly comatose observer—and to contemporary viewers who have increasingly experienced a routinization of population control—this kind of headline is readily understood: fears of a plague like menace have materialized, widespread panic has ensued, and civilians have become prisoners in a war zone. Seeking refuge in a church, Jim comes upon a scene of horror: hundreds of blood-smeared corpses strewn across the floor. A priest comes towards him—but to represent threat, not salvation. An infected, he lopes at Jim, whose instinct for survival takes over. Knocking the priest down, he escapes the church but is pursued by several more carriers of the deadly virus, finally to be rescued by two more survivors, Selena (Naomie Harris) and Mark (Noah Huntley), who fire bomb the infected in scenes that call to mind photographic images of the burning bodies in motion of Hiroshima or napalmed victims of the Vietnam War.

Like the visual inversions of the opening shots, the next several scenes follow a dynamic that reverses the journey of the romantic hero, which typically follows his departure towards the unknown, slaying of a monster, and return home, as Jaguar Paw did in *Apocalypto*. In this case, the journey begins with Jim's return home, is followed by *his* rescue by a "maiden", and concludes with their departure to the unknown. Plot-wise, this unfolds because, despite Selena and Mark's explanation of what has happened and their conviction that his parents are no doubt already dead or infected, Jim insists on going home to find them. The three set out, only to discover that his parents have managed to kill themselves in time to avoid the virus. The couple lie together in conjugal embrace upon their bed, with Jim now witness to a primal scene of parental demise rather than conception, which symbolically sets up his ineffectuality as heroic warrior. In the next scene, an infected Mark attacks Jim and it is Selena who comes to his rescue by slaying her ferociously rabid friend.

From this point forward, the two of them are the hero and heroine of a post-apocalyptic romance—but which one functions as hero and which as heroine shifts several times along the way. Further complicating the traditional romance formula, they soon join forces with Frank (Brendan Gleeson) and his daughter Hannah (Meghan Burns), all four in search of a safe haven from the virus. The next stage of their journey begins because Frank has heard radio broadcasts from soldiers who proclaim they have the "answer to infection". Together in Frank's car, their exodus juxtaposes scenes of urban horror as they leave London and momentary pastoral harmony as they make their way towards Manchester. So too, there is a juxtaposition of Selena and Jim's opposing ethical perspectives. Selena declares herself willing, as she has amply demonstrated, to kill anyone who threatens her, "in a heartbeat". Jim, by contrast, expresses his willingness to help others even at risk to himself. Selena's position is actually less stark than her insistence, since she has already come to Jim's rescue, which involved personal risk, and she is soon seen as valiantly protective of Hannah, who loses her father to the infection, making the three of them a blended family. In other words, Jim's empathy needs to be balanced by more willingness to save himself in order for him to become more heroic, and Selena's fierce individualism needs more empathy for her to become more human.

As with *Apocalypto*, a central feature of threat and hope in *28 Days Later* focuses on women's capacity to reproduce the species. Once the new "family" reaches the military outpost that has been established by nine soldiers under the command of Major Henry West (Christopher Eccleston), this conflict becomes paramount. Initially it seems that the soldiers will aid them, but soon it becomes clear that these men are themselves a threat. The beauty and order of their seized estate, turned fortress, becomes increasingly ominous as Major West explains to Jim his desire to "start again". Escorting him though the kitchen, we see the male cook adorned in a pink apron, with West describing the kitchen as "the belly of the house, the hearth, the first step toward civilisation". In blatant reinforcement of this fascist sense of so-called civilization, he next shows Jim the household "pet", an infected black man named Mailer, chained like a dog to a post. Like the chimp at the outset, this man is the object of cruel study for the sake of a cure; West wants to see how long he will live with the virus if starved to death.

It is soon apparent that Selena and Hannah are to be forced into sexual slavery and breeding by the soldiers. Or, as West puts it, he has "promised them women" because "women mean a future". It is the threat of their rape that propels Jim towards rebirth as masculine warrior. But first he is cast yet again as inept. Attempting to come to Hannah and Selena's aid against sexually menacing soldiers, he is knocked to the ground and put under guard. He is then taken out to be executed. Like Jaguar Paw, he manages to escape just at the edge of death, and—quite improbably, given his previous physical weakness—races through the forest, breaks into the house, and releases Mailer, the chained up infected, killing several soldiers along the way in order to rescue Hannah and Selena, who are being forced to put on seductive dresses for their sexual subjugation.

Thus traditional gender roles are momentarily reinserted. Jim has become a full-fledged warrior and Selena the maiden in need of rescue. Jim's necessary brutality is signified by a return to eye imagery. The reddened eyes of the rage virus are supplanted by his methodical and brutal gouging out of a soldier's eyes with his thumbs thrust deep into the sockets. This reinforces the shot of his wide-opened bright eye upon coming out of the coma. His vision is clear—it is necessary for him to accept his role as destroyer of the enemy.

Initially his bloody act leads Selena to think he has become infected—but, contrary to her earlier insistence to kill him if this should occur, she cannot bring herself to do it. This shift in her ethical vision and his assurance that he is uninfected has an aphrodisiac effect, and Selena and Jim passionately embrace for the first time in the film. A split second of comic relief follows: Hannah comes in, thinks an infected Jim is biting Selena, and knocks him back to save her friend.

Hence the return to traditional gender roles is short-lived. The three run to a car to escape, but Major West is hiding in the back seat and shoots Jim in the side, giving him a Christ-like wound, and rendering him dependent on Selena once again. Hannah, moreover, emerges as newly valiant by taking over the wheel and ramming the car through the gates. A reversal of race accompanies the gender-reversal in which the women are the heroes. Mailer attacks Major West just after he has shot Jim, dragging him from the car and beating him to death. The final shot we see of the estate turned fortress is of Mailer standing in the threshold, sole proprietor of the landed manor.

Another cut: another 28 days later. The film circles back to the hospital where we have first seen Jim, but this time what jumps out is a frenetic and bloody scene, with Selena and Hannah desperately attempting to save his life as his wounded side bleeds profusely. Again, Jim re-wakens and viewers realize that he is dreaming about how he was saved, and is again slowly waking up, this time in a quaint cottage bedroom, light gently spilling in through the window behind his bed. Selena is another room, contentedly sewing. Hannah is outside, in a beautiful rolling hill landscape. The idyll imagery is provisionally broken with images of a few infected still slowly dying—but their location is someplace else. Hannah runs into the cottage, announcing "It's coming!" and all three rush out to spread a huge billowing white cloth. As the sound of an aircraft grows closer, the camera eye provides an aerial shot of the new family standing on the last letter of their homemade message, HELLO. Selena looks back, smiling at the others as she asks: "Do you think they saw us this time?" The final words of the film are delivered from within the jet, but in Finnish. Thus the message remains ambiguous for most viewers at the time (an internet discussion provides a translation, "Would you send a helicopter?").[3] Because the words are not English, viewers recognize that earlier hints about the virus being contained to England must be true; other nations have avoided it and the quaran-

tine appears to be coming to an end. As in *Apocalypto*, an outside
force has entered the post-apocalyptic world to suggest an imminent
transformation in the life the protagonists have forged. Jim looks to
the horizon.

The final scene of *28 Days Later* also resembles the final moment
of *Apocalypto* in terms of the family unit as the sign of hope for
continuing life against ongoing threat. Yet the differences between
what comprises that family are at least as significant. Whereas Gibson's
film reveres the "natural" nuclear family, Boyle's film gives homage
to a bricolage family unit. In *Apocalypto*, Jaguar Paw remains heroic
in terms of traditional gender expectations. Seven has shown herself
to be brave, but her courage is marshalled on behalf of her children.
In *28 Days Later*, what has been achieved is a blending of gender
roles for each of the three remaining characters. Sexual relations are
not really alluded to and thus remain indefinite. Race difference goes
unspoken and appears irrelevant. What is most at stake is that each
one of the three survivors has achieved a clearer, more balanced
ethical vision in terms of individual and collective well-being, manifest by egalitarian relations. In this reordering of the traditional romance motif, what counts is an ethics of equality, regardless of gender
and race. Whether it will be achieved remains unresolved. While
there is, therefore, a questionable utopian dream emerging implau-
sibly from the apocalyptic nightmare, no resolution occurs. What the
film suggests is a better way to live is clear enough, but such an ethical orientation would not thwart viral apocalypse. More coherently,
irresolution reigns.[4]

Aspiration for a new ethical vision coupled with irresolution concludes *Children of Men* as well. Of the three films, it provides the
clearest social critique and presents the most insightful perspective
on how a society slides into chaos. Furthermore, its blend of apocalyptic imagery and elements of romance is the most coherent. Director Alfonso Cuaron achieves this more even-handed treatment
by placing an ironic mantle over the shoulders of the romance genre.
Ironic romance should be distinguished from both ironic apocalypse
and traditional romance. In regard to the first distinction, ironic apocalypse portrays an already post-apocalyptic world in which nothing
can be done. The irony comes from knowing this and yet having to
endure it. Bleakness overrides the terrain, with apathy the only sane
response (Quinby 1994: xvi). Traditional romance, as I have already
indicated, depicts heroes whose actions of bravery are beyond usual

human ability and which culminate in revenge against the enemy and rescue of an endangered heroine. When irony is added to the mix, the heroics bend towards pessimism and can at times veer into depicting the hero as an absurd figure who nonetheless strives to achieve his quest. The ineffectuality of Jim in *28 Days Later* draws on irony in this way, but then erratically shifts back into customary heroics at various points. With *Children of Men*, the irony remains consistent, startling, and worthy of deeper reflection about how to live ethically within travail.

The film turns a dystopian screw to affix a scene just familiar enough to contemporary western society to suggest that it can indeed happen here. Taking place in 2027, it opens in a London coffee shop where the protagonist Theo Faron (Clive Owen) stands in line as a television announcer reports that the world's youngest member has just been killed in a brutal stabbing by a disgruntled autograph seeker, who was then himself beaten to death by a furious mob. Thus celebrity culture goes on even though human generation does not, and savagery is endemic to both situations. We are further informed that the victim, "Baby Diego," was 18 years, 4 months, 20 days, 16 hours and 8 minutes old. As with the tag line of *28 Days Later*, the days are numbered, and the widespread desperation resulting from this unexplained loss of human fertility is soon reinforced by a bomb that explodes on the street, nearly killing Theo. Here apocalypse is cast as slow decline, punctuated by everyday acts of post-apocalyptic brutality.

The bomb attack is said to be the work of "The Fishes", a radical group whose mission is to combat governmental oppression of refugees who have poured into Great Britain precisely because, as the governmental media declares, "The world has collapsed. Only Britain soldiers on." Despite the Christian allusion, The Fishes hardly hold to turning the other cheek. The bomb may indeed be theirs, and viewers are soon made aware that the goals of some of the group's members are as ruthless and authoritarian as the British government. The leader of the group, it turns out, is Theo's ex-wife, Julian (Julianne Moore), whose efforts do seem to be more idealistic, since she is committed to getting a young woman who is found to be pregnant out of the country and on to a ship called *Tomorrow*, which is to transport her to the Human Project, where a group of scientists are seeking a way to reverse infertility.

The dynamic of the film is that of a political thriller as Theo takes over the role of getting Kee (Claire-Hope Ashitay) to the ship. Once again, then, the issue of fertility becomes the thread through which the story of loss of order, inhumanity, and the possibility of any future is woven. And once again, it is women's fertility that is accented. As with *Apocalypto*, a woman's pregnant belly is, literally and figuratively, front and centre. In contrast to Jaguar Paw's bravado and Jim's bursts of "manly" courage, Theo is an enervated man, ironically employed as a bureaucrat in the Ministry of Energy. Loss of fertility, it is symbolically suggested, corresponds to a loss of imagination about how to transform a world without children, a world without hope.

Further irony surrounds the romance's maiden-in-distress figure— the "key"—who is to serve as the hope of humanity. Not a virgin, nor the whitened Madonna of western Christian imagery, Kee is a sexually active adolescent of African descent. She has no idea which of her many sexual partners has impregnated her. *Children of Men* thus turns the Christian story inside out to suggest that salvation will not come from divine intervention but, rather, human involvement in transforming humanity (it is noteworthy that the film was released on Christmas Day). That transformation, in the purview of the film, is exemplified by Theo's own shift from moral debilitation to ethical commitment. The intimation of divinity in his name Theo thus resonates with the play on his last name, Faron, to suggest not only the need to be fair, but also that he will have to pay the fare of sacrifice.

As ironic hero, Theo does not seek a quest; it befalls him. Julian offers him £5,000 if he will obtain travel permits to the cordoned off coast. The back-story to their estrangement is significant in explaining why he would act on her request, beyond the money. This is filled in when Theo visits an old couple, Jasper (Michael Caine) and his disabled wife, who has apparently suffered physical debilitation because of political torture. A former political cartoonist, Jasper has since retreated to his house in the woods, his most political act of resistance now limited to selling pot to neighbours, including a shady police officer, Sid (Peter Mullan), who works at a prison camp filled with refugees, and who will later become the means by which Theo gets Kee to the coast. It turns out that Theo was once a political activist but lost his determination when his son Dylan died from the flu pandemic. As with *28 Days Later*, then, *Children of Men* draws attention to particular fears endemic to contemporary society about the deadly spread of diseases. In this case, Theo's political and ethical will has ebbed with his departed son, the signifier of his physical and spiritual infertility.

What spurs Theo to action is Julian's death, when she is shot in the throat, as it turns out, by one of her own group. She becomes the first of several sacrificial figures in this ironic romance. Unaware of the group's sabotage, Theo, Kee and Miriam (Pam Ferris), who is to serve as Kee's midwife, flee to The Fishes' country house. This is where Theo is informed of Kee's pregnancy. The handling of the revelation is worth noting. As viewers, we see the astonishment and awe on Theo's face as he beholds her pregnant belly. The camera eye then shifts from his perspective so that we too see her eight-month fullness along with him, through his eyes, as it were. A second revelation occurs when Theo discovers The Fishes' plot to use Kee to forward their political agenda, and to kill him. Theo resolves to save their lives.

Theo's ability to act as hero, however, mocks the traditional romance in which the valiant warrior possesses exceptional prowess. Far from prodigious, Theo rescues Kee and Miriam in a comedic chase scene in which he has to push their car down a hill in an effort to get its engine going. Further sacrifices ensue, first with Jasper and his wife and later Miriam. Finally, it is only Theo and Kee on a journey to *Tomorrow*. One of the most profound moments of ironic commentary on the traditional romantic hero is when Theo becomes midwife to Kee as she gives birth to her daughter. In an abandoned warehouse, on a stained mattress on the floor—the film's version of the stable where Mary delivers Jesus—he spreads his coat for her to lie on as she begins her labour and helps talk her though the pain of contraction and pushing.

Far more than the heroics of escorting Kee and her baby though the war zone of the prison camp that soon follows, this scene captures what is for me the film's acute metaphor for ethical agency amidst turmoil: midwifery. What is emphasized here is the interaction of the act. To be in attendance to others in order to preserve life is offered not only to counter the traditional concept of the hero, diminished these days as a Rambo warrior, but also to offset the totality of sacrifice which exempts all other acts of aid. As the one who gives birth, Kee is indeed the key to this preservation of life, but it is her courage and fortitude in the face of danger that is at stake at least as much as her "natural" capacity as a reproductive female.

Moreover, that this is a white man helping a black woman deliver her baby furthers the film's vision of racial solidarity, making manifest what is necessary to alter the course of history signified by the brutality against refugees who are caged, forced into prison camps and tortured (as the often-noted scene that replicates Abu-Grahib makes clear).

As with the other two films, uncertainty suffuses the ending of *Children of Men*. Bobbing about in a small rowboat, Kee, her baby grasped close, and Theo await the coming of the ship. She discovers that he, like Jim in *28 Days Later*, has been shot in the side. Again, the Christ motif is brought to bear. But, contrary to Jim, it remains unclear whether Theo will live—and there is certainly no utopian scene to follow. Unlike the story of Christ, there is no death or resurrection either. Only a foggy light and glimpse of *Tomorrow* before the screen cuts to black. Sounds of children's voices and laughter can be heard as the credits begin to roll. Are these the memories of ruined world or the promise of what is to come? The answer remains ambiguous.

What is known is that Kee has decided to name the new baby Dylan, after Theo's dead son, a tribute to the love and courage he has found again within himself and the mark of her personal transformation into an individual capable of caring for the new life she has brought into the world. Perhaps most crucial in *Children of Men* is that both Theo and Kee are cast as ordinary individuals who confront extraordinary circumstances. He is not the super warrior that Jaguar Paw is. Nor does he suddenly erupt into unexpected prowess as Jim does. Although like Seven, Kee is initially defined by her motherhood, by the end, there is no retreat into the nuclear family as the sole hope for humanity, as with *Apocalypto*. And, in contrast to the utopian new family at the end of *28 Days Later*, Kee and Dylan gesture to a new tomorrow, but one in which the only certainty in an uncertain world is the necessity of being able to strive for a better world.

Unlike apocalyptic films in which the upshot is the Final End as justified punishment, post-apocalyptic scenarios trade-in the perennial alarmist card in order to get across a different message, more attuned to the particular perils of contemporary life: since we have brought these dangers and hostilities about, it is a political and ethical imperative that we find ways to diminish their power for harm. Rather than the full-blown spectacle of the End, post-apocalyptic films beseech us to seek endings to human-made suffering and to forge new ways to imagine actions of courage and conviction that have been too narrowly defined under the traditional romance of the hero.

Notes

1.   With a nod to Tina Pippin (1999) who points to the figure of Jezebel as a "vamp/ire" because of the way she is recurrently cast as menace to men, posing the query of whether the figure of Jezebel can be revamped.

2.   A number of critical responses that argue about the film's historical errors are readily available on an all-purpose site like Wikipedia, and are no doubt worth attention, but I am not engaged in that debate here.

3.   http://en.wikipedia.org/w/index.php?title=28_Days_Later&printable-yes

4.   On 11 May 2007, the sequel *28 Weeks Later* was released. The ambiguity of the first film allowed for the logic of another to follow. I have not seen it as the time of this writing.

References

Mervyn F. Bendle, "The Apocalyptic Imagination and Popular Culture," *Journal of Religion and Popular Culture*, XI (2005), online at Http://www.usask.ca/relst/jrpc/art11-apocalypticimagination.html

Norman Cohn, *Cosmos, Chaos, and the World To Come: The Ancient Roots of Apocalyptic Faith* (New Haven, CT: Yale University Press, 1993).

Mel Gibson, "Mel Gibson Criticizes Iraq War at Film Fest", Associated Press (2006), online at: http://www.msnbc.msn.com/id/15001985/

Anthony Lane, "Under the Volcano," *New Yorker*, 8 January 2007, pp. 83–4.

John W. Mertens, *The End of the World: The Apocalyptic Imagination in Film & Television* (Winnipeg, Canada: J. Gordon Shillingford, 2003).

Tina Pippin, *Apocalyptic Bodies: The Biblical End of the World in Text and Imagination* (New York: Routledge, 1999).

Lee Quinby, *Anti-Apocalypse: Exercises in Genealogical Criticism* (Minneapolis, MI: University of Minnesota Press, 1993).

Lee Quinby, *Millennial Seduction: A Skeptic Confronts Apocalyptic Culture* (Ithaca, NY: Cornell University Press, 1999).

Eugene Weber, *Apocalypses: Prophecies, Cults, and Millennial Beliefs Through the Ages* (Cambridge, MA: Harvard University Press, 1999).

Films Cited

28 Days Later (dir. Danny Boyle, 2002)
Apocalypto (dir. Mel Gibson, 2006)
Children of Men (dir. Alfonso Cuaron, 2006)
Dr Strangelove or: How I Learned to Stop Worrying and Love the Bomb (dir. Stanley Kubrick, 1964)
On The Beach (dir. Stanley Kramer, 1959)
Planet of the Apes (dir. Franklin J. Schaffner, 1968)

Making Things New
Regeneration and Transcendence in *Anime*

Mick Broderick

Perhaps one of the most striking features of anime *is its fascination with the theme of apocalypse.* (Susan Napier)

Introduction

As *anime* scholar Susan Napier (2005) suggests, apocalypse is a major thematic predisposition of this genre and mode of national cinema. Many commentators (for example, Helen McCarthy, 1993; Antonia Levi, 1998) on *anime* have foregrounded the "apocalyptic" nature of Japanese animation, often uncritically, deploying the term to connote annihilation, chaos and mass destruction, or a nihilistic aesthetic expression. But which apocalypse is being invoked here? The linear, monotheistic apocalypse of Islam, Judaism, Zoroastrianism or Christianity (with its premillennial and postmillennial schools)? Do they encompass the cyclical eschatologies of Buddhism or Shinto or Confucianism? Or are they cultural hybrids combining multiple narratives of finitude? To date, Susan Napier's work is the most sophisticated examination of the trans-cultural manifestation of the Judeo-Christian theological and narrative tradition in *anime*, yet even her framing remains limited by discounting a number of trajectories apocalypse dictates. However, there are other possibilities. Jerome Shapiro (1994), for example, argues convincingly that the millennial imagination, as a subset of apocalyptic thought, is closer to the Japanese spiritual understanding of heroic mythology.

To develop this thesis the following chapter reads key *anime* not covered in Napier's lengthy critique through various strains of apocalyptic discourse, namely *Spriggan* (1998) and *Appleseed* (2004), while referencing others in the genre (e.g. *Akira*, 1988). It considers the utopian teleology of the chaotic, transitional period each narrative heralds (the "middest" as Kermode describes it) that creates a pathway to a new order, or returns balance to a corrupt and moribund world, often through trans-humanist, technological hybridity or psychic/supernatural human evolution.[1] While catastrophic imagery of wholesale destruction and vengeful violence is certainly present in these works this chapter will consider the often ignored, complementary apocalyptic themes of regeneration and renewal that are drawn from both Japanese and Western mythic or religious traditions.

Anime, Eschatology and Secular Apocalypse

One of the most consistent and perceptive analysts of *anime*, Philip Brophy (2005, 2007), has produced pioneering work on aesthetics and form, in particular recuperating the work of Tezuka (*Tetsuan Atomu/Astro Boy*) for Western audiences, and demonstrates a critically nuanced and sensually (aural and visual) sophisticated appreciation of *anime* as art, commercial product and as transnational culture. Over the past 15 years Brophy has demonstrated how the influence of the atomic bombings of Hiroshima and Nagasaki can be traced throughout *anime*'s post-war development and aesthetic sensibilities—from the ocular flash contained in *kawaii* cartoon eyes to the radiating beams and explosive detonations of energy weapons in *mecha* (Brophy and Ewington, 1994). Yet Brophy also underplays the importance of regeneration and renewal in what he repeatedly describes as the apocalyptic, post-apocalyptic and hyper-apocalyptic in Japanese animation.[2] Similarly, writers such as Alan Cholodenko (1991), Pauline Moore (2007), Jane Goodall (2007), Freda Freiberg (1996) and Ben Crawford (1996), like Brophy, all foreground the post-nuclear Japanese experience as radically informing the thematic, formal and aesthetic concerns of *anime*, including its apocalyptic dimension.[3] However, each author relies on predominantly secular Western understandings of apocalypse to connote and conflate what is essentially an *eschatological* perspective (i.e. the study of finality). Collectively, the critical concern of these analysts is in the destructive, explosive and mutational form and theme of the medium and its national-historical contexts (and, importantly its seduction and/or phenomenological appeal).

Susan Napier, on the other hand, while embracing the cultural impact of the atom bombings, also recognizes the origins and re-visioning of indigenous Japanese variations on apocalypse, and at least foregrounds the possibility of transcendence or rebirth. Her complex reading of the most popular genres of *anime* finds them dominated by apocalyptic visions (Napier, 2005: 251). Napier also acknowledges "one of the basic paradoxes is that apocalyptic destruction is both feared and welcomed" (*ibid.*: 253) but doesn't expand on this millennial desire for retribution and annihilation, one that is in fact embraced by Brophy's eloquent and lyrical discourse but can be traced back to Susan Sontag's seminal essay "The Imagination of Disaster" (1965), Frank Kermode's (1967) *The Sense of an Ending* and Norman Cohn's (1957) *The Pursuit of the Millennium*.

While considering the social and cultural responses to the recent millennium, Krishan Kumar (1995: 205) identifies significant difference between past and present "doomsayers". Regardless of their sense of oppression and bleak prognoses, earlier prophets of doom, according to Kumar "generally retained something of the messianic or millennial hope that out of the ruins would come regeneration" (*ibid.*). Following Hans Enzensberger's argument concerning the interdependent *yin* and *yang* of apocalyptic and utopian thought, (i.e. without catastrophe, no millennium; without apocalypse, no paradise), for Kumar, "What we seem to have today is the apocalyptic imagination without hope but also, more strikingly, a kind of millennial belief entirely emptied of the conflict and dynamism that generally belong to it. It is a millennial belief without a sense of the future" (*ibid.*).

So what is missing from this picture? By principally accentuating the secular apocalyptic nature of *anime* narratives, these critics and theorists mostly articulate a nihilism or ambivalence concerning the catastrophic destruction rendered in these works which negates the traditional dual nature of apocalyptic *telos*—to restore harmony for a millennium or transcend human time and space into a divine realm. Equally significant is the discounting of Japanese religious influences and traditions that inscribe both the aesthetic composure and sensibility of *anime*'s form and content. Limiting the exploration of *anime* to the application of Western apocalypse in this way forecloses analysis of the remaining organizing principles of this chiliastic theology, such as the role and figuration of messiah and antichrist, the battle of Armageddon, saving of an elect, day of judgement and the afterlife. These tropes are evident in *anime*'s hybrid appropriation of this Western master narrative of legitimation, recirculated within the globalized medium of international animation. Indeed, much *anime* explores, if not challenges the postmodern malaise identified by Kumar by envisioning "hope" in the form of *surviving* apocalyptic change, from planetary renovation to species evolution/hybridization, to individual psychic and emotional transcendence.

Hybrid Apocalypse, *Masse* or *Mappo*?

Many commentators on Japanese society stress the fundamentally secular nature of daily life and culture (see Aoki and Dardess, 1981; Kitagawa, 1990; Reischauer and Jansen, 1995). Reischauer and Jansen (1995: 203) recognize the importance of religion "in the Japan of old" but suggest the type of secularism extant within the West "dates back at least three centuries in Japan". Religious thought in post-war Japan remains essentially hybrid, combining Confucianism, Buddhism and Shintoism. Just as Kumar and Kermode determine Judeo-Christian apocalyptic tropes and traditions are evident in the secular West, there remain lingering, centuries-old traditions of Shinto (animistic worship of the nature and environment, whether animate or inanimate objects), Buddhism (transmigration of the soul, salvation and fulfilment in paradise) and Confucianism (ethical values informing moralities of governance, education, and loyalty to family and employer). Christianity impacts Japanese society to a far lesser degree (less than 2 per cent of the population), however, it retains a large influence on the educated elite.[4]

Increasingly Japanese are attracted to popular movements assuming "new religions" status, of which several hundred have achieved official recognition and now claim membership in the tens of millions (*ibid.*: 214). Most are themselves hybrid with elements drawn from older Shinto, Buddhism and Chinese folk rites. Their popularity also stems from these new religious movements (NRMs) and sects providing a social space for individuals outside of conventional and formal religious institutions. Regardless of the secular society and ambivalent agnosticism, Japanese society ostensibly remains organized around religious observances. The thousands of shrines across the islands, domestic altars and public festivals, performative marriages with Christian or Shinto ceremonies and elaborate Buddhist funerals, all contribute incongruously to the daily *secular* life of the 70–80 per cent of Japanese who "do not consider themselves believers in any religion" (*ibid.*: 215).

From a Western perspective it may be difficult to comprehend how the Japanese can simultaneously accommodate all three (or four, if Christianity is included) major religions, in an amalgamation of beliefs, without apparent contradiction or sectarian conflict. Pragmatism and compromise is intrinsic to the history of Japanese religion (and society) according to Joseph Kitagawa, evident in the early hybridity of Shinto and Buddhism, with "practical coexistence between the two religions" well established in the Heian period (794–1185), during which time: "Buddhism absorbed the optimistic world-affirming attitude of Shinto so that the traditional motifs of Buddhism, a quietistic view of Nirvana and a negative outlook regarding life and the world, were greatly modified" (Kitagawa, 1990: 68–69).

Susan Napier does explore and acknowledge, to varying degrees, the Japanese religious undercurrents of apocalyptic approximation. Indeed, of the three principal modes of *anime* that she delineates, both the Elegiac and Carnival have clear relevance to the third mode, the Apocalyptic. Yet, by 2005 Napier finds an "absence of major apocalyptic series or film" *anime*, curiously discounting *Metropolis* (2001) as "retro apocalypse" and nihilistic (Napier 2005: xv).[5] It is odd in this context that Napier addresses neither *Appleseed* nor the "steam-punk" *Steamboy* (2004), two significantly "apocalyptic" *anime* of recent years.

Just as several critics (Zamora, 1989; Norris, 1995; O'Leary, 1998) of postmodern Western eschatology observe, Napier (2005: 251–52) finds colloquial slippage from the original meanings of apocalypse and its contemporary "common understanding" which she describes as "something on the order of global destruction". Fully aware of its original Greek meaning as "revelation" or "uncovering", Napier emphasizes that this context of disclosure remains present "even though it is lost to conscious usage [...] so many of our images, ideas, and stories about the end of the world continue to contain elements of revelation" (Napier, 2005: 252). More significantly, as a process intrinsic to apocalyptic discourse, she asserts:

> the anticipation of the revelation of "secrets" or "mysteries" is an important narrative technique in all the apocalyptic texts examined [...] In many works of anime, much of the narrative tension is not from "waiting for the end of the world" but from the revelation of how and why the world should end. Given the distance between Japanese religion and Christianity, it is fascinating that present-day Japanese notions of the end of the world echo much in Revelation (*ibid.*).

Amongst these traces she includes exaggerated visions of death and desire, messianic figures offering revenge fantasies and a hostility towards history and temporality.

Napier suggests that the process of animation itself contributes to "developing a distinctively Japanese notion of apocalypse", which partly draws from the Buddhist doctrine of *mappo* with its concept of "a fallen world saved by a religious figure" and based on the 'latter days of the Law', the final 1,000-year phase of decadence and decline following the Buddha's death (*ibid.*). Yet Japanese historian of religion, Kitagawa, recognizes that this apocalyptic heritage and lineage is a more extensive and complex one, where the:

> yearning of the Japanese people to restore the idealized state of the golden days, coupled with the notion of the identity of religion and politics (*saisei-itchi*), has often developed a messianic fervor, especially during political crises. The ethnocentric, messianic restoration implicit in the indigenous religious tradition of Japan received further stimulus from the apocalyptic notion of Buddhism known as *mappo* (the coming of the age of degeneration of the Buddha's Law) as well as from the "immanental theocratic" motif of Confucianism, as exemplified by the messianic motif of Nichiren's teaching in the thirteenth century, respectively. Many observers sense the similar ethnocentric, messianic motif in [...] many other postwar new religions that present the "old dreams" of Japan as the "new visions" of the coming social and political order. (Kitagawa, 1990: 339)

While Napier recognizes the importance of apocalyptic cults in Japan that she finds evident since the nineteenth century, other commentators have shown how millenarian movements and ideologies can be traced to the tenth century, if not before, with various charismatic shamans and messianic cult leaders appearing to the present day (see Kitagawa, 1990; Hall *et al.*, 2000; Stone, 2000). In Japanese history, as much as its representation in *manga* and *anime,* such sects and cults emerged regularly and, as with the West, frequently espoused radical ideology announcing the end of days.

Most famously in recent Japan, Aum Shinrikyô, the messianic cult led by Ashara Shokô, responsible for the 1995 sarin gas attack on the Tokyo subway, was preparing for the end of the world and its members were avid consumers of "apocalyptic manga and anime" (Napier, 2005: 8). Indeed, six years earlier, with the international film release of *Akira,* following its successful *manga* serialization, a doomsday cult is depicted at the margins of the narrative. Napier comments that, despite the emphasis on the spectacle of disaster, "appropriate to the basic ideology of apocalypse, most works, even the apparently nihilistic *Akira,* include such elements as an explicit criticism of the society undergoing apocalypse and why this society should be encountering such a fate. These reasons are almost always related to human transgression" (*ibid*.)

In the *Akira manga* the psychic sect leader, Lady Miyako, is a major character, however, in the *anime*, this role becomes marginal and acquires an indeterminate gender, appearing as a fanatical devotee of the evolutionary super or post-human, Tetsuo and Akira. In the film's penultimate scenes of urban conflict Tetsuo approaches Akira's subterranean cryogenic vault. When advancing anti-government demonstrators observe the telekinetic Testuo deflect an exploding tank shell and reappear unscathed, they (mistakenly) declare him "Lord Akira" and shout, "It's the Great Awakening", but a protester admonishes the new devotees: "Don't be fooled. This isn't the Rapture. He's a false messiah!" The assembled Army attacks the demonstrators and the "crazy cult" followers with laser weapons. As the old monk is carried by disciples through the smouldering chaos s/he chants manically:

> Oh, flames of purity, raze this corrupt city. Burn all the unclean believers of our time. Give yourselves into the flames, children, you will all be born again. Consume our hearts. Wash our unclean hearts in the eternal fire. Your bodies will be purified with flames.

Nevertheless, as Tetsuo's psychic wrath obliterates the armed forces in retaliation, the cultist and his/her followers are perfunctorily

dispatched as collateral damage, while Testuo remains either oblivious or ambivalent as to their abrupt fate. Remarkably this brief sequence manages to evoke Buddhist and Judeo-Christian messianic prophecy, the antichrist, Adventist disconfirmation, Shintoesque purification and karmic transcendence. Hence, overt millenarian ideology and cant neither aids nor abets Tetsuo or Akira; it is shown to be ultimately irrelevant to their apocalyptic agenda and agency.

Most ancient societies and religions conceived their creation and destruction myths via a combination of animism and astrology, constructing elaborate calendars drawn from the fertility cycles of the changing seasons and/or the immutable course of solar, lunar, planetary and celestial rotations (Eliade, 1971; Campbell, 1991). Frequently, these cycles contain defined linear periods or epochs which proceeded inevitably from one to another, initiating in a bountiful golden age and then degenerating successively into periods of exponential decline until these societies are destroyed and reborn in the ensuing cycle. Shapiro cites the importance of Shinto and later Japanese religious paradigms that privilege nature and seasonal cycles as essential to how Japanese culture perpetuates its distinctiveness from the West (Shapiro 2002: 256). As Damian Thompson suggests:

> The purpose of these historical schemes is to align human behavior with the divine plan [...] the theme of epochs brought to an end by human wickedness, and of closeness to the End, emerges as the common denominator of the world's historic religions. Belief in moral decline is an inevitable accompaniment to the nearly universal belief in original paradise. (Thompson, 1996: 9).

This theme is readily apparent in post-holocaust *Akira*, when Colonel Shikishima descends into the frozen crypt that contains the dismembered remains of the psi-warrior Akira (who later appears like a child Buddha), he has a flashback to an earlier conversation with the scientist, Doctor Ônishi, bemoaning the decadence that has befallen Neo-Tokyo:

Shikishima: Scientists are a bunch of romantics. Military men on the other hand always consider the risks first. Over thirty years it's taken. We've come so far crawling up from the rubble ...

Ônishi: But I've always felt that you held a resentment, even a hatred, for this city, Colonel.

Shikishima: The passion to build has cooled and the joy of reconstruction forgotten. Now, now it's just a garbage heap made up of a bunch of hedonistic fools.

Such an exchange recalls Frank Kermode's observation that to some intellectuals the Great War would "abolish a worn-out world and introduce a new one. But the apocalyptic optimism with which many men, and perhaps especially artists, responded to the prospect of battle could not survive the experience of the following four years, and when hoped failed the sense of decadence returned" (1995: 258). So too we find the world-weary twenty-first-century military man, Colonel Shikishima, apocalyptically desiring the destruction/renovation of Neo-Tokyo, just as the previous cityscape was destroyed 20 years earlier. The wish for regeneration that Kermode identifies in *fin-de-siècle* excess is soon fulfilled in *Akira's* extensive, violent yet transcendent denouement.

Writing in *Atomic Bomb Cinema: the Apocalyptic Imagination on Film*, Jerome Shaprio finds the Buddhist *mappo* tradition in Japanese cinema and *anime* complemented by another arcane institution, *masse*. Conceptually, the latter is closer to an apocalyptic narrative than the former: "*masse* describes the complete end of the world, and the beginning of an entirely new one" (Shapiro, 2002: 257). This is an important distinction in terms of both *Spriggan* and *Appleseed* and qualifies the Japanese apocalyptic further as there is not so much a continuity or salvation of an elect in this schema, as in Western tradition, but the closure of one narrative and the beginning of another. In *Spriggan*, a human machine hybrid (i.e. cyborg) attempts to annihilate all life on the planet and start afresh with newly designed creatures, whereas in *Appleseed*, artificially augmented human clones (bioroids) are created to harmonize warring homo sapiens but are themselves positioned to be the inheritors of Earth once humanity is "euthanazed".

From a Japanese perspective there should be no surprise in these apocalyptically bricolage plots. Shapiro strongly emphasizes the impact of Post-Meiji modernization and influence of Western mythologies and narratives in contemporary Japanese cinema and *anime*, an impact he reinforces by quoting "Japan's leading clinical psychologist, Hayao Kawai", who stresses this influence "cannot be underestimated" (*ibid.*, 254). For Shapiro this is another form of social ambivalence, ambiguity and cultural hybridity: "Almost paradoxically, the Japanese are infatuated with the new, disdain anything outdated, and are not sentimental about revising, amending, or discarding 'tradition'" (*ibid.*: 257).

What Japanese films exhorting the apocalypse achieve distinctively is "a passion, both serious and playful, for living in accord with the natural world—in all its beauty and terror" (*ibid.*: 255–56). The notion of playfulness is a serious one for Shapiro and one largely missing from Napier's textual readings, and can be equally found in *mono no aware*, a point Shapiro takes eminent Japanese film scholar Donald Ritchie to task over (and by implication Napier) as fundamentally misreading this Buddhist tradition (*ibid.*: 264–67). Equally, the influence of traditional, pre-cinematic modes of art such as Haiku (championed by Gerald Vizenor) requires the skilled reading/mastery of interpretation. As in the hermeneutics required for biblical exegesis in such rich apocalyptic texts as Revelation, appreciating Haiku requires a "transcendent oneness" in the act of contemplation that seeks to harmonize and find balance in any reading. Yet harmony and balance also informs Western theological interpretation and practice. As Frank Kermode argues, following Helmut Gerber's assertion that "genuine decadence *is* a renaissance", apocalyptic transition requires the balance of both decadence and renovation or renaissance, and is often indistinguishable and/or at least contemporaneous (Kermode, 1995: 258).

Shapiro further delineates the Buddhist canon: "*masse* signifies an age of moral decadence, and in ancient times it also meant a retributive event that guides humanity", but unlike Judeo-Christian apocalypse, it assumes an eschatological stature, not Revelation's consummation of history into a single, linear teleology. "Rather than connoting rebirth or the battle of good and evil, *masse* simply denotes punishment for crimes rather than sin. *Masse* does not include a cosmic reorganization [...] rather the world ends, and then something else takes its place" (*ibid.*: 341, n. 19). In this way, *masse* complements the concept of *mono no aware*, in that it embodies a sense of sorrow for the loss and transience of all things. According to Shapiro, it also "expresses a profound sympathy which is more difficult to define" (*ibid.*: 264).

Apocalyptic *anime* is well suited to interrogating this transcendent feeling, momentarily closing the rupture between what *is* and what *will* be, linking the *here* with "what lies beyond". In order to demonstrate these influences I have selected two major Japanese animated productions, *Spriggan* and *Appleseed,* both from serialized *manga* origins that engage thematically with apocalyptic concerns but have yet to receive significant critical attention. Unlike the soteriological impulse of Western apocalypse, the advocates and potential instigators of Armageddon in *Spriggan* and *Appleseed* neither seek the salvation nor the perpetuation of humankind. These *anime* entertain narratives of *mappo* and *masse* as myths of decadence and decline, which are ultimately rejected in both films with the messianic intervention of deliver-heroes. For all of its failures, moral exhaustion and its capacity for self-destruction, humanity is saved or granted a reprieve in both productions by protagonists rejecting false gods and prophets, or by embracing advanced transhumanist ideals that complement and compensate for human flaws.

Spriggan

This OAV (original *anime* video) was also released theatrically in a number of international territories and is a curious amalgam of many hybrid thematic and iconographic references to biblical apocalypse. As in many *anime*, such as *Akira*, *Spriggan* is set in a future realm not too indistinguishable from today. It is a world under ecological threat where humankind seems pre-ordained for extinction, punished in a quasi-biblical, technological deluge that conflates Buddhist *masse* tradition with Old Testament prophecy to encompass renewal or evolutionary progress.

After the death of a classmate who is an unwilling suicide bomber under post-hypnotic command with the words "Noah will be your death" scrawled across his chest, Yu Ominae, the impulsive and eponymous "Spriggan" confronts his supervisor, Mr Yamamoto of ARKAM, a covert global intelligence organization. As a high school senior, Yu is the youngest spy working for ARKAM and is later revealed to be a genetically enhanced product of military experimentation and indoctrination. Peering out of his office window at the myriad skyscrapers before him, the camera pans upward while Yamamoto quotes from Old Testament scripture, his pale cigarette smoke slowly ascending and dispersing in a neat visual metaphor of transcendence and transformation:

> "And the Lord saw that the wickedness of man was great and His heart was filled with grief. And the Lord said 'I will destroy man whom I have created from the face of the Earth. And behold, I myself am bringing floodwaters on the Earth to destroy from under heaven all flesh in which is the breath of life and all that is on the Earth shall die."

This ponderous sequence works typologically to recall and anticipate the catastrophic deluge, both as historical myth and an antediluvian prophecy of future calamity. It is the Spriggan's cryptic introduction to a battle that will take place atop Mt Ararat in Turkey, where one of two competing secret armies has located the Ark and battle for access. As Norman Cohn has comprehensively demonstrated, the near universal mythologies of flood act as a precursor to

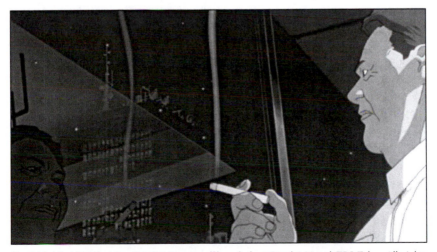

Biblical apocalypse (Cohn, 1999). Punitive Deluge is a mini-narrative of end-time that demonstrates rebirth and suggests something cyclical, yet is contained within Judeo-Christian theology as a linear and teleological movement. Arguably both Shinto and Buddhist purification rituals employing water contribute to this rich tradition of deluge mythology, especially given the Japanese archipelago's ongoing assault by tsunami and typhoons (Kitagawa, 1990: 13).

In his appropriately titled book, *Strange Weather,* Andrew Ross suggests the mythic resonances of deluge (and other "violent" acts of Nature) is due to their ubiquitous effect:

> Instances of prolonged meteorological abnormality expose popular and official anxieties about the economy of change and consistency that regulates our everyday lives. Historical weather events, no matter how singular or prolonged, are remembered as material instances of radical abnormality long after contemporaneous political or social events and upheavals have faded from the popular memory [...] the longstanding endurance of these popular memories is no doubt partly due to the perception that, unlike remote political events, natural hardships, at least in principle, effect everyone almost equally. (Ross, 1991: 231)

Indeed, as Ross maintains, such anthropomorphizing of nature and spectacular weather continues from the pre-modern into the post-modern world, as we find in *Spriggan* and other *anime*. The biblical Flood attains the dimension of micro-apocalypse, or a rehearsal for the complete point of *eschaton*, with the apocalypse, in the immanent future. Hence, even seemingly linear and singular myths of decline and rebirth hold cyclical and repeated motifs, that exegete Northrop Frye calls type and antitype (Frye, 1983: 25).

Such mythologies are germane to *Spriggan*. In a clandestine Pentagon operation, the US Machine Corps sends a telekinetic child cyborg, Colonel MacDougall, and two appropriately named assassins, Fat Man and Little Boy, on a 'black op' to gain control of the Ark, having obtained a triangular entry key from another alien artefact excavated from elsewhere. Inside the ARKUM laboratory atop Mt Ararat the diminutive Col. MacDougall forcibly wrests control from an elderly scholar-scientist, Dr Meisel. After briefly downloading/absorbing Meisel's linguistic computer data, MacDougall translates the alien glyphs for those present, explaining that the Ark is a giant machine controlling the Earth's weather by manipulating ozone and carbon dioxide in the upper atmosphere and adjusting the global intake of ultraviolet radiation:

I am the Lord of the sky. He who awakens me shall have dominion over that which enfolds the earth, the mighty shield that protects all. When evil runs rampant on the Earth I will change the blessings of heaven to the curses of hell and the children of God shall be once more destroyed and created anew.

With this interpretation MacDougall immediately dispatches his Pentagon minder and assumes control himself, informing the doctor and his assistant Margaret that "it wasn't man who set me on this course … it was God who selected me". Like many self-anointed prophets of NRMs, MacDougall expresses not just his witness to apocalyptic predeterminism, but demonstrates his active agency in fulfilling its teleology.

Inside the Ark, Dr Meisel, Margaret and the child cyborg MacDougall locate the giant machine's alien operating system, known as "Noah". The sequence is a stunning one. As the scientists decipher the central control panel, a cavernous hemisphere of rotating Mandela and arcane hieroglyphs radiate across a massive internal canopy, resembling an astronomical and astrological map of the cosmos. All present are in awe of the sublime spectacle unfolding before them. MacDougall enthuses:

"It's incredible! With the Cold War over, the greatest single threat to the Earth is destruction of the environment. Acid rain, ozone depletion, global warming—with Noah in our hands we could eliminate

all of these problems in a heartbeat. My country thinks it has to lead the world in all things. They'd do anything to get their hands on this. That's why the Machine Corps sent me here, with this kind of power at their command, they'd have every government in the world at their feet." But the doctor protests: "Noah is too dangerous to be activated" warning that it could destroy MacDougall's own country in the process.

This sequence is intercut with Spriggan Ominae in the twilight periphery surrounding the Ark's core, trying to locate the three protagonists while travelling through a liminal dimension that bends and distorts time and space. In this weird, quantum realm he encounters enormous dinosaurs, frozen in stasis, alongside scores of other fantastic creatures both reptilian and mythological.

MacDougall continues: "I don't doubt that Noah could have helped create the ice age that destroyed the dinosaurs, but I always felt that it might have had another function beside simply changing the atmosphere [...] I don't think those creatures were just collected by Noah, I think they were *created* here. I think they are experimental prototypes for the next generation of animals to walk the earth." As Ominae searches deeper into the alien zone the creatures appear more incredible and bizarre and MacDougall's scientific exposition attains a millenarian rant. "Noah doesn't just control the weather, it's a *creator* of life! [...] it might even be possible that the entire human

race began here in the Ark of Noah. Forget about saving the old world doctor, together you and I can create a *new* one [...] The entire human race is a *mistake* of history doctor. We have the chance to correct God's only creative *failure* [...] He's giving us the chance to *correct* all that is wrong in the world! That's why I brought you here. That's why *He* brought you here. Please. Work with me." Incredulous at the demagoguery, the doctor emphatically declares, "Never!"

Unappeased by Meisel's categorical refusal to cooperate, MacDougall activates the Ark in retribution: "I've just triggered the global warming function doctor. In minutes hurricanes and typhoons will begin forming in unprecedented numbers. The polar ice caps will melt and the levels of the ocean will begin to rise. At last, the *second* flood has begun! It's the end of the world as you knew it ..." The three watch the global climatic rupture from within the heart of the Ark as a montage of satellite views of spiralling storms, ice sheets tearing asunder, flooded cities and giant tsunamis forming, with MacDougall adding: "Why wait forty days and nights when you have tidal waves".

But in a selfless act of messianic heroism Spriggan Ominae manages to intervene and rescue Meisel and Margaret, temporarily overcoming MacDougall. Perplexed, the cyborg colonel laments: "I don't understand. Why would anyone want to turn down the chance to

work with a God?" before commanding Ominae to leave the Ark, calling him a "cockroach" who's presence is despoiling his "holy temple". Yet, ultimately unable to defeat Ominae, the dying MacDougall initiates the Ark's self-destruct sequence destabilizing the "alien time/space stasis" that maintains the massive structure. The machine implodes in a massive climatological inversion resembling hurricane, tornado and collapsar into which all matter (including the maniacal McDougall) is sucked, disappearing at the event horizon.

The sublime atmospheric contortions and turbulence subsides. Despite widespread destruction the process of ecological apocalypse is averted. MacDougall—anti-christ, false prophet and deceiver—is vanquished and annihilated. The film concludes with two Spriggans (Ominae and his French counterpart) united after escaping the Ark. The pair have prevented the wannabe cyborg deity from obliterating *homo sapiens* and replacing them with his new creations. The camera tracks backward to reveal celebrations atop the newly flattened Mt Ararat, with its smoking cavity instead of a summit. Over an angelic choir the diegesis moves to a god's-eye-view. The camera slowly zooms out, dissolving to a macro view of Turkey and its continental neighbours, before revealing the full globe of the Earth from space. A triumphal orchestration signals the finale. Global harmony and balance restored.

Appleseed

If *Spriggan* succeeds in retelling and reinterpreting biblical mythology of decadence, decline and deluge by conflating a postmodern secular narrative with apocalyptic and millennial tropes and characters, the more recent *Appleseed* instantly foregrounds its literally apocalyptic agenda with an introductory title and passage from Revelation 12:4.

> And his tail drew the third part of the stars of heaven, and did cast them to the earth; and the dragon stood before the woman which was ready to be delivered, for to devour her child as soon as it was born.[6]

At first this passage appears unrelated to the *mecha* fury of urban battle we are about to witness, rendered by live motion-capture within 3D CG, as well as the segue only minutes later from this maelstrom of Armageddon to the utopian city of Olympus.[7] Yet the New Testament quotation foregrounds the centrality of the female protagonist in an apocalyptic battle between forces of entropic human genocide and those who would protect the "future perfect" by making things anew. Significantly, *Appleseed's* characters and locations also draw from classical Greek myth and literature in nomenclature and its overall dialectical narrative interrogation of historical, progressive decline and decadence which, while tangential to Judeo-Christian apocalypse, is far closer to concepts of *mappo* and *masse*.

The opening sequence establishes the catastrophic, post-holocaust terrain inhabited by guerilla fighters and their mechanized military opponents. A lengthy firefight ensues inside the shell of a decaying multi-storey building where resistance fighter Deunan Knute is captured by the elite ESWAT (Extra Special Weapons and Tactics) team airdropped in to the ruined city. Knute awakens to find herself in the new "utopia" of Olympus, a majestic twenty-second-century metropolis populated by genetically engineered human-hybrid clones called "bioroids" that now govern the remnant functioning world. One of the next generation of bioroids, Hitomi, introduces the bewildered Knute into the socio-political history of the city: "In Olympus, mankind has finally achieved a state of utopia, in a fair and balanced society".[8]

As the pair speed towards the capital's central district along gleaming highways on a gravity-controlled floating car, Hitomi continues to brief the war-weary Knute, new to the city, explaining that the bioroids: "are not just 'ordinary' clones but an advanced hybrid

species made from the highest quality components". Knute expresses bemusement at Hitomi's politically correct rhetoric until Hitomi proudly reveals her own bioroid status: "while our composition may be superior to yours, bioroids in no way attempt to control human beings. Our role is to stabilize an otherwise turbulent society. We're facilitators of balance and peace".[9] Like Klaatu and the robot "policeman", Golt, patrolling the universe in *The Day the Earth Stood Still* (1951), this exchange suggests that an elect of human society has achieved the millennium of harmony and peace only by delegating governance to a more advanced form of artificial life.

Emerging from a long tunnel we see the astonishing Tartaros and Daidalos, twin massive ringed metal and glass structures that house the enormous Intelligence Network "brain" that oversees Olympus, nick-named Gaia. Despite Olympus being governed solely by a bioroid council and led by a bioroid Prime Minister Athena, who supervises ESWAT, the regular army is human and commanded by General Uranus and his faithful Colonel Hades. However, it is revealed that all final authority ultimately rests with Gaia and its decision is irrevocable.

Hitomi explains that Gaia is a self-expanding network that monitors all aspects of daily life in the city: "Particularly the bioroid interaction with humans" since "humans are ruled by unstable emotions. Their inherent anger often leads to war but in bioroids emotional

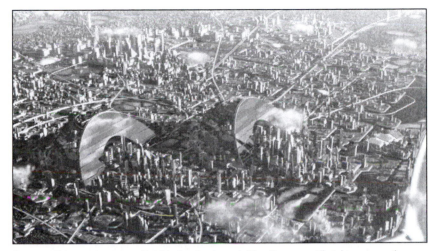

reactions are suppressed. We harbour no anger or jealously towards other people and that's how we've been able to keep the peace." Maintaining this utopian existence, however, requires a form of biological Mutual Assured Destruction (MAD) as deterrent. Atop of Daidalos is "D-Tank", containing a genocidal virus that if ever released, would "wipe-out all bioroid existence". Resigned to this ever-present threat, Hitomi relates: "I know it's man's need for self-preservation [and] it's vital to maintain a balance between us; that's why Gaia also monitors the emotional effect of bioroids on humans".

Arriving inside the giant complex Hitomi introduces Knute to the Olympus Elders, seven nonagerians who hover about the transparent domelike container of Gaia's fluctuating neural plasma, like a giant version of Dr Onishi's scientific display monitoring the godchild in *Akira*.

Hitomi relates that the will of Olympus is decided through a form of Socratic dialectics involving "debate between Gaia and the seven elders". [10] One by one, the elders explain Gaia's function and the genocidal Olympus fail-safe mechanism. Gaia is a "collection of the wisdom and acumen of the scientists who designed it", a machine, perfect in its stability that will never waver, with no capacity for human sentiment. "By adding our seven minds to its collective understanding of humanity we give Gaia's thinking a measure of flexibility."

The Elders continue: "Co-existence between man and bioroid is the last remaining hope for the survival of our species" with Gaia "ever watchful of that balance". Another explains, "The bioroids are vastly different life forms from human beings". And like the brief, in-built life span of the Tyrell Corporation's replicants in *Blade Runner* (1982), in *Appleseed* bioroid reproductive functions "remain inactive so they can produce no offspring [and] must periodically undergo a life extension process". The wizened septet of orbiting Elders surmise, "since emotions such as love and hate are controlled, desire and enmity are almost non-existent [...] This is how we differentiate the bioroid species from our own."

However, all is not well in paradise. At first *Appleseed*'s utopian community appears like post-millennial elect but smouldering interspecies conflict suggests this is only a brief apocalyptic interregnum of relative peace prior to an imminent and decisive battle. After a terrorist attack by rebel factions of *human* soldiers decimates the bioroid's preservation technologies inside the heavily fortified Daidalos, the Olympus parliament convenes in emergency session. One elder informs the assembled council that the genocidal attack on bioroid life-extension "imperils the future of humanity as well". Announcing to the chamber that Gaia has willed that all reproductive functions will be permanently restored to the bioroids, the humans present (mostly regular army) are incensed. Speaking simultaneously to the parliament and live to all Olympians, the Elder trumpets with emphatic confidence: "Bioroid reproductive capabilities will be restored and they will evolve into a new race of man and create a shining paradise for us all". But this millennial prophecy only masks a more insidious plot hatched by the Elders.

An unwitting pawn in an apocalyptic game, Deunan Knute retrieves vital data for the expedient and complicit Elders. Bioroids, they explain, as a new form of life could help us save humanity: "Man was doomed, but coexistence gave us all a glimmer of hope. Even so, the human race could not suppress its violent nature. Mankind despises those that are different. Once again man has succumbed to hatred and anger [...] and he no longer has the ability to maintain this planet." Echoing the terminal prognosis of Colonel MacDougall in *Spriggan*, the Elders attempt to justify to Deunan their devious manipulations via apocalyptic logic and rhetoric: "Gaia has made an accurate prediction, that the human race is doomed to annihilate itself and destroy the world in three generations. Deunan, *our* time has passed. The human race must step aside [...] if the world is to survive we have no choice but to relinquish the future to the bioroids."

The decrepit men next reveal the truth about D-Tank, contradicting Hitomi's earlier "fail-safe" narrative of bioroid genocide, like an updated genetic Doomsday Device recalling *Dr Strangelove* (1963):

> When the tank is destroyed the virus will make the entire human race permanently infertile. We swore that no human life would be taken. And so it won't—instead we will slowly close the book on human history. The last chapter will be the euthanasia of mankind [...] even utopia could not quell man's need for violence. Once again he became embroiled in a global war and reduced the world to ashes. And now Olympus too has been marred by the sins of humanity [...] The bioroids will create a new species, and mankind will be eradicated from the planet.

Deunan protests that the Elders deceived her and manipulated Gaia's data, forcing it to make a spurious decision. Unrepentant one Elder asserts with dogmatic certainty: "It is humanity's destiny [...] we accept the fate of our race and intend to perish along with the rest", but just as another is about to press the red doomsday button releasing the infertility virus, the bioroid Prime Minister, Athena, enters with her personal guard and aborts the global genocide.

But the city's automated self-defence system does activate and seven massive robotic "spiders" raze the city as they converge on D-Tank, pre-programmed to release the devastating virus. Amid the mayhem, as buildings are levelled and bridges crushed, Knute and her ESWAT colleagues race to prevent the genocide from being unleashed. With seconds to spare, Knute ascends the lead "spider" and disarms the program with the mystical intervention of her dead mother, Dr Gilliam, who's spirit seemingly inhabits Gaia's software, like the Shinto *kami* or *tama,* residing inside all things, a true ghost in the machine (Kitagawa, 1990: 12–15).[11] Knute prevails and halts the genetic holocaust, granting humanity immunity from an inexorable euthanasia.

Having earlier rendered the Elders' controls inactive, Athena again reminds them all of the bioroids' primary function: "To ensure the survival of the human race", ironically confirming the previous public prophecy by her seemingly defiant intervention: "We are no longer the bioroids you created but members of a *new* race".

Appleseed concludes with this triumphant declaration. Partly by design and possibly by chance, the superior bioroids are shown to have already attained "enlightenment", advancing to a higher realm of (co)existence with *homo sapiens.* In this brave new world, under the watchful eye of the artificial intelligence network Gaia, human women and female bioroids unequivocally usurp the exhausted ideology of patriarchy moments before it set about unilaterally extinguishing all human life.

An Ending

According to apocalyptic scholar Malcolm Bull:

> Popular-secular apocalyptic feeds on the same images of nuclear holocaust, ecological catastrophe, sexual decadence and social collapse that inspire contemporary religious millenarianism. But unlike the religious variety, secular apocalyptic—which is found in many areas of popular culture, but most notably in science fiction, rock music and film—is not usually intended to influence public opinion in favour of social or political objectives such as nuclear disarmament or environmental regulation, but in many cases the language of apocalyptic is deployed simply to shock, alarm or enrage. (Bull, 1995: 4–5).

Japanese animation has frequently been accused of exploitation and gratuitous excess. Yet what any number of *anime* are successful in achieving is rendering and evoking the "inconceivable". Instead of halting at Armageddon's denouement, apocalyptic *anime* glimpses beyond the cataclysms of radical renovation. The demolished metropolis, felled buildings, spent ordinance, devastated urban populaces and planetary topographies riddled with explosive craters, smoking fissures, molten frameworks, and blasted terrains from heaving overpressure; the cacophonies of battle, mass evacuation, blinding light, searing rays, nuclear detonations, psychic energy pulses and the corresponding silences of affect—these are the chaotic processes that announce and produce the violent but necessary *transition* from one state of existence to the next, often as evolutionary development, or as a counterforce to nihilistic agendas, or to *usurp* and *prevent* entropy, hubris or the destructive interventions from internal or external parties.

Regardless of the recent preponderance of secular apocalypticism that critics such as Malcolm Bull target, *anime* texts that adopt apocalyptic, messianic or millenarian tropes frequently do so as an organizing principle of their hybrid narratives as well as their aesthetic processes. The glib or cynical postmodern self-reflexivity Bull finds amongst cultural circulation is largely eschewed in *anime*. There is no apocalyptic MacGuffin here, momentarily trotted out to expediently explain or justify or motivate plot and character.[12] The films discussed above are nuanced and sophisticated interpretations that engage in "revelation" while adopting the poetic, linguistic and iconographic excesses of biblical *ecriture* applied to the specifics of the animated film medium, Japanese tradition and a globalized market.

Notes

1. "Balance" and "harmony" are vital to the understanding of Japanese art and culture and perform a deep structural platform for aesthetic expression.

2. Brophy's excellent and poetic BFI handbook, *100 Anime*, for example, is full of abridged summaries of major works frequently described as apocalyptic, post-apocalyptic or hyper-apocalyptic (e.g. *Ai City, Akira, Barefoot Gen, Doomed Megalopolis, Giant Robo, Roujin-Z, Demon City Shinjuku, Fist of the North Star, Neon Genesis Evangelion, Space Adventure Cobra, Steamboy, Urotsukidoji, Violence Jack*).

3. I am in no way attempting to discount the veracity of these authors' scholarship, or homogenize their critical work as "secular". While this may seem a pedantic (or semantic) issue, the continued figuring of *anime* in terms

of Judaeo-Christian theological tradition is deeply problematic and imprints a Western reading and epistemology on Japanese (no matter how globalized) cultural production.

4.   "Christians are strongly represented among the best-educated, leading elements in society and have therefore exerted a quite disproportionate influence. Another factor is that Christianity, as an important element of Western civilization, has attracted general attention. Most educated Japanese probably have a clearer concept of the history and basic beliefs of Christianity than they do of Buddhism" (Reischauer and Jansen, 1995: 213).

5.   Indeed, *Metropolis* is no more "retro" that Miyazaki's earlier *Laputa: Castle in the Sky* (1986).

6.   In the accompanying DVD audio commentary, director Aramaki Shinji explains that although the film begins with this biblical quote, "it was not absolutely necessary here but it had atmosphere, and it was phrase that put everything into place, and I had strong feelings about it".

7.   As Arakami outlines in the director's commentary, the visceral and kinetic violence of the opening sequence is deliberately chaotic and confusing, to disorient the viewer: "You don't really get a good sense of what's going on".

8.   As Jerome Shapiro (2002: 265) reminds us, "In Japanese philosophy and culture, especially its aesthetics, *balance* is a fundamental principle. Balance, however, is something fluid, dynamic and transient".

9.   To confirm this seemingly automated exposition, Hitomi concludes with the Central Planning Bureau's motto for Olympus design: "The basis of all design is human-centred and user-friendly. Conceptual simplicity and structural complexity achieves a greater state of humanity."

10.   These old men are deeply ambiguous if not duplicitous characters, and revealed to be complicit in several homicidal schemes, ranging from individual murder (Knute's mother, Dr Gilliam), through to "speciescide". The seven may also allude to the myth of the assault on Thebes—its seven gates and the seven soldiers who led an army against the city. The allusion is further strengthened in the *anime* when the seven spider-like defence robots are activated by the Elders to destroy D-Tank and usher in the end of *homo sapiens*.

11.   Such technological "ghosts" are replete in apocalyptic *anime*, particularly the Magi system in *Evangelion Neon Genesis Evangelion* television series and films (1995 onwards) and the three *Ghost in the Shell* films and TV series (1995, 2004, 2006).

12.   MacGuffin is a term Alfred Hitchcock coined to describe essential but superfluous plot exposition that gave context for the plot direction and seemed important but merely serves as a catalyst for action/themes of much more interest to the filmmaker and audience (e.g. jealousy, surveillance, murder, sexual dysfunction). Shapiro (2002: 60–2) finds that nuclear plots are often

little more than MacGuffins in the majority of what he has called "atomic bomb cinema", yet he recognizes that some bomb films deploy apocalyptic narrative to, as Kermode would have it, make sense of the end.

References

M. Y. Aoki and M. B. Dardess (eds), *As the Japanese See It: Past and Present* (Honolulu, HI: University of Hawaii Press, 1981).

Mick Broderick, *Anime's Apocalypse: Neon Genesis Evangelion as Millennarian Mecha*. *Intersections*. No. 7, March 2002. At <http://wwwsshe.murdoch.edu.au/intersections/issue7/broderick_review.html>

Philip Brophy, *100 Anime* (London: British Film Institute, 2005).

Philip Brophy, "Sonic—Atomic—Nuemonic: Apocalyptic Echoes in Anime". In Alan Cholodenko (ed.) *The Illusion of Life 2: More Essays on Animation* (Sydney: Power Publications, 2007), pp. 191–208.

Philip Brophy and Julie Ewington (eds), *KABOOM! Explosive Animation from America and Japan* (Sydney: Museum of Contemporary Art, 1994).

Malcolm Bull, "On Making Ends Meet". In Malcolm Bull (ed.) *Apocalypse Theory and the Ends of the World* (Oxford: Blackwell, 1995), pp. 1–17.

Joseph Campbell, *The Masks of God*, Vols 1–4 (London: Penguin, 1991).

Alan Cholodenko (ed.), *The Illusion of Life: Essays on Animation* (Sydney: Power Publications, 1991).

Alan Cholodenko (ed.), *The Illusion of Life 2: More Essays on Animation* (Sydney: Power Publications, 2007).

Norman Cohn, *The Pursuit of the Millennium: Revolutionary Millenarians and Mystical Anarchists of the Middle Ages* (New York: Oxford University Press, 1957).

Norman Cohn, *Noah's Flood: The Genesis Story in Western Thought* (New Haven, CT: Yale University Press, 1999).

Ben Crawford, "Emperor Tomato Ketchup: Cartoon Properties from Japan". In Mick Broderick (ed.), *Hibakusha Cinema: Hiroshima, Nagasaki and the Nuclear Image in Japanese Film* (London: Kegan Paul International, 1996), pp. 75–90.

Edwin O. Reischauer and Marius B. Jansen, *The Japanese Today: Change and Continuity*, 3rd Edition (Cambridge, MA: Belknap Press, 1995).

Mircea Eliade, *The Myth of the Eternal Return: Or, Cosmos and History* (Princeton NJ: Bollingen, 1971).

Freda Freiberg, "*Akira* and the Postnuclear Sublime". In Mick Broderick (ed.), *Hibakusha Cinema: Hiroshima, Nagasaki and the Nuclear Image in Japanese Film* (London: Kegan Paul International, 1996), pp. 91–102.

Northrop Frye, *The Great Code: The Bible and Literature* (London: Ark Paperbacks 1983).

Jane Goodall, "Hybridity and the End of Innocence". In Alan Cholodenko (ed.) *The Illusion of Life 2: More Essays on Animation* (Sydney: Power Publications 2007), pp. 152–70.

John R. Hall, P. D. Schuyler and S. Trinh, *Apocalypse Observed: Religious Movements and Violence in North America, Europe and Japan* (London: Routledge, 2000).

Frank Kermode, *The Sense of an Ending: Studies in the Theory of Fiction* (Oxford: Oxford University Press, 1967).

Frank Kermode, "Waiting for the End". In Malcolm Bull (ed.) *Apocalypse Theory and the Ends of the World* (Oxford: Blackwell, 1995), pp. 250–63.

Joseph M. Kitagawa, *Religion in Japanese History* (New York: Columbia University Press, 1990).

Krishan Kumar, 'Apocalypse, Millennium and Utopia Today'. In Malcolm Bull (ed.) *Apocalypse Theory and the Ends of the World* (Oxford: Blackwell, 1995), pp. 200–26.

Antonia Levi, *Samurai from Outer Space: Understanding Japanese Animation* (Chicago, IL: Open Court, 1998).

Helen McCarthy, *Anime! A Beginners Guide To Japanese Animation* (London: Titan, 1993).

Helen McCarthy, *The Anime Movie Guide—Japanese Animation since 1983* (London: Titan, 1996).

Pauline Moore, "When Velvet Gloves Meet Iron Fists: Cuteness in Japanese Animation". In Alan Cholodenko (ed.) *The Illusion of Life 2: More Essays on Animation* (Sydney: Power Publications, 2007), pp. 119–50.

Susan Napier, *Anime from Akira to Howl's Moving Castle, Experiencing Contemporary Japanese Animation* (New York: Palgrave Macmillan, 2005).

Christopher Norris, "Versions of Apocalypse: Kant, Derrida, Foucault". In Malcolm Bull (ed.) *Apocalypse Theory and the Ends of the World* (Oxford: Blackwell, 1995).

Stephen O'Leary, *Arguing the Apocalypse. A Theory of Millennial Rhetoric* (New York: Oxford University Press, 1998).

Edwin O. Reischauer and Marius B. Jansen, *The Japanese Today: Change and Continuity* (Cambridge, MA: Belknap Press, 1995).

Andrew Ross, *Strange Weather: Culture, Science and Technology in the Age of Limits* (London: Verso, 1991).

Jerome F. Shapiro, "Does Japan have a Millenary Imagination?" *Kyoto Daigaku Sôgôningengakubu Kiyô*, July 1994: 133–45.

Jerome F. Shapiro, *Atomic Bomb Cinema: The Apocalyptic Imagination on Film* (New York: Routledge, 2002).

Susan Sontag, "The Imagination of Disaster". In Mick Broderick (ed.), *Hibakusha Cinema: Hiroshima, Nagasaki and the Nuclear Image in Japanese Film* (London: Kegan Paul International, 1965/1996), pp. 38–53.

Jon R. Stone, *Expecting Armageddon: Essential Readings in Failed Prophecy,* (London: Routledge, 2000).

Damian Thompson, *The End of Time* (London: Minerva, 1996).
Lois Zamora, *Writing the Apocalypse: Historical Vision in Contemporary US and Latin American Fiction* (New York: Cambridge University Press, 1989).

Films Cited

Akira (Dir: Otomo Katsuhiro, 1988)
Appleseed (Dir: Aramaki Shinji, 2004)
Blade Runner (Dir: Ridley Scott, 1982),
Dr Strangelove or: How I Learned to Stop Worrying and Love the Bomb (Dir: Stanley Kubrick, 1963)
Ghost in the Shell (Dir: Mamoru Oshii, 1995)
Ghost in the Shell 2: Innocence (Dir: Mamoru Oshii, 2004)
Ghost in the Shell: S.A.C. (Dir: Kenji Kamiyama, 2006)
Metropolis (Dir: Rintaro, 2001)
Neon Genesis Evangelion (Dir: Hideaki Anno, 1995-6)
Spriggan (Dir: Kawasaki Hirotsugu, 1998)
Steamboy (Dir: Otomo Katsuhiro, 2004)
The Day the Earth Stood Still (Dir: Robert Wise, 1951)

Selling Faith Without Selling Out
Reading the *Left Behind* Novels in the Context of Popular Culture

Jennie Chapman

> We all sense we are a part of something God is doing, and we are delighted he is using these books. (Bill Anderson, President of Christian Booksellers Association)
>
> Does having a book in Wal-Mart really matter to God? (Rick Christian, President of Alive Communications literary agency).[1]

Introduction

Tim LaHaye and Jerry B. Jenkins's *Left Behind* novels are a cultural phenomenon of profound importance. They have sold in their multi-millions; spawned a lucrative cottage industry of related merchandise and persuaded, according to the authors, many thousands of Americans to accept Jesus Christ as their saviour as the impending end of the world casts its inexorable shadow over history.[2] Yet despite their popularity, much of the public discourse on the novels, itself sporadic and sometimes spurious, characterizes them at best as a negligible footnote in the story of recent American culture, and a thoroughly bizarre one at that. One bemused commentator writing in the British *Daily Telegraph,* for example, could only describe as "science fiction" the rapture theory on which the plot of *Left Behind* hinges, adding with some relief that "[t]o many pious Protestants and Catholics, this sounds completely bananas".[3] And it is not only the secular press that has trivialized the novels; even those with a vested interest in religious developments, be they practising Christians, faith leaders or scholars of religion, are often only vaguely aware of the apocalyptic novels which have proved so popular and influential across the Atlantic.

Despite the paucity of serious discourse, academic or otherwise, acknowledging the cultural significance of *Left Behind*, the novels' status as a highly salient feature of an increasingly diverse American cultural landscape can hardly be refuted. As such, it is the aim of this chapter to assess, question and problematize the popularity of the *Left Behind* novels. First, I will examine some of the existing theories of popular culture, and suggest that *Left Behind* poses a challenge to this corpus by exceeding and disrupting such categories as "popular culture", "mass culture", "subculture" and "mainstream". I will then explore some of the reasons—commercial, political, and cultural— for the novels' success and popularity, in spite (or, indeed, because) of their polemical religious tone. Finally, I will attend to the texts themselves, in order to examine the relationship between evangelicalism and popular culture posited by the authors, and to consider how this fictional representation of the American cultural terrain resonates with the reality beyond *Left Behind*'s pages. My central argument is that the phenomenon of *Left Behind* provokes us to re-evaluate the ways in which we think and speak about popular culture, religion, and the complex and often fraught relationship between the two.

Dispensationalism, the Rapture, and *Left Behind*

Left Behind is a series of apocalyptic "rapture fiction" published between 1995 and 2007. Conceived by Christian Right activist and prophecy student Tim LaHaye, and penned by writer-for-hire Jerry Jenkins, the original series consisted of 12 novels, though the writing partners have recently supplemented the franchise with three prequels and a sequel.[4] Though it has been translated into 113 languages, *Left Behind* nevertheless remains a distinctly American phenomenon, enjoying the vast majority of its commercial success in the United States, drawing upon specifically American religious, cultural and rhetorical traditions, and depicting what the authors take to be the quintessential "American experience" as universal and normative.[5]

The eschatological framework and rationale for the series is provided by the doctrine of premillennial dispensationalism, a rather singular exegesis of prophetic scripture introduced to the States in the mid-nineteenth century by the Irish dissenter John Nelson Darby, and later popularized by the *Scofield Reference Bible*, first published in 1909. Darby's literalist hermeneutic divided history into discrete periods, known as dispensations. These were differentiated by the particular way in which God dealt with his human subjects: thus, in each dispensation humanity would be tested, each test inevitably resulted in failure, and a new dispensation would begin. The present era is described as the church age, during which God momentarily turns his attention from his chosen people—the Jews—to those who have accepted Christ as their saviour—the Church. The church age represents a "great parenthesis" between the previous dispensations (which pertained to Old Testament prophecies relating to the Jewish people) and the millennium (when Christ would return to reign on earth, and God would return to his previous task of dealing with the earthly problems of Israel). During this period of eschatological stasis, and in contrast to preceding dispensations, no more biblical prophecies will be fulfilled. Indeed, the prophetic clock cannot start ticking again until the occurrence of a supernatural event which dispensationalists eagerly await, and which provides the opening scene in the first installment of LaHaye and Jenkins's series.[6]

The "rapture" is a central element of dispensationalist doctrine based upon an interpretation of 1 Thessalonians 4:16–17 which, according to Darby, describes the true church being physically "caught up … in the air" to join Christ in the heavens. The bulk of the narrative delineates the seven-year "Tribulation" period of apocalyptic judgement and suffering which befalls those "left behind" in the rapture, finally concluding with the return of Christ and the onset of His millennium. The dispensational Tribulation technically begins with the post-rapture signing of a covenant between the Antichrist and Israel (a parody of Israel's covenantal relationship with God); therefore, the *Left Behind* novels, which open with the rapture, begin shortly before the start of the Tribulation proper, although the conditions that characterize that period are certainly established at the outset.

Left Behind thus depicts a world plunged into chaos following the abrupt disappearance of millions across the globe. Though the cause of this event is initially a mystery to most of the novels' inhabitants, spiritually astute readers will immediately recognize it as the beginning of the prophesied end-times. As the world struggles to come to terms with the vanishings, an obscure Romanian leader named Nicolae Carpathia emerges from anonymity, wooing the masses and the political elite alike with his seeming compassion, intelligence and charisma. Though Carpathia promises to bring peace and order to a world on the brink of anarchy, he is in fact the Antichrist, the "great deceiver" who exploits the widespread confusion instigated by the disappearances in order to seize global control and institute a terrifying totalitarian regime. As if this wasn't enough, the Tribulation is also marked by the wrath of God, who inflicts biblical punishments—including locust plagues, earthquakes, freak weather and the transformation of rivers into blood—upon those who fail to accept Christ as their saviour. *Left Behind*'s protagonists, meanwhile, are a group of newly converted evangelicals who see the error of their spiritual ways after being "left behind". Naming themselves the Tribulation Force, they spend the years preceding the Second Coming engaged in a divinely inspired battle to win souls for Christ and thwart the efforts of Satan.

Considering the specificity of the doctrine espoused in *Left Behind*, the series has proved remarkably popular. Some 65 million copies have now been sold, and the last six novels all attained the number one position on best-seller lists including *New York Times, Publishers Weekly, Wall Street Journal* and *USA Today*.[7] Though many readers of the series are evangelicals, a significant number—around three million, according to a 2001 survey—are outside of this tradition. The Barna Research Group, which conducted this study, found that almost one in nine American adults had read at least one of the LaHaye and Jenkins novels. The survey director concluded that the series constitutes one of the most widely experienced religious teaching or evangelistic tools among adults who are not born-again Christians, reaching a larger and more diverse audience than, say, radio or television ministries.[8]

Stylistically, the novels emulate the thriller genre, but also incorporate aspects of romance, conspiracy and war fiction in their quest for broad generic appeal. Their artistic aspirations are often overshadowed, however, by their political polemicism. The novels are unashamedly right-wing: "big government" is castigated, multilateralism condemned as a ruse of the devil, pacifism rejected as futile and possibly diabolical, and liberalism, secularism and cultural pluralism interpreted as sure signs of Satan's growing influence on earth. Commentators in the media and in some sections of the academy have consequently read the *Left Behind* project as a platform for the more extremist agendas of the religious right, frequently characterizing the series as bizarre, alien and possibly dangerous.[9] This aspect of the novels is only one of several which have attracted negative attention. The series' literary merit has been the target of several critics: Amy Johnson Frykholm, a perceptive and sympathetic authority on *Left Behind*, nonetheless finds the protagonists "flimsy and ill developed, the plot contrived, and the writing thin"; religion scholar Glenn W. Shuck similarly describes the prose as "banal" and the characterization as "poorly sustained", adding that a sensitive analysis of the series is frustrated by the fact that "[n]onevangelical readers will likely find the novels offensive in numerous ways".[10] Meanwhile, many mainline Christian critics accuse the series of making unbiblical and unethical departures from the true gospel, claims which have been bolstered by concerned commentators from other faith groups, as well as secular parties involved in gay and women's rights, environmental campaigns and the political left, to name a few examples.[11]

Despite these oft-articulated misgivings, the books nevertheless occupy a central position in American popular culture: a fact which, given the caveats listed above, is both extraordinary and intriguing. As it can hardly be argued that every reader of the franchise is a right-wing, homophobic, misogynistic zealot (with a poor taste in literature at that), we must look to other explanations in our analysis of the complex and apparently confounding popularity of *Left Behind*. This problem will be taken up in later sections of this chapter, but before doing so it is necessary to foreground our analysis by working towards a definition of popular culture which can accommodate religious discourses such as those articulated by LaHaye and Jenkins.

Cultural Categories and the Problem of *Left Behind*

The notion of culture is notoriously difficult to determine, and is especially so in relation to a product such as *Left Behind*. The language we have developed to describe and classify cultural products—which includes such terms as popular, mainstream, subculture, mass culture, counter-culture, high-/middle-/low-brow—suddenly seems reductive when confronted with LaHaye and Jenkins's dispensational fiction. Despite its extraordinary sales figures, *Left Behind*'s atypical subject matter and seemingly pre-defined, tightly delineated audience seems to preclude its designation as "mainstream".[12] At the same time, it doesn't quite fit into the category of "subculture" either, given the romantic associations of resistance, transgression and heroic disenfranchisement the term conjures. It would seem a stretch indeed to postulate a correlation between the conservative, reactionary themes of *Left Behind*, and the radical punks or mods so vividly described by scholars such as Dick Hebdige and other members of the "Birmingham school".[13]

At first glance, then, the theories of subculture that emerged from Birmingham appear to have little relevance to *Left Behind*, or indeed, to other examples of evangelical cultural engagement. Hebdige's classic study, *Subculture: The Meaning of Style*, while recognizing that "[t]he meaning of subculture is always in dispute", nonetheless describes subcultures as grass-roots, youth-oriented, deviant movements which signal a "refusal" of the dominant order—a model which appears at odds with Christian culture on several levels.[14] However, when one examines *Left Behind* through Hebdige's interpretive framework, certain affinities do emerge. For many commentators, *Left Behind* cannot be categorized as "mainstream" because it commits what Hebdige calls "a crime against the natural order", presenting a worldview which differs radically and unsettlingly from dominant, normative, "rational" notions of reality.[15] To this extent, *Left Behind*'s subversive, "alien" content is consonant with the dominant view of subcultures as estranged, exotic and potentially threatening. Yet the novels, with their conservative ideological perspective and primarily white, middle-aged, female audience, hardly conform to the typical model of youthful, anarchic dissidence either. *Left Behind* problematizes the dominant discourse because it appears to be *at once* aberrant, subversive and disruptive *and* conservative, reactionary and archaic.

Left Behind demonstrates that the subcultural aesthetic can be radically reappropriated for various ideological ends; it also shows how assumptions about subcultures posited by the dominant culture might apply to a variety of movements with vastly different goals, values and beliefs. LaHaye and Jenkins's rapture novels thus expose the profound problems of categorization where cultural movements are concerned. In *American Culture, American Tastes*, historian Michael Kammen argues persuasively that cultural orthodoxies, such as notions of high, low, mass and popular culture, are no longer convincing in the current age of mass media communication, in which almost every cultural form has been subject to commodification, and in which traditional "taste" boundaries formed in relation to class, ethnicity, race and religious belief are frequently transcended. Despite this suspicion of categories, however, Kammen continues to find a marked disparity between popular culture—which he characterizes as specific, local, and grass-roots (much like Hebdige's subculture)—and mass culture, which is conversely homogeneous, national/global, and commercial.[16]

Perhaps because the relationship between religion and popular culture has largely been ignored until recently, Kammen does not attend to phenomena such as *Left Behind*: had he done so, he may have found his distinction between popular and mass culture somewhat troubled. *Left Behind* is indeed a profitable commodity and, one might therefore surmise, a thoroughly incorporated "mass culture" product which bears little resemblance to Kammen's idea of popular culture. In another sense, however, the world of end-times prophecy belief from which *Left Behind* emanates does bear comparison to the grass-roots cultures delineated by Kammen and Hebdige. As Paul Boyer demonstrates in his study of contemporary prophecy belief, *When Time Shall Be No More*, dispensationalism is a "theology of the people".[17] In the time-honoured tradition of subcultural movements, it is a dissident worldview which is prone to rejection and stigmatization, both by the dominant secular culture and "mainline" Christianity. Therefore, those who shaped the doctrines that informed *Left Behind* did so in a subterranean milieu which circumvented the institutional structures of the church, the seminary and the publishing house. It would appear, then, that dispensationalist culture is "popular" in Kammen's sense of being grass-roots and anti-institutional. Certainly, this status is often played upon by believers themselves, whose rhetoric emphasizes the renegade, marginal nature of their faith.

Yet while it is true that dispensationalism is often rhetorically situated upon the peripheries of American culture—both by those inside *and* outside the faith—the history of American evangelicalism presents a somewhat more nuanced picture which challenges this orthodoxy. In the 1970s Hal Lindsey's book *The Late Great Planet Earth* provoked widespread interest in the subject of prophecy, while *Newsweek* went so far as to name the year of President Jimmy Carter's election, 1976, the "Year of the Evangelical", reporting that some 50 million Americans shared the new president's "born again" faith in Jesus. Evangelical prophecy continually makes significant interventions into that very "mainstream" which seeks to relegate it to the "lunatic fringe", changing the meaning of the "mainstream" in the process.

The success of *Left Behind* has done much to disprove conventional theories of marginality, which, rather than acknowledging the actual significance of evangelical culture in the larger story of American culture, tend to serve the interests of a secular "mainstream" seeking to maintain its own cultural hegemony. *Left Behind* occupies a nebulous hinterland between subculture and the "mainstream", grass-roots popular culture and commercial mass culture. It thus demands of scholars a careful consideration of the place *Left Behind* occupies in the American cultural landscape—not to mention a reappraisal of what we mean, and indeed what is at stake, when we invoke the conventional terminology of cultural studies.[18]

Selling Faith Without Selling Out

We have seen that in a number of ways *Left Behind* disrupts our preferred paradigms for thinking about culture. The following section considers how the series, and dispensationalism in a more general sense, interacts with one particular theory of popular culture which has become almost paradigmatic in modern cultural studies discourse. The theory of incorporation was developed by British academics, including Stuart Hall, Tony Jefferson, and, of course, Dick Hebdige, in the 1970s. Influenced by Gramsci's application of Marxian economic theory to the examination of culture, it proposes that subcultures follow a more or less standard trajectory in which they are eventually "made safe" for mainstream public consumption. According to this process, the subculture is initially met with shock and condemnation; however, over the course of time, and through the constitutive discourse of the media, the subculture is sanitized and domesticated, purged of its anti-social and transgressive elements. Though subcultures "begin with a crime against the natural order", they are eventually "incorporated, brought back into line, located on the preferred 'map of problematic social reality'". By this logic, as Henri Lefebvre notes, "that which yesterday was reviled today becomes cultural consumer-goods".[19] While this theory does allow for the exercise of personal agency by consumers of popular culture, it nevertheless acknowledges the power of the dominant culture at any given epoch to curb the potentially disruptive effects of such movements.

Subcultures are thus absorbed by the dominant culture through a process of incorporation, by which the subculture is tamed and made publicly acceptable. Both Hebdige and Kammen ascribe this process to the mass media, through which subcultures/popular cultures become, almost inevitably, mainstream. As we know, *Left Behind* has achieved notable "crossover" success as a "mainstream" product. One may well view this success as evidence of the series' incorporation by the dominant culture. Unusually, however, this mainstreaming of *Left Behind* has *not* been accompanied by the attenuation of transgressive content which ordinarily accompanies incorporation. In spite of *Left Behind*'s visibility in the marketplace, its explicitly, often polemically evangelical message has not been tempered. Heather Hendershot writes in her study of evangelical culture:

> a subtle or absent salvation message is the hallmark of much of the media that finds financial success beyond the Christian market. The wildly successful LaHaye and Jenkins books are more the exception than the rule; they are filled with evangelical fervor and are hardly subtle.[20]

Left Behind has been able to retain its explicit religious imperative even as it is absorbed by the popular fiction market, thus simultaneously conforming to and confounding extant models of cultural accommodation.

It is finally worth noting briefly that *Left Behind* not only unsettles our assumptions about cultural stratification in the general sense, but also disrupts the norms of production in the realm of specifically Christian culture. Jonathan Cordero identifies a prevailing Christian fiction aesthetic which guides and limits the kind of fiction acceptable to the Christian publishing industry's target market.[21] If a particular novel is to be successful, Cordero observes, the imperative to entertain should dominate the imperative to minister; religious messages should be implicit rather than explicit; and a generic Christianity is preferable to a particular Christianity. LaHaye and Jenkins's series breaks with all of these directives. Pages of exhortation, often including lengthy quotes from scripture, continually intersperse the action, one might say at the latter's expense. As Hendershot notes, the religious message in *Left Behind* has in no way been blunted, concealed or allegorized—it is overt, insistent and unapologetic. Moreover, this message is extremely particularistic. Far from extolling vague, uncontroversial Christian values such as love, forgiveness and compassion, *Left Behind* is rooted in the specifics of dispensationalism, a peculiar form of end times belief that would confound many

Christians *within* the evangelical tradition, let alone a secular audience. In many ways, then, *Left Behind* has ploughed its own cultural furrow. Its success defies both the logic of cultural incorporation by the "mainstream", and the specific precepts of cultural production in a Christian context.

The Pleasure of the Text

Much has been written in cultural studies on the economies of pleasure that inform subjective reading experiences. Popular literature in particular is assumed to operate within such an economy: genres such as the romance novel, the action thriller, or the hardboiled detective story, are conventionally thought to evoke pleasure through the use of familiar forms which do not make intellectual demands upon the reader. Roland Barthes identifies this rather prosaic experience as *plaisir,* as opposed to the ecstatic pleasures of stylistic invention to which he ascribes the term *jouissance.*[22] As I have briefly suggested, *Left Behind* borrows its style, motifs and devices from the established repertoires of popular genres such as those listed above. Stylistically, it is, like other popular literature, largely formulaic and predictable. However, while romances or detective stories might be experienced as titillating moments of escapism from the quotidian routine of ordinary life, the *Left Behind* books seek to be more than just lightweight entertainment. They also demand to be read as a lesson, a warning, an exhortation. The events depicted on the pages *will happen,* the authors tell us, and the various trials of the characters exemplify how Christians should conduct themselves in a time of tribulation, be it the actual Tribulation of the end times, or what LaHaye describes as the "pre-tribulation tribulation" of our current era.[23]

The novels thus fracture traditional notions about popular literature, because their clearly pedagogical intent seems at odds with the kind of effortless, undidactic enjoyment afforded by other popular genres. Whereas other popular literature is self-effacing about its ideological imperatives, *Left Behind* wears its ideology on its sleeve. Moreover, the "pleasure" it invokes exists in intimate relation to, rather than in spite of, this ideology. The pleasure the reader experiences depends significantly upon his or her own ideological perspective, and its relation to the message of the novels. Consequently, the types of pleasure the novels elicit are diverse and sometimes surprising. This variety of pleasures experienced by readers from divergent religious, cultural and ethnic backgrounds goes some way to explaining why the novels have found success with audiences who may not ordinarily engage with dispensational culture.

As one might expect, evangelical readers of *Left Behind* report a classic experience of pleasure in the texts. Frykholm notes the prevalence of food and eating metaphors in such readers' descriptions: many alternately describe "savouring" and "devouring" the novels, often comparing them to chocolate, a food typically associated with the "guilty", even *verboten* pleasure also evoked by the consumption of popular literature.[24] The novels additionally serve to affirm and accentuate readers' sense of their own evangelical identity. Unlike typical pleasure reading, which is a private, personal activity, *Left Behind* is often experienced in the context of community. Books are passed around congregations and Bible studies, often without the express approval of that body's leadership, providing reading communities with a common focus, a topic for debate, a shared experience. Frykholm contends that, whereas other types of reading take place in solitude, "[r]eading *Left Behind* is better understood ... as an act of social connection".[25]

Glenn Shuck has suggested that *Left Behind* seeks to create just the right amount of tension between evangelicals and the rest of the world: when the balance is correct, evangelicals feel different enough from the world to maintain their own specific identity, yet have enough in common with it to meaningfully participate in its affairs.[26] On the one hand, then, the novels play upon and possibly exacerbate the existing cultural anxieties of evangelical readers, who often perceive themselves as liminal figures in a largely secular world which tends to trivialize or ridicule their beliefs and values. Within the narrative, this paranoid worldview is figured through motifs such as the "mark of loyalty", a microchip inserted under the skin and demarcated by a tattoo, which evangelical readers will recognize as the "mark of the beast" described in Revelation.[27] As Carpathia has made the mark mandatory, the dissension of believers forces them to adopt the uncertain and risky status of fugitives, enemies of the state who must remain constantly alert to deceit, betrayal and infiltration in order to ensure both their own survival and that of their fellow believers. This exiled status only affirms the protagonists' conviction that they can never feel truly at home on earth until Christ's return.

"We are aliens in this world," one believer tells another in *Desecration,* "homeless if anyone is".[28]

Such a sense of paranoia and displacement mirrors in exaggerated terms evangelical readers' sense of persecution in *this* world, and, through this mimesis, legitimizes such an outlook. However, the novels do not simply reaffirm evangelical perceptions of marginality—this would be overly dystopian and would fail to provide the narrative resolution that readers expect. As Stephen D. O'Leary notes, in evangelical end-times belief (unlike its secular equivalents) apocalyptic fear must always be counterbalanced by millennial hope.[29] Thus the novels posit an imaginative resolution to the persecution of Christians it perceives in both the post-rapture world of the novels *and* present day America. Knowing the biblical prophecies to be infallible, the characters (and sympathetic readers) observe with self-satisfaction the suffering of those who have opposed them, safe in the knowledge that "in the end, we win".[30]

In this sense, *Left Behind* performs a similar function to other forms of popular literature: it offers a "compensatory solution" to problems encountered and anxieties experienced by readers in their day-to-day lives. As Janice Radway finds in her ethnographic work with readers of romance fiction, readers temporarily substitute themselves for the heroines in the story. Whereas in real life the reader's various trials, difficulties and disappointments may not be resolved satisfactorily, her fictional proxy claims a singular and decisive victory over such obstacles.[31] Such a trade-off, as we have seen, also occurs in *Left Behind.* The novels simultaneously reflect the "real" world the reader inhabits, and offer an escape from it.

Different Readers, Different Reading Pleasures

While many of *Left Behind*'s readers include themselves in the evangelical flock, there are an estimated three million—a considerable minority—who do not. Why do such readers engage with *Left Behind,* especially given the authors' apparent desire to exclude them through the narrow, even cliquish worldview their novels portray? One might suggest that another type of reading pleasure comes into play when we attempt to analyse the motivations of such readers. Non-dispensationalists may experience an inverse sort of pleasure through their rejection of, and nonidentification with, the novels. In this way, identity is affirmed negatively—non-sympathetic readers galvanize their own sense of self in their refusal to relate to the characters, in their recognition that "that is not me".[32] Some readers "enjoy" the novels, then, precisely because they violently disagree with them, as did one of Frykholm's subjects. This particular reader read the first three books even though she was irritated by their politics, their tone and, especially, their representation of women. "Pleasure and anger are not contradictory, in Samantha's case, but feed into one another," writes Frykholm, "so that anger allowed her to continue to find some pleasure in reading the books."[33]

Yet others have different motivations for reading the novels. Many read them on the recommendation of evangelical friends or family members, who often harbour the hope that the novels will encourage a conversion; others still pick up the books simply because the cover or title attract them, or because they have been positioned in shops alongside other (not necessarily religious) titles which they may have already read and enjoyed—as we shall see, the distribution of *Left Behind* to supermarkets, drugstores and bookstore chains has broken down previously existing boundaries between Christian and secular fiction, making LaHaye and Jenkins's books potentially available to a far more diverse audience than the products of their predecessors, which were sold almost exclusively through Christian retailers. For a range of reasons, then, a substantial number of nonevangelical readers have engaged with the novels to an extent not seen before within the realm of Christian culture.

Explaining the Popularity of *Left Behind*

LaHaye and Jenkins's novels have been singular in their ability to combine commercial success with an overt religious message. Although I will argue later that the novels become more "niche" as the series unfolds, their general popularity is difficult to deny, and their success as Christian fiction is certainly unprecedented. What are the conditions that have allowed *Left Behind* to succeed so spectacularly where other similar examples have (comparatively) failed?

One factor in LaHaye and Jenkins's success is simply the savvy marketing of the series, demonstrating the growing sophistication of the Christian culture market. Unlike its predecessors, *Left Behind* is sold not only in Christian bookstores but also mainstream book chains such as Barnes and Noble and Borders. Indeed, even supermarkets such as Wal-Mart and Costco, and airports across America have stocked the title. Many of these do not simply sell the novels but actively market them: Wal-Mart, for example, gave away copies of the first chapter of the final instalment, *The Glorious Appearing,* as part of a major promotion of the series.[34] Additionally, a massive array of *Left Behind* spin-off products, which include a movie trilogy, a board game, a music CD, graphic novels, children's fiction, a computer game, prequels, sequels and even an instructional video to be viewed by those left behind in the event of the rapture, has greatly increased the market presence of the *Left Behind* brand.

The reputation of the authors has also been instrumental to their product's success. Tim LaHaye has long been a prominent figure in American evangelicalism, and was a key instigator of the movement's politicization in the 1970s. In 2001, the *Evangelical Studies Bulletin,* published by the Institute for the Study of American Evangelicals, named Tim LaHaye the most influential Christian leader of the last 25 years.[35] Before publishing the *Left Behind* novels, LaHaye wrote extensively on a range of themes, gaining some notoriety for his unabashedly provocative views on homosexuality (*The Unhappy Gays,* 1978), secular humanism (*The Battle for the Mind,* 1980), psychology (*The Spirit-Controlled Temperament,* 1966) and, of course, biblical prophecy (*Are We Living in The End Times?,* 2000). Jenkins is perhaps less well-known, but nonetheless has some notable credentials, as the biographer of several Christian sports stars, former editor of the premillennialist *Moody Magazine,* and founder of the Christian Writers Guild. He has recently produced his own end times trilogy independently of LaHaye, entitled *Soon.* The celebrity status of *Left Behind*'s writing team has no doubt assisted the series' promotion. In particular, LaHaye's candid political views have garnered attention from cultural conservatives outside the evangelical fold, while his outspokenness on a historically stigmatized aspect of the Bible has piqued the interest of Christians whose churches have deemed eschatological teachings irrelevant or even heretical.[36] Indeed, many mainline Protestant ministers and theologians accept vicarious responsibility for the popularity of dispensationalism and *Left Behind*, noting that the neglect of the prophetic books of the Bible by moderate churches has led some Christians to look elsewhere for teachings on the end of history. *Left Behind* is one popular source of such information, even though that information may well be, according to many ministers, theologically suspect. As one Lutheran pastor regretfully observed:

> [p]eople are hungry to have some information about what the Bible says about the future. And if you don't give them something good to eat, they'll eat junk food. And the *Left Behind* series are kind of the Twinkies and Hostess Cupcakes of the theological world.[37]

The novels have additionally both benefited from, and contributed to, the increasing visibility of evangelical culture in America since the 1970s. The high profile of evangelical figures such as Jerry Falwell, Jesse Helms, Pat Robertson, John Ashcroft, and indeed former President George W. Bush, has focused America's attention on this ever-present, but not always so conspicuous aspect of American culture. Simultaneously, Christian popular culture has pervaded the marketplace: Christian rock music, broadcasting networks, radio programmes and even PC operating systems are now commonplace, along with a plethora of so-called "Christian kitsch" including bumper stickers, trinkets and "witness wear".[38] Both Heather Hendershot and Colleen McDannell describe these phenomena as constituting an alternative or parallel Christian culture, but these designations are not quite accurate.[39] They imply separation, another world which is "out there" but which is nonetheless inaccessible and somewhat mysterious. On the contrary, bumper stickers which read "In case of rapture, this car will be unmanned" and T-shirts which proclaim that Jesus, not Coca-Cola, is the "Real Thing", are highly visible markers of faith. They do not designate a separate, parallel culture, but rather intrude upon and change the landscape of mainstream American culture.

The timing of the novels' release was undoubtedly advantageous. *Left Behind*'s launch in 1995 dovetailed with the approaching millennium and the end times fervour it fomented. The terrorist attacks of 11 September 2001, served to heighten such apocalyptic anxieties, with a corresponding increase in eschatological explanations of the attacks. According to a survey of 500 bookstores, sales of *Left Behind* increased by an astonishing 71 per cent in the eight weeks following 9/11, in comparison to the eight weeks preceding it.[40] As Americans asked searching questions about the disaster, dispensationalism provided ready answers, along with the concomitant assurance that that terrible day, far from being random and meaningless, was part of God's plan. As one reader of prophecy paperbacks explained, "I'm settled on the fact that this happened for a reason, and God was trying to get our attention".[41] The subsequent war in Iraq did little to dampen this apocalyptic expectation; indeed, the connection dispensationalism discerns between events in the Middle East and the end times proved even more provocative to prophecy interpreters. The stories told in *Left Behind* offered a comforting, not to say compelling antidote to the existential uncertainties that emerged during the height of the series' popularity.

We should finally bear in mind that dispensationalism itself has always been popular (in Kammen's sense of the word) by nature. Given its anti-institutional and often anti-intellectual stance, it is not surprising that this doctrine should find its most effective expression in generic, easy-to-read novels rather than through ecclesiastical structures and "high" theology. Moreover, it is incorrect to read *Left Behind*, as many observers have, as something totally unprecedented. As noted earlier, Hal Lindsey's dispensational tract, *The Late Great Planet Earth*, has sold some 28 million copies since its publication in 1970, while Don Thompson's rapture movie, *A Thief in the Night* (1972), was seen by as many as 100 million evangelicals in churches, youth groups and camp meetings.[42] *Left Behind* is thus part of a long tradition of "rapture fiction", which is in turn one aspect of a broad range of Christian literature that includes everything from Christian romances, thrillers, epics and historical novels, to self-help manuals, relationship guides and autobiographies. In a sense, the series is simply the latest—albeit by far the most visible and successful—incarnation of a culture which has been flourishing at a subterranean level for decades, if not centuries. After all, ever since the Wesleys' innovative use of print and popular hymns, American evangelicalism has thrived precisely because of its willingness to utilize new communications methods—and the infrastructure of popular culture—as tools for evangelism.

From Niche Culture to Popular Culture and Back

It should be borne in mind that there are 16 novels in LaHaye and Jenkins's series: it does not seem unlikely that further additions will appear in the future. Therefore, the function of the novels and their relationship to their audience may not remain uniform over the course of the series. From the launch of the first novel in 1995, to the pub-

lication of the most recent in 2007, I would argue that the relationship between the novels and mainstream culture changes significantly.[43] While the first novel appears to attempt to garner a fairly
broad audience through the use of recognizable motifs borrowed
from the repertoire of popular literature—the use of stock characters, the presence of conspiracy, a mystery to solve, an incipient romance—by the middle of the series one observes a shift in the tone
and perspective of the narrative.

Rather than seeking to attract new readers, the later novels aim to
consolidate their existing reading community and foster that
community's sense of collective identity, thus tending towards an
increasingly insular perspective. Whereas the earlier novels stress the
importance of evangelism, characters in later instalments barely interact with nonbelievers except as enemies to be vanquished. The
boundaries between the "us" of the Tribulation Force and the "them"
of Carpathia sympathizers and the undecided, become increasingly
rigid and impermeable as the series progresses. Moreover, while the
earlier books are more willing to utilize the apparatus of popular
culture—and perhaps soften somewhat their polemical tone—in order to attract a diverse audience, this imperative becomes less of a
priority as the series develops and the audience narrows. Certainly
from the eighth book, *The Mark*, onwards, the authors are less shy of
exhortation, including lengthy quotes from scripture, employing increasingly specialist terminology, and giving voice to more hard-line
and potentially offensive views. Although the authors certainly heed
the imperatives of the popular cultural economy initially, these are
finally trumped by the theological and cultural views of the authors,
and the perceived needs of a narrowly delineated audience who
already identify with the doctrines presented in the texts. *Left Behind*, then, seeks to attract a broad popular audience at the outset,
but by the end of the series preaches mainly to the choir.

Popular Culture at the End of History

Left Behind occupies a paradoxical position in American popular
culture, simultaneously engaging with and defining itself against it.
On the one hand, the series follows a highly specific theology which
many outside the dispensational subculture may find unintelligible.
On the other, however, it taps into familiar American mythologies
which are readily identifiable to many readers in the United States.

Bruce David Forbes suggests that Left Behind capitalizes upon a range of themes which permeate American culture. For example, the struggle between good and evil that the books delineate is hardly peculiar to rapture fiction, but is pivotal in a range of American narratives, from Disney stories and the Western, to science fiction and superhero comics. Moreover, this good-versus-evil motif is played out in very specific ways: evil always comes from the outside ("we" are not the problem); people are either good or evil, not both; the solution is the destruction of the evil-doers, or redemption through violence; and in the end, good vanquishes evil.[44] These are the motivating principles at work both in *Left Behind* and a good deal of "mainstream" American culture. In this way, these seemingly incongruous rapture fictions aren't so strange after all. Their success lies partly in their ability to blend—in just the right measure—the specifics of dispensationalism, and the general themes of good versus evil that are so prevalent in the wider culture.

Left Behind, then, does not simply appropriate the mechanisms of popular culture in a commercial or material sense. It also engages with popular culture at a textual level, guiding evangelical readers through their own interactions with a modern, mediated America, and instructing them, through the examples of the protagonists, how to be "in the world but not of the world". It offers imaginative solutions to the quandaries in which contemporary evangelicals find themselves, as they attempt to reconcile their faith to the secular consumer society they—as primarily white middle-class Americans—unavoidably find themselves a part. Far from rejecting outright, as some of their fundamentalist predecessors have, the modern reality of malls, movie theatres and money, LaHaye and Jenkins instead indicate to readers that they can have it both ways. They can be evangelicals *and* consumers, believers in both the saving grace of Jesus and the principles of the free market, engaged with the gospel message as well as the latest films, fashions and celebrity gossip. By depicting the end times as both "now" and "not yet" (as Timothy Weber puts it), the authors counsel their readers to expect the rapture to take place at any moment, but to nevertheless continue to live as though it will not.[45] In other words, otherworldly expectations must be tempered by a continued and meaningful engagement with the world in which evangelicals, for the time being, must remain. This negotiation is played out in *Left Behind*, in which the characters enjoy a comfortable, technologically advanced American lifestyle, whilst remaining mindful of the even more abundant (even more "American"?) world beyond.

The presence of popular culture in LaHaye and Jenkins's fictional milieu is pervasive. From the opening gambit of the rapture, we see characters attempt to understand and rationalize events through the lens of the popular imagination. For example, one of *Left Behind*'s central characters, Tribulation Force member Buck Williams, is convinced that the vanishings must have been caused by some "technology that could remove people from their clothes and make them disappear", a notion more fully expressed by a minor character who remarks that the "[o]nly thing I can compare it to is the old *Star Trek* shows where people got dematerialized and rematerialized". When the novels' hero, Rayford Steele, speculates whether "some world power" has done it "with fancy rays", the idiom of science fiction is conjoined with another popular motif—conspiracy.[46] These examples admittedly read rather awkwardly, especially out of context. It is nevertheless important to recognize the authorial intent—as far as it is possible to gauge such a thing—that informs these allusions. By making explicit and sometimes heavy-handed references to popular culture, LaHaye and Jenkins attempt to place their characters, and by extension, their readers, squarely in the modern world. This has two intended effects: first, it anchors the narrative in a familiar spatial and temporal location (America, the 1990s) through the use of easily decoded cultural signposts; second, and more importantly, it attempts to challenge stereotypes of evangelicals which paint them as reactionary, unsophisticated rubes who find themselves ill-at-ease in the contemporary environment. *Left Behind*'s Christian characters are instead savvy, technologically adept and self-consciously modern.

The novels' strategic use of the language of popular culture is often manifested in innovative ways. The authors invoke popular culture, for example, to demonstrate their awareness that their beliefs may seem somewhat incredible to the uninitiated:

> Nothing could be scripted like this, Buck thought, blinking slowly. If somebody tried to sell a screenplay about millions of people disappearing, leaving everything but their bodies behind, it would be laughed off.[47]

Of course, Hollywood has undoubtedly produced far stranger fare than the scenario Buck outlines. The intended effect of this remark is to foreclose possible criticisms concerning the novels' plausibility, by anticipating and articulating those criticisms within the narrative itself. The fact that this deflection is performed through the language of popular culture, an unmistakable signifier of modernity, demonstrates the authors' desire to engage with contemporary trends, ideas and idioms, even if these attempts sometimes seem a little inept and incongruous. Similar tactics are at work in the novels' extensive use of jargon and specialist language, such as "computerese". The following passage in *The Mark* is a typical example:

> This thing will literally intercept the impulses being relayed from point to point in the processor, carrying them to the power source, whether battery or AC, and drawing the current into the motherboard itself.[48]

It should be noted that the preceding passage is incidental to the plot and contributes little to the action. What it does do is announce—rather ostentatiously—that the authors are as *au fait* with modernity as any secular maligner who might sneer at their seemingly primitive beliefs.[49] Such language could also be read as a strategic rearticulation of popular fiction genres such as the techno-thriller, which the authors "poach", to use Michel de Certeau's terminology, for their own ideological purposes.[50]

There are abundant examples of such artful reappropriations of popular cultural discourse in *Left Behind*, too numerous to fully recount here. The main point is that the series does not reject and condemn popular culture outright, as some of its predecessors have, but rather selects the aspects of popular culture that buttress most effectively the dispensational message. This pragmatic, almost utilitarian approach to worldly engagement has long influenced American evangelicals, in their enigmatic quest to remain in the world but not of it.[51]

Conclusion

This chapter has sought to use *Left Behind* as an illuminating example of the problems inherent in the traditional interpretive frameworks of cultural studies. As we have seen, the novels affirm existing cultural paradigms to some extent, but equally, exhibit some important departures from them. They have been commercially successful without being fully "incorporated", yet the public perception of the books still casts them as a niche cultural product. They make ample use of motifs, imagery and structures mined from popular culture, while espousing an idiosyncratic eschatology which would only make sense to those schooled in the tenets of dispensationalism. In many ways *Left Behind* seems a strange anomaly, refusing the labels of popular culture, mainstream culture or even evangelical culture, and instead occupying an indeterminate space in between.

It is, then, perhaps most useful to analyse *Left Behind* not as a product of any of these categories, which implies the impermeability and discreteness of such classifications, but rather as an example of the long-standing reciprocity of Christian and secular forms of the apocalyptic imagination. Gary DeMar, author of a theological critique of *Left Behind*, argues that the series is not, as LaHaye claims, an interpretation of biblical prophecy, but an interpretation of the *popular interpretation* of biblical prophecy.[52] It does not analyse directly the books of Revelation, Daniel, Ezekiel and Matthew, but filters them through layers of Darbyite dispensationalism, Hal Lindsey, disaster movies, action novels and political populism. As such, DeMar suggests, the novels are unbiblical and misleading, because they take their cues from the popular apocalyptic consciousness rather than from their original source—scripture.

Whether or not DeMar's observation is correct, his contention demonstrates the hybridity of apocalyptic visions in contemporary Western culture, as well as the heterogeneity and flexibility of cultural forms and classifications more generally. Evangelical culture, popular culture and mass culture merge in *Left Behind,* as the authors inevitably draw upon the traditional Christian *and* contemporary popular images of the end of time that are deeply inscribed into their cultural milieu. As occupiers of the present world of American consumerism, media and politics, and anticipators of the heavenly millennial kingdom beyond, the authors and readers of *Left Behind* necessarily occupy and negotiate a liminal terrain. By re-examining the scope and relevance of traditional cultural categories, scholars might evolve a language with which to make this territory legible.

Acknowledgements

I would like to thank my supervisors, Crawford Gribben, Peter Knight, and Brian Ward, for their advice and encouragement in the writing of this essay and others.

Notes

1. Quoted in Steve Rabey, "No Longer Left Behind: An Insider's Look at How Christian Books are Agented, Acquired, Packaged, Branded and Sold in Today's Marketplace," *Christianity Today*, 46: 5 (22 April 2002), pp. 26–33, p. 28, p. 30.

2. See http://www.leftbehind.com/channelinteract.asp?pageid=824& channelID=80

3. Christopher Howse, "What's all this about Rapture?" *Daily Telegraph*, News (24 April 2004), p. 36.

4. The *Left Behind* prequel trilogy, collectively entitled *Countdown to the Rapture*, comprises *The Rising: The Antichrist is Born* (2005); *The Regime: The Rise of the Antichrist* (2005); and *The Rapture: In the Twinkling of an Eye* (2006). The sequel, *Kingdom Come: The Final Victory* was published in 2007.

5. Translations figure taken from Loren L. Johns, "Conceiving Violence: The Apocalypse of John and the *Left Behind* Series," *Direction*, 34: 2 (2005), pp. 194–214, p. 194; for a discussion of *Left Behind's* myopic nationalism, see Amy Johnson Frykholm, "What Social and Political Messages Appear in the *Left Behind* Books? A Literary Discussion of Millenarian Fiction," in Bruce David Forbes and Jean Halgren Kilde (eds), *Rapture, Revelation and the* Left Behind *Series* (New York and Basingstoke: Palgrave Macmillan, 2004), pp. 167–95.

6. My summary of dispensationalist tenets here is necessarily brief, and it should be noted that there are several variations of this rather complex exegetical system—for further elaboration, see Craig A. Blaising and Darrell L. Bock, *Progressive Dispensationalism* (Wheaton, IL: Bridgepoint, 1993); Ernest Sandeen, *The Roots of Fundamentalism: British and Amercan Millenarianism, 1800–1930* (Chicago, IL and London: University of Chicago Press, 1970), chapter 3

7. Bruce David Forbes, "How Popular are the *Left Behind* Books ... and Why? A Discussion of Popular Culture," in Bruce David Forbes and Jean Halgren Kilde (eds), *Rapture, Revelation and the* Left Behind *Series*, pp. 5–33, p. 8.

8. http://www.barna.org/FlexPage.aspx?Page=BarnaUpdate&Barna UpdateID=100. Page accessed 3 June 2007.

9. For scholarly criticism of this type, see Darryl Jones, "The Liberal Antichrist—Left Behind in America," in Kenneth G. C. Newport and Crawford Gribben (eds), *Expecting the End: Millennialism in Social and Historical Context* (Waco, TX: Baylor University Press, 2006), pp. 97–112; Kevin Phillips, *American Theocracy: The Peril and Politics of Radical Religion, Oil and Borrowed Money in the 21st Century* (New York: Viking, 2006); Michael Standaert, *Skipping Towards Armageddon: The Politics and Propaganda of the* Left Behind *Novels and the LaHaye Empire* (Brooklyn, NY: Soft Skull Press, 2006). For

media criticism, see Nicholas D. Kristof, "Apocalypse (Almost) Now," *New York Times,* Editorial (24 November 2004), p. A23.

10. Amy Johnson Frykholm, *Rapture Culture: Left Behind in Evangelical America* (Oxford: Oxford University Press, 2004), p. 89; Glenn W. Shuck, *Marks of the Beast: The* Left Behind *Novels and the Struggle for Evangelical Identity* (New York: New York University Press, 2005), p. 15, p. 20.

11. See, for example, Barbara Rossing, *The Rapture Exposed* (Boulder, CO: Westview, 2004); Carl Olson, *Will Catholics Be Left Behind?* (Fort Collins, CO: Ignatius, 2003).

12. I choose to use the term mainstream in quotation marks because I believe it is a problematic term which effaces the multivocity of the cultural milieux it describes. Nonetheless, as it continues to be invoked in cultural studies discourse as a way of designating the dominant cultural order, I also use the term, though with significant reservations.

13. The so-called Birmingham scholars were led by Richard Hoggart, who founded the Centre for Contemporary Cultural Studies (CCCS) in 1964. Its cohort includes Stuart Hall, Paul Willis, Dick Hebdige, Tony Jefferson and Angela McRobbie. The centre adopted a broadly Gramscian approach to the study of popular culture which, with its emphasis on agency and resistance in ordinary cultural life, remains the dominant analytical paradigm in this field today.

14. Dick Hebdige, *Subculture: The Meaning of Style* [1979] (London and New York: Routledge, 1991), p. 3.

15. Dick Hebdige, *Subculture,* p. 3

16. Michael Kammen, *American Culture, American Tastes: Social Change and the 20th Century* (New York: Basic Books, 1999).

17. Paul Boyer, *When Time Shall Be No More: Prophecy Belief in Modern American Culture* (Cambridge, MA: Belknap Press, 1992), p. 304.

18. I am grateful to Crawford Gribben for encouraging me to address the problematic conceptualization of evangelical marginality in mainstream discourse.

19. Dick Hebdige, p. 3, p. 94, p. 92.

20. Heather Hendershot, *Shaking the World for Jesus: Media and Conservative Evangelical Culture* (Chicago, IL: University of Chicago Press, 2004), p. 200.

21. Jonathan Cordero, "The Production of Christian Fiction," *Journal of Religion and Popular Culture,* Vol. 6 (Spring 2004), http://www.usask.ca/relst/jrpc/art6-xianfiction.html. Accessed 20 May 2007)

22. Roland Barthes, *The Pleasure of the Text,* trans. Richard Miller (New York: Hill and Wang, 1975).

23. Susan Harding, "Imagining the Last Days: The Politics of Apocalyptic Language," in Martin E. Marty and R. Scott Appleby (eds), *Accounting for Fundamentalisms: The Dynamic Character of Movements* (Chicago, IL: University of Chicago Press, 1994), pp. 57–78, p. 69.

24. Amy Johnson Frykholm, *Rapture Culture*, p. 8.

25. Ibid., p. 40.

26. Glenn W. Shuck, p. 4.

27. Revelation 13: 16–18.

28. Tim LaHaye and Jerry Jenkins, *Desecration: Antichrist Takes the Throne* (Wheaton, IL: Tyndale House, 2001), p. 95.

29. Stephen D. O'Leary, *Arguing the Apocalypse: A Theory of Millennial Rhetoric* (New York and Oxford: Oxford University Press, 1994), p. 217.

30. Tim LaHaye and Jerry Jenkins, *Armageddon: The Cosmic Battle of the Ages* (Wheaton, IL: Tyndale House, 2003), p. 282.

31. Janice Radway, *Reading the Romance: Women, Patriarchy and Popular Literature* [1984] (Chapel Hill, NC: University of North Carolina Press, 1991).

32. See "The Margins of *Left Behind's* Readership," in Amy Johnson Frykholm, *Rapture Culture*, pp. 67–88.

33. Ibid., p. 71.

34. David D. Kirkpatrick, "In 12th Book of Best-Selling Series, Jesus Returns," *New York Times*, National Desk (29 March 2004).

35. http://www.worldnetdaily.com/news/article.asp?ARTICLE_ID=23070. Accessed 24 November 2008.

36. The "elective affinities" (to use Max Weber's term) between the *Left Behind* novels and neoconservativism have been well documented. However, there are more empirical connections, such as those fostered by LaHaye's Council for National Policy, which brings together secular and Christian conservatives such as Tom DeLay, Oliver North, Ralph Reed and Pat Robertson. See Hugh Urban, "Bush, the Neocons and Evangelical Christian Fiction," in *Counterpunch* (18 November 2004), www.counterpunch.org/urban11182004.html. Page accessed 18 May 2007.

37. Bruce David Forbes, p. 20.

38. The open-source Linux distribution, Ubuntu, launched a Christian version in 2006. It includes Bible study software, scripture quote-of-the-day, virtual rosary, and redesigned icons, such as a church symbol in place of the "home" button. For a thoughtful analysis of the uses of "Christian kitsch", see Colleen McDannell, *Material Christianity: Religion and Popular Culture in America* (New Haven, CN and London: Yale University Press, 1995), pp. 163–97 and pp. 222–69.

39. Heather Hendershot, p. 28, p. 36; Colleen McDannell, p. 268.

40. Kevin Sack, "Apocalyptic Theology Revitalized by Attacks: Calling 9/11 a Harbinger of the End Times," *The New York Times*, National Report Pages (23 November, 2001).

41. Ibid.

42. Randall Balmer, *Mine Eyes Have Seen the Glory: A Journey into the Evangelical Subculture in America* (New York and Oxford: Oxford University Press, 1989), p. 62.

43. Unfortunately, the Barna Survey does not indicate whether its respondents from various religious backgrounds have read all, some, or just one of the *Left Behind* books. Such information would offer more concrete insights into the series' transitional relationship with the mainstream.

44. Bruce David Forbes, p. 24.

45. Timothy Weber, *Living in the Shadow of the Second Coming: American Premillennialism 1875–1925* (New York and Oxford: Oxford University Press, 1979), p. 48.

46. Tim LaHaye and Jerry Jenkins, *Left Behind: A Novel of the Earth's Last Days* (Wheaton, IL: Tyndale House, 1995), p. 17, p. 20.

47. Ibid., p. 79–80.

48. Tim LaHaye and Jerry Jenkins, *The Mark: The Beast Rules the World* (Wheaton, IL: Tyndale House, 2000), p.185.

49. Although many secular critics perceive dispensational belief as primitive, it has in fact only been extant for around 150 years, making it a relatively novel exegetical model.

50. Michel de Certeau, *The Practice of Everyday Life,* trans. Steven F. Rendall (Berkeley, CA and London: University of California Press, 1984).

51. See George Marsden, *Understanding Fundamentalism and Evangelicalism* (Grand Rapids, MI: William B. Eerdmans, 1991).

52. Gary DeMar, *End Times Fiction: A Biblical Consideration of the* Left Behind *Theology* (Nashville, TN: Thomas Nelson, 2001), p. xx–xxi.

"The Shadow of the End"
The Appeal of Apocalypse in Literary Science Fiction

Roslyn Weaver

But the day of the Lord will come like a thief. The heavens will disappear with a roar; the elements will be destroyed by fire, and the earth and everything in it will be laid bare. Since everything will be destroyed in this way, what kind of people ought you to be? You ought to live holy and godly lives as you look forward to the day of God and speed its coming. That day will bring about the destruction of the heavens by fire, and the elements will melt in the heat. But in keeping with his promise we are looking forward to a new heaven and a new earth, the home of righteousness.

(2 Peter 3:10–13 [NIV])

Our end-determined fictions ... are placed at what Dante calls the point where all times are present, *il punto a cui tutti li tempi son presenti*; or within the shadow of it. It gives each moment its fullness. And although for us the End has perhaps lost its naïve *imminence*, its shadow still lies on the crises of our fictions; we may speak of it as *immanent*.

(Frank Kermode [1967: 6])

Introduction

Apocalypse has been an enduring and popular theme in science fiction literature, appearing in texts from the nineteenth century (for example, Mary Shelley's *The Last Man* [1826], H. G. Wells' *War of the Worlds* [1898]) to contemporary times (e.g., Margaret Atwood's *Oryx and Crake* [2003], Cormac McCarthy's *The Road* [2006]), and inspiring many films based on literary narratives of catastrophe (e.g., P. D. James' *The Children of Men* [1992], Richard Matheson's *I Am Legend* [1954]). Such visions of the future attribute the causes of devastation to a range of factors, including nuclear weapons (e.g., Walter M. Miller Jr's *A Canticle for Leibowitz* [1959], Simon Brown's *Winter* [1997]) and environmental and health issues (e.g., George R. Stewart's *Earth Abides* [1949] and George Turner's *Beloved Son* [1978]). Apocalyptic science fiction literature reveals a dark future and serves to situate current events "under the shadow of the end", to use Frank Kermode's term (1967: 5), acting as a counterpoint to more utopic visions.

While one might imagine these apocalyptic warning tales have a positive function in that they presumably seek to avoid real-life future disasters, some critics have argued that apocalypse in fact functions as a tool for dominant groups to oppress and persecute those in minorities. This suggests that its use in science fiction can be problematic. These theorists argue that apocalypse is itself violent and too easily adaptable for hostile purposes. Yet while some critics highlight the negative features of apocalypse, there are others who point out its potential as a literature of dissent. This chapter surveys some of the key contributions in the field in order to discuss the ongoing appeal of apocalypse and its ability to critique a range of viewpoints and agendas, and argues that the apocalyptic paradigm offers writers a powerful framework for the interrogation of dominant and oppressive groups and practices. Biblical apocalypse, for instance, has been enormously influential on secular apocalyptic works, and such texts were from minority groups themselves. The potential for critique is especially appealing in science fiction, itself a literature that often imagines future disaster in order to expose and warn of the dangers of contemporary political and ethical scenarios.

Apocalypse

Apocalypse means revelation, disclosure, uncovering what is hidden, but contemporary practice uses the term broadly, and most often to denote a general disaster of some kind. Current usage most often describes a catastrophic event, usually involving human deaths and widespread destruction of land or the urban environment. The disaster might be natural: environmental or geological; or it might be deliberate and of human origin: a war, a chemical weapon such as a virus, or, often, nuclear weapons. The concept can also refer to a danger to humankind, a cataclysmic event that threatens the continued existence of humans. Regardless of the context and the background, people often view the resulting destruction as apocalyptic.

The common identification of apocalypse as disaster means that the term has shifting meanings. For Jacques Derrida (1984: 34), the identification of catastrophe as apocalypse creates an "apocalypse without apocalypse, an apocalypse without vision, without truth, without revelation". Yet the fact that one can understand the term in different ways suggests a flexibility of definition. Malcolm Bull (1999: 48) argues against too narrow or restrictive a definition of apocalypse, because "the terminology of apocalyptic is, or at least appears to be, meaningfully used in other contexts". Commentators have used apocalyptic labels to describe events ranging from the advent of atomic weapons to the 11 September 2001 terrorist attacks in the USA, and from the World War Two Holocaust to the 2004 Asian tsunami.[1] On the other hand, James Berger (1999: xii) writes that people often consider apocalypse in terms of a break in history: "historical events are often portrayed apocalyptically—as absolute breaks with the past, as catastrophes bearing some enormous or ultimate meaning: the Holocaust, for example, or Hiroshima, or American slavery, the American Civil War, the French Revolution, the war in Vietnam and the social conflicts of the 1960s". Gary K. Wolfe (1983: 1) has argued that the fictional equivalent of real-life apocalypses such as concentration camps or the industrial revolution refer not to the literal end of the world, but rather to "the end of a way of life, a configuration of attitudes, perhaps a system of beliefs". Bull (1995b: 5) suggests that one may categorize apocalypse in one of four ways: as high-religious or -secular, or popular-religious or -secular apocalypse. Within the secular types, high-secular apocalypse imagines a progressive view of history while popular-secular visions "discern little purpose in the world, except in its ending" (Bull, 1995b: 5), instead focusing on "images of nuclear holocaust, ecological catastrophe, sexual decadence and social collapse" (Bull, 1995b: 4). It is clear, therefore, that writers and readers can understand and in fact use apocalypse in a multitude of ways with different meanings.

The relationship between apocalypse and science fiction is very close. Science fiction reveals imagined glimpses of a different reality, straying from the status quo and the world readers know and disclosing something new. W. Warren Wagar (1982: 9) defines science fiction in the same way as speculative fiction, as "any work of fiction … that specializes in plausible speculation about life under changed but rationally conceivable circumstances, in an alternative past or present, or in the future". Van Ikin and Terry Dowling (1993: xv) have noted that science fiction can allow the alteration of the reader's perception, for "we are made to see the world, our lives, our blinding reality, with new eyes". This has an exact consonance with the revelatory aspect of apocalypse, for apocalyptic literature also reveals new perspectives to the reader. The underlying truth of cata-strophic threats—arms races, viral agents, environmental disasters, terrorist threats and indigenous suffering—also serves to undercut the fictional nature of apocalyptic narratives, with the result that writers blur the line between what is fictional and what is, or could be, real.

While apocalypse is frequently understood in terms of disaster, there are both positive and negative aspects of the term, the utopic and dystopic,[2] that appear to various extents in literary science fic-tion texts. In line with the popular imagination's association of apoca-lypse with disaster, many novels use apocalypse in its negative sense, focusing on disaster and destruction, while others use apocalyptic imagery and themes in positive ways, and still others negotiate a path between the two extremes. Therefore, even while a large number of apocalyptic fictions utilize a dystopic setting, depicting catastrophes and horror without the accompanying hope, there is also the potential for writers to use apocalypse to generate positive meanings.

The Appeal of Apocalypse

Critics have linked the appeal of apocalyptic narratives to their seem-ing relevance to current situations. Frank Kermode (1967), for ex-ample, has argued that apocalyptic literature, with its emphasis on sequence and endings and beginnings, encourages readers to "imag-ine a significance for themselves" (4) and helps give sense to people's lives (7). In his influential study on the genre, *The Sense of an Ending: Studies in the Theory of Fiction* (1967), he looks at "the ways in which fictions ... satisfy our needs. So we begin with Apocalypse, which ends, transforms, and is concordant" (5). Kermode writes that the book of Revelation has "a vitality and resource that suggest its consonance with our more naïve requirements of fiction" (7). He makes the point that the continued popularity of apocalyptic fictions— a "brooding on apocalypse" (11)—means that while there may be less belief in an imminent end of the world, there is now a sense that it is "immanent" (6). The end is pervasive, and this results in a cli-mate of "perpetual crisis" (28). Apocalypse, Kermode argues, is re-silient because its meanings are fluid and open to interpretation. "Clerkly scepticism" is one of the features of apocalypse (10), and it entails caution about exact predictions:

Its predictions, though figurative, *can* be taken literally, and as the future moves in on us we may expect it to conform with the figures. Many difficulties arise from this expectation. We ask such questions as, who is the Beast from the Land? ... The great majority of interpretations of Apocalypse assume that the End is pretty near. Consequently the historical allegory is always having to be revised; time discredits it. And this is important. Apocalypse can be disconfirmed without being discredited. This is part of its extraordinary resilience. It can also absorb changing interests, rival apocalypses ... It is patient of change and of historiographical sophistications. It allows itself to be diffused, blended ... (8)

The genre proves so fluid, in fact, that even when time proves that various interpretations and guesses about Christ's return are incorrect, people can dismiss the calculations as "error" (9) and the power of apocalypse endures.[3]

Wagar (1982) concurs with Kermode's belief that apocalypse appears relevant to a society that has a sense of living at the end of things. He suggests that apocalypse is "one way in which a dying culture—in this case, the national-bourgeois culture of the post-Christian West—has chosen to express the loss or decline of its faith in itself" (Wagar, 1982: xiii). The loss of confidence means that apocalyptic fictions appeal to our sense "that we do indeed live in an endtime, an era in history marked by the collapse of the traditional civilizations of the non-Western world and by the senescence of the national-bourgeois social order in the West" (Wagar, 1982: xiii).

Stephen D. O'Leary (1998: 14) argues that part of the attraction of apocalypse is its perceived status as a solution to the "problem of evil", suggesting that apocalypse is essentially a rhetoric designed to persuade its audience; a rhetoric that is made up of three themes: time, evil and authority. The construction of time is one of the crucial elements of apocalyptic discourse, for rhetoric must convince its hearers that they are, indeed, living at the end of history, and if people view themselves at the "end", they are reassured that there will be a final conclusion to evil (O'Leary, 1998). Apocalyptic rhetoric attempts "to situate its audience at the end of a particular pattern of historical time; to the extent that people adhere to apocalyptic claims, their perception of time is altered" (O'Leary, 1998: 13). The authority theme is significant in that apocalyptic discourse must be convincing to its audience (O'Leary, 1998: 51), constructing the prophecies as logical, feasible extrapolations of the current state of society.

Other commentators suggest that narratives of disaster are appealing because of their articulation of fears or desires, offering a vicarious experience for readers. Susan Sontag (1965: 225), for instance, suggests that viewing fictional catastrophe in science fiction films can "normalize what is psychologically unbearable, thereby inuring us to it". She suggests that the events of the Second World War and the Cold War amplified the fears about society and the world that are reflected in catastrophe films. The anxieties that underpin apocalyptic fiction do not necessarily negate the appeal of the genre, however, but rather may actually add to the allure. Similarly, Rosemary Jackson (1981) has also noted the possibility that the fictional expression of anxiety may act to alleviate that fear. Jackson (1981: 9) argues that the fantastic genre contains "impulses towards transgression". The textual (vicarious) expression of these elements may neutralize them for the reader, or the works may retain their "existential disease" (*ibid.*). While neither Sontag nor Jackson refers specifically to science fiction literature, their points are still applicable because of the way in which the reading of fictional catastrophe may in some way alleviate the real-life fear of it. As both critics observe, it is possible that the textual expression of disturbing images and events can work to mitigate the feeling of anxiety. In this respect, the appeal of apocalyptic fiction is ambivalent. Many apocalyptic science fiction texts offer worst-case futures, extrapolating contemporary fears to cataclysmic endings. Yet the prediction of a bleak future can conversely offer hope for those that heed the warnings, or even merely for the readers whose real world is better than the fictional one.

Biblical Apocalypse

However, the appeal of apocalypse for science fiction writers can be far more significant than simply revealing or alleviating cultural anxieties. Apocalypse can also become a tool for critique, one that offers a powerful critical framework for science fiction writers because it enables writers to imagine present systems of society coming to an end or illustrate how a new, revised world might be after a catastrophic event. The potential for apocalypse to operate as a critical voice is attractive, and has a long tradition that owes much to early biblical apocalyptic accounts. Secular apocalyptic fictions retain significant connections to biblical apocalypse, and many of the themes and images from both the Old and New Testaments of the Christian

Bible reappear in and inform secular fictions. While our understanding of apocalypse owes much to the Book of Revelation in the Bible, there are other biblical apocalyptic texts, such as Daniel and Zechariah, as well as the prophecies in Isaiah that speak of revealing "new things, of hidden things unknown to you" (Isa. 48:6).

The apocalyptic messages of books such as Revelation and Daniel offer a consistent message that persecuted groups will overcome their oppressors at a future stage. L. L. Morris (1962) suggests that apocalypse in the Bible includes several key features:

> Characteristic of apocalyptic is the thought that God is sovereign, and that ultimately He will intervene in catastrophic fashion to bring to pass His good and perfect will. He is opposed by powerful and varied forces of evil, and these are usually referred to symbolically, as beasts, horns, *etc*. There are visions; angels speak, there is the clash of mighty forces; and ultimately the persecuted saints are vindicated. (Morris, 1962: 1093)

The dreams of future events predict invasions and oppression from powerful and corrupt rulers seeking to persecute God's people, using beasts and creatures as symbols for human empires and kingdoms. The visions show a cosmic conflict between God and figures representing the Antichrist, and give numerical accounts of when the events will occur. In Biblical apocalypse, there will be great trials, judgement for those who defy God, the second coming of the messiah, the Christ, in all his glory, the promise of "everlasting life" (Dan. 12:2) and deliverance from pain and sorrow for the faithful in a renewed, remade world; God himself will "wipe every tear" away (Rev. 21:4).[4]

The "day of the Lord" is a refrain throughout both the Old and New Testaments (for example, Joel 2:31, Zech. 14:1, 2 Thess. 2:2), effectively giving God's faithful a perspective of human history approaching a significant rupture, for "the end of all things is near" (1 Pet. 4:7). Andrew McNab (1962: 1140) writes that in New Testament texts "the coming of the Lord which would mark the close of the age was believed to be imminent". Apocalyptic discourse in the Bible insists that a time is rapidly approaching when God will judge all. He will reward those who follow his ways while those who have rejected him will face the consequences of their rebellion.

Apocalypse in the Bible, then, can be a language for the oppressed faithful of past and present times, a discourse that foretells disaster in the future yet nonetheless offers hope and the promise of better things to come. God will ultimately reward the faithful who persevere and endure with future glory in the new world: New Jerusalem, Zion. One of the main purposes of these revelations is therefore encouragement, for the writings and prophecies often occurred during times of oppression. The context of future blessing and restoration gives meaning to the destruction and catastrophe:

> Then I saw a new heaven and a new earth, for the first heaven and the first earth had passed away ... I saw the Holy City, the new Jerusalem, coming down out of heaven from God ... And I heard a loud voice from the throne saying, "Now the dwelling of God is with men, and he will live with them. They will be his people, and God himself will be with them and be their God. He will wipe every tear from their eyes. There will be no more death or mourning or crying or pain, for the old order of things has passed away." (Rev. 21:1–4)

In the biblical narrative, the visions of disaster focus on the promise of a new world for believers, as seen in the concluding sections of apocalyptic texts, which emphasize the expectation of the new heavens and the new earth (for example, Isa. 65:17–19; Rev. 21:1–4).

One can briefly summarize biblical apocalypse, then, in the following ways. First, it is a revelation about the world, a new perspective uncovering something that was previously hidden. Second, the revelation usually concerns the future, and this knowledge enables the readers to see their present circumstances more clearly and in context. Third, the purpose of the revelation is to provoke a response in its receivers; the vision of the messiah's coming in the future served as encouragement to the faithful as well as inspiring a response of right living in the present. The revelation includes a darker side of warnings of judgement, seen in terms of global catastrophes that signal the end of the present world. The apocalyptic vision thus reveals not only the future hope for the faithful, but also a warning of the destruction awaiting those who do not turn to God. Finally, biblical apocalypse includes a promise of a new, better world after the disaster. Apocalypse offers a voice for those who suffer, giving hope of their restoration.

Apocalypse in Literary Science Fiction

Given that biblical apocalypse offers the promise of future freedom from current troubles, it is perhaps unsurprising that its themes prove so appealing for a secular audience. Typically, science fiction authors locate their secular apocalypses in the future, essentially functioning as prophets who warn of a forthcoming event. Much as Revelation foretells future judgement to elicit appropriate responses, apocalyptic fictions can depict grim futures intended to provoke action now.

The images and themes from the biblical apocalyptic writings permeate secular apocalypse, demonstrating a lasting legacy and congruence with the visions in the Bible, even while non-religious writing usually excises the supernatural elements. Northrop Frye (1957: 141) suggests that "the Biblical Apocalypse is our grammar of apocalyptic imagery", while Derrida (1984: 25) argues that the apocalyptic "tone" or discourse that intimates the end is near "always cites or echoes [*répercute*] in a certain way John's Apocalypse". David Ketterer (1974: 333) writes that even the most secular of apocalyptic fictions retains the "religious element", no matter how "displaced, [or] disguised". This can mean, for example, that in a secular text a nuclear war might substitute for Judgement Day (Brians, 1987: 54). Ketterer (1974: 123–24) argues that the basic plot of science fiction disaster literature follows the sequence of events in Revelation, with four stages: first, dystopia; second, the warning or experience of a disaster; third, life post-disaster; and finally, the establishment of a new world. He writes that the revelatory aspect of apocalypse occurs because the new worlds envisioned leave the reader's viewpoint challenged and "expanded" (16), thereby revealing "the *present* world in new or other terms" (38).

The language and imagery of biblical apocalypse are pervasive and apt to appear again and again in contemporary science fiction literature, even if with different motivations and from secular perspectives. Wagar (1982: 53) points out that "Revelation is a warehouse catalogue of calamities" with its "natural disasters, such as earthquakes, storms, and droughts. Pestilence does its worst, along with monsters". The scenes of environmental destruction in particular have provided contemporary fictions with a template for imagining disaster: "There was a great earthquake. The sun turned black like sackcloth made of goat hair, the whole moon turned blood red, and the stars in the sky fell to earth, as late figs drop from a fig tree when shaken by a strong wind. The sky receded like a scroll, rolling up, and every mountain and island was removed from its place" (Rev. 6:12–14). Revelation's four horsemen of the apocalypse, the seven seals, plagues, scrolls, the woman and the dragon, the heavenly city and its garden containing the tree of life, and especially the notion of a promised land, a new world, are all references that reappear in works that use the terms without any of the divine meaning of the original visions. It should be no surprise that secular writers with no interest in God often adopt and adapt apocalypse, for the natural disasters of Revelation in particular lend themselves to secular appropriation even if the authors ignore the divine foundations of the apocalypse.

While dramatic imagery is particularly exploited in science fiction cinema and television (e.g., *The Day After Tomorrow,* 2004; *Supervolcano,* 2005), literary science fiction also frequently describes worldwide catastrophes, especially in relation to ecological cataclysms. For instance, Ian Irvine's *The Human Rites Trilogy* (2000–2004) narrates the catastrophic effects of a looming ice age on the world, caused by global warming. In the second novel, *Terminator Gene* (Irvine, 2003), half the world's cities are under water due to sea levels rising 6 metres, and the story features the flooding of New Orleans following a major hurricane.[5] The media reports the event as "Armageddon … a forerunner of what is to come for all of us" (Irvine, 2003: 412). During the third novel, *The Life Lottery* (Irvine, 2004), governments plan to avert the ice age by detonating thousands of nuclear bombs to create the Panama Seaway between the Atlantic and Pacific Oceans. This act means that "huge earthquakes are going to destroy Central America. Mountains will fall down. Millions will die" (Irvine, 2004: 471). By the conclusion of the book, the two main characters, Irith and Bragg, are on an aeroplane over the Pacific Islands when they notice that below them "the sea seems to be boiling":

> there came a pale flash, distantly and below them. It was followed by a red flare that became a fireball, spreading in all directions. Someone screamed from the back of the plane … The fireball grew rapidly, as though the whole atmosphere was on fire, exploding towards them in a vast, raging sphere like a photographic image of the surface of the sun. Suddenly the whole plane went quiet. "Nature is the biggest terrorist of all," she [Irith] said thoughtfully. "It creates with the most painstaking labour, then tears it all to pieces in an instant." (Irvine, 2004: 529–30)

These descriptions of the natural world appear to have close links to the desolations in Revelation, even while the divine elements are absent. Irvine's trilogy warns of a future ecological collapse, an enormously popular theme in recent times that intersects with real-life concerns about global warming.

Wagar (1983: 170) suggests that "stories of man-made catastrophes continue the ancient tradition of prophetic warning, by which sinful man is reminded of his disobedience and the wrath to come that his wrong-doing has earned". Authors might construct the catastrophe as a judgement of humanity, such as apocalyptic events that are, for example, nuclear or technology-themed, in which the disaster that befalls humans is clearly the result of their own corruption and greed for power, even if God is absent from the text. Other texts suggest that apocalyptic cataclysms reveal the worst impulses of humanity. For example, in Sean McMullen's *The Greatwinter Trilogy* (1999–2001), a science fiction series of novels set after nuclear bombs have devastated the world, the ability to predict a second nuclear winter is seen as "lucky" because it offers the opportunity for profit and power from disaster, rather than the chance simply to avert catastrophe and save lives (1999: 68).

Science fiction literatures, then, despite their frequent disavowal of the divine, nonetheless demonstrate the influence of the imagery and themes of biblical apocalypse. However, there are two significant departures from the religious paradigm within science fiction. The first major development is that secular versions of Revelation frequently over-emphasize disaster and judgement, ignoring or displaying less interest in the themes of blessing and mercy that are of greater significance in the Bible. Their visions of apocalypse, that is, often conclude with the end of the world and are unable or unwilling to anticipate or imagine a new world. Far from being a literature of encouragement, such tales often suggest pessimism about the world, although authors can channel this negativity into critiques of society. Literary science fiction often magnifies the aspect of destruction as the primary interest. Ketterer (1974: 94) suggests that secular fictions frequently adopt the "negative aspect" of apocalypse, "with its emphasis on destruction, Hell, and chaos", while Edward James (2000: 50) notes that despite the preponderance of secular references to Armageddon or Doomsday, in most contemporary fictions such terms are "not even a token reference to the Book of Revelation, but merely a common shorthand for a man-made catastrophe, particularly a devastating war". As Ketterer (1974: 133) points out, in apocalyptic writing "a dystopian situation and the end of the world go hand in hand as thematic aspects of the same 'bad scene'".

Krishan Kumar (1995: 205), meanwhile, notes apocalypse's connection with utopia and argues that one aspect of apocalypse is "a
sense of hope, of something constructive emerging from the ruins",
and that this parallels the expectation in utopianism that "a great
disaster ... must precede the emergence of the millennial kingdom
or the good society". He notes that contemporary apocalypse is often missing the vision of a new world, and questions why the modern "sense of an ending [is] so flat, so lacking in *élan*? Why have we
truncated the apocalyptic vision, so that we see endings without new
beginnings?" (212). Kumar argues that "we need both millennium
and utopia" (212), for the former offers hope while the latter provokes desire: "The one tells us that change is possible, the other why
we need to make the change, what we might gain if we do so"
(214). Yet he suggests that modern apocalypse does not tend to exhibit this hope for a better future. Instead, the contemporary "low-
keyed" apocalypse (211) constitutes what he calls a "debased
millenarianism, without a compensating utopian vision" (212). Kumar
considers that this debased millenarianism is evident in declarations
of the end of history, such as in Francis Fukuyama's *The End of
History and the Last Man* (1998), because any sense or belief that
modern society has achieved progress and "peace and plenty"
(Kumar, 1995: 205) lacks genuine pleasure in such developments
and is in fact "profoundly negative" (Kumar, 1995: 215).

Often, there is no hope of a new world in apocalyptic literary
science fiction, which promises the destruction without the new
heaven and new earth, and imagines not utopia but dystopia. This is
evident to varying degrees in two key science fiction works from the
mid-twentieth century: Miller's *A Canticle for Leibowitz* (1959) and
Nevil Shute's *On the Beach* (1957), both of which depict a world
that has been devastated by nuclear war. Miller's novel is set in
America after a nuclear war, where grotesque survivors of radiation
live in a desolate earth. Over time, society appears to progress and
rebuild itself. Eventually, when the threat of atomic war appears once
again, the assumption is that humanity has learned from its devastating mistakes in the past:

> We all know what *could* happen, if there's war ... Back then ... maybe
> they didn't know what would happen. Or perhaps they did know, but
> could not quite believe it until they tried it ... They had not yet seen a
> billion corpses. They had not seen the still-born, the monstrous, the
> dehumanized, the blind. They had not yet seen the madness and the

murder and the blotting out of reason … Now—*now* the princes, the presidents, the praesidiums, now they know—with dead certainty … they cannot do it again. Only a race of madmen could do it again. (Miller, 1959:277-78)

Despite the horrors of the past, humans seem unable to learn from previous mistakes and a second nuclear war occurs, effectively re-peating history. While *Canticle* suggests that humanity has an inher-ent flaw that makes apocalyptic events inevitable, the novel nonetheless ends with some measure of hope as a group of people leave Earth in a starship to begin life elsewhere. In contrast, Shute's *On the Beach* withholds from its readers even that small comfort. Narrating the gradual extinction of all life after nuclear bombs have devastated the globe and radiation is slowly covering the planet, Shute's novel offers the suggestion that despite the inevitable end of all human life, "It's not the end of the world at all … It's only the end of us. The world will go on just the same, only we shan't be in it" (Shute, 1957: 79). Yet these two works leave the reader only with death rather than restoration, and the end of the world rather than the hope of another. Both novels offer bleak assessments of humanity's ability to progress, suggesting that future disaster is inescapable. Miller and Shute use apocalypse in these instances to warn of the dangers of nuclear weapons in the hands of flawed humans; presumably in a desire to transform readers' perspectives and effect changes. How-ever, the texts lack substantial alternatives or ideas how to avoid such grim futures, and moreover, as Wagar (1982: 128) notes, apocalyp-tic science fiction has thus far had limited success in actually averting real-life catastrophes.

While the focus on destruction rather than restoration is one de-velopment from biblical apocalypse, the second key point of differ-ence from apocalypse's origins is that some secular narratives subvert the original context of apocalypse as a language for the oppressed to instead use apocalyptic rhetoric to dominate and justify the persecu-tion of minority groups. Many critics have highlighted this possibility, and it is worthwhile considering some of the key arguments on the subject. For instance, Richard Dellamora (1994: 3) notes that society has often negatively associated homosexuality in particular with end times. He suggests that while apocalyptic thinking is in itself neither positive nor negative, it is nonetheless easily adaptable for negative ends:

Among dominant groups apocalyptic narratives have often been invoked in order to validate violence done to others. Among subordinate groups apocalyptic thinking is frequently an effect of the pressure of persecution. Apocalyptic narratives have been mobilized to justify the imprisonment, torture, and execution of the subjects of male-male desire. (Dellamora, 1994: 3)

It is therefore important to be wary of apocalyptic discourse. Dellamora's discussion centres upon homosexuality and apocalypse, but his comments are also applicable to other minority groups in that those in power can use apocalyptic rhetoric to justify their persecution of minorities. Indeed, literary science fiction can reflect this tendency. David Seed (2000a: 12) notes that authors can utilize "the apocalyptic paradigm" in many different ways for any number of agendas, but Bull (1995b) suggests that while apocalypse may be open to different agendas, writers do not always realize this potential:

Unlike the religious variety, secular apocalyptic—which is found in many areas of popular culture, but most notably in science fiction, rock music and film—is not usually intended to effect personal spiritual transformation. It may be designed to influence public opinion in favour of social or political objectives … but in many cases the language of apocalyptic is deployed simply to shock, alarm or enrage. (Bull, 1995b: 4–5)

Other critics have read apocalypse as a negative genre, or one that is open to the worst uses. Kermode (1967: 13) notes that a range of groups can appropriate the genre for their own ideological purposes, even the rhetoric of Nazism, a point that Norman Cohn (1957: 286) echoes, who highlights the fact that historical figures such as Hitler and Lenin have adopted apocalypse in its extreme form.

The target in science fiction may be any minority group. Edward James (2000: 53) points out that the holocaust scenario appears utopic to some readers, who see in such fictions the opportunity to "cleanse the world of its corrupting forces (liberals, feminists, homosexuals, and blacks) and restore the good old masculine values". Similarly, Wagar (1982: 109) writes that the evolutionary and natural selection tenets of science meant that fictions could "rationalize warfare between the races of mankind, or the extermination of inferior races … Once the idea was abroad that great life-and-death conflicts are inevitable and, for that matter, enjoined by laws of nature, imagining racial, class, or national wars of eschatological proportions was an easy next step". Marlene Goldman (2005: 26) claims that violence is at the "heart" of apocalypse and that it can facilitate the persecution of minorities because:

> Revelation, in keeping with its name, unveils a secret, and that its hidden message, predicated on violence and absolute destruction, is politically charged ... the originary apocalyptic violence that engendered the nation-state typically involved the subordination and commodification of women, Native peoples, ethnic minorities, and the landscape. (Goldman, 2005: 25)

Robert Plank (1983: 36) similarly argues that apocalyptic works can demonstrate malice and hostility, while Catherine Keller's (1996: 28) examination of gender and apocalypse argues that apocalypse is "a quintessentially male product" that cannot be divested of its "toxic misogyny" (29), thus making it a problematic trope for feminist uses.

While these critics argue that apocalypse can facilitate the persecution of minorities, others have pointed out that apocalypse in fact allows minority groups to instead subvert this and present radical critiques of society in their science fiction works. Indeed, using apocalypse for negative ends is arguably a perverted use of a literature that itself emanated from the persecuted Jewish or Christian peoples, who faced oppression from the ruling authorities of the day. While dominant systems have since appropriated apocalyptic rhetoric, apocalypse was originally a narrative for the oppressed and therefore resolutely critical of the major powers in society.

O'Leary (1998) notes that there are multiple uses of apocalypse, and suggests that apocalypse is limited neither to conservatism nor rebellion, but instead offers a framework for either stance depending on the rhetoric. He claims that apocalypse can be subversive because it is based on Revelation, which was highly anti-authoritarian in its stance, although he also writes that "eschatalogical narrative can be used to legitimate, as well as subvert, political authority" (O'Leary, 1998: 56). In a similar way, Derrida (1984) also suggests that apocalypse can have multiple meanings and purposes. In his discussion of the persuasion and rhetoric of apocalyptic discourse, Derrida refers to the "narrative sending" of apocalypse, that is, the "ruses, traps, trickeries, seductions" (27) that apocalypticists use to convince their hearers. The apocalyptic tone persuades others of hidden things, of secret truths and revelations:

> Whoever takes on the apocalyptic tone comes to signify to, if not tell, you something. What? The truth, of course, and to signify to you that

it reveals the truth to you; the tone is the revelatory of some unveiling in process. Unveiling or truth, apophantics of the imminence of the end, of whatever comes down, finally, to the end of the world ... Truth itself is the end, the destination, and that truth unveils itself is the advent of the end ... Then whoever takes on the apocalyptic tone will be asked: with a view to what and to what ends? In order to lead where, right now or soon? The end is beginning, signifies the apocalyptic tone. But to what ends does the tone signify this? The apocalyptic tone naturally wants to attract, to get to come, to arrive at this, to seduce in order to lead to this ... The end is soon, it is imminent, signifies the tone. I see it, I know it, I tell you, now you know, come ... We're the only ones in the world. I'm the only one able to reveal to you the truth or the destination. (Derrida, 1984: 24–25)

Derrida claims that "nothing is less conservative than the apocalyptic genre" (29), yet points out that the apocalyptic tone "can be mimicked, feigned, faked. I shall go so far as to say *synthesised*" (10). This can mean, of course, that science fiction authors may use apocalyptic discourse to justify oppression, as discussed earlier. If anyone can use and adopt and fake apocalypse, it is open to any agenda, and Derrida suggests that because apocalypse is "an apocryphal, masked, coded *genre*, it can use the detour in order to mislead another vigilance, that of censorship" (29), hiding its message to evade detection: "We know that apocalyptic writings increased the moment State censorship was very strong in the Roman Empire, and precisely to catch the censorship unawares. Now this possibility can be extended to all censorships, and not only to the political, and in politics to the official" (29). However, apocalypse's ambiguities, the "mixing of voices, genres, and codes" (Derrida, 1984: 29), can result in multiple meanings and interpretations, and even the misinterpretation of the message. As Dellamora (1994) points out, Derrida's argument has two significant aspects, the "analytic" which insists that we must examine apocalypse in order to "resist the manipulative use", and the "affirmative" which facilitates the use of the genre "on behalf of subordinated individuals and groups" (Dellamora, 1994: 26).

This chapter suggested earlier that apocalypse can function as a language for the oppressed, operating as a genre of critique for authors of science fiction. Cohn (1957) writes that the apocalyptic pattern focuses on the eventual overthrow of tyranny, leaving the persecuted group the ultimate victors:

> The world is dominated by an evil, tyrannous power of boundless de-
> structiveness—a power moreover which is imagined not as simply hu-
> man but as demonic. The tyranny of that power will become more and
> more outrageous, the sufferings of its victims more and more intoler-
> able—until suddenly the hour will strike when the Saints of God are
> able to rise up and overthrow it. Then the Saints themselves, the cho-
> sen, holy people who hitherto have groaned under the oppressor's
> heel, shall in their turn inherit dominion over the whole earth. (Cohn,
> 1957: 21)

Other critics have emphasized this, suggesting that apocalypse can
act as a protest genre against systems and politics in society. For example, Lois Parkinson Zamora (1989: 3–4) suggests that "novelists
who use apocalyptic elements, like the biblical apocalyptists, are often critical of present political, social, spiritual practices, and their
fiction entertains the means to oppose and overcome them". This
reflects Revelation and the "subversive vision" of the narrator who is
"outside the cultural and political mainstream" (Zamora, 1989: 2).
Noting that apocalyptic fictions increase "during times of social disruption and temporal uncertainty" (177), Zamora's implication is that
the times of change create an environment particularly conducive
to social critique. Berger (1999) also suggests that the subversive element of apocalypse has inspired a range of anti-authoritarian stances:

> The desire to see the old order disintegrate links such religiously and
> politically disparate apocalypticists as the romantic anarchist Henry Miller,
> the poststructuralist theorist Michel Foucault, 1970s Punks, more re-
> cent cyberpunk science fiction writers, and Christian New Right theo-
> logians like Hal Lindsay. For all of these, the world is poised to end and
> is so suffused with moral rottenness and technological, political, and
> economic chaos and/or regimentation that it should end and must end,
> and it must end because in some crucial sense it *has* ended. This weird
> blend of disgust, moral fervor, and cynicism helps explain the enor-
> mous, ecstatic, fascinated pleasure many people in late-twentieth-
> century America feel in *seeing* significant parts of their world destroyed
> [in disaster films]. (Berger, 1999: 7)

For Berger (1999: 7), "apocalyptic and post-apocalyptic representations serve varied psychological and political purposes. Most
prevalently, they put forward a total critique of any existing social
order".

A recent example of the use of apocalypse in science fiction as
political interrogation is Andrew McGahan's *Underground* (2006),

set in the dystopic near-future of Australia during a time of economic disaster and frequent terrorist attacks. In the novel, Australia's capital city, Canberra, is demolished after the detonation of a nuclear device, ushering in "Armageddon on a whole new level" (30). Islamic terrorist groups are held responsible for the bomb, and they are subsequently persecuted and effectively banned from practising their religion. The ensuing state of emergency and martial law sees an increase in police, intelligence and military forces. Yet it appears that the bomb was actually the work of American groups, sanctioned by the Australian Government, which also fosters terrorist groups in order to maintain a perpetual state of crisis and retain power, using disaster for their own gain. The novel offers a sustained condemnation of contemporary Australian (and American) politics, particularly the "war on terror" and its effects on civil liberties: "the outlawing of refugees ... security laws passed time and time again, each regime more oppressive than the last ... organisations banned. Protesters locked away. Freedoms disappear. Coercion legalised" (275). McGahan's work argues that a nation that is so intent on protecting and defending its freedom at any cost risks sacrificing that very freedom because of a loss of integrity and the erosion of civil rights. *Underground* closes with the narrator comparing the Australian situation with the fall of the Roman Empire, warning of the apocalyptic consequences of focusing on protectionist policies at the expense of liberty:

> If—in this blind pursuit of security above all else—we poison our own society, and so decline, and fall, then we will be more culpable than even the Romans were before us. And such a fall, I suspect, would be followed by an Age so terrible, compared with the knowledge and the light which preceded it, that it wouldn't merely be called Dark. It would be called Black. (McGahan, 2006: 294)

Apocalypse proves an attractive choice for McGahan's purposes because of the way depicting future disaster can encourage readers to re-evaluate their own real-life culture and politics. Science fiction allows writers to develop the notion that present circumstances can or will lead to future catastrophe.

Another potential area of critique for apocalypse is that of empire and colonialism. Kermode (1967: 29) has argued that there are several themes that appear in apocalypse, including decadence and renovation, progress and catastrophe, and empire. He suggests that there is a strong connection between apocalypse and the idea of imperialism (10), where apocalyptic "doctrines of crisis, decadence, and empire" (14) allow societies to read nations, wars and empires in terms of the end of the world. Goldman (2005) argues that apocalypse is highly critical of imperialism because "Revelation's fundamental aim lies in challenging its readers to resist the Roman Empire and to remain faithful to the teachings of Christ" (17). She writes that apocalypse is a central theme in Canadian fiction because it provides an appropriate template for that nation's experience, although writers tend to challenge and "rewrite" the apocalyptic narrative rather than celebrate it, presenting instead an adaptation of apocalypse where "Canadian exploration more often invoked apocalyptic visions of hell than of paradise" (3). Goldman suggests that "Canadian writers, recalling the visions of apocalyptic writers at mid-century … stress the links between apocalyptic violence and the creation of the Canadian nation-state" (25). Her study notes that the apocalyptic "Canadian perspective" is "ex-centric" (27), focusing on the damned rather than the elect. Reading Revelation in terms of the Roman Empire, Goldman proposes that "simply put, early apocalypses are disaster narratives registering the impact of Roman imperialism and colonialism" (17), and contemporary fictions can also use the genre for similar purposes.[6]

In the context of the associations of apocalypse with empire, it is possible to see that science fiction writers can use an apocalyptic discourse to speak against imperialism and shadow a nation's experience. For example, writers can adopt the genre in order to examine cultural issues, such as Archie Weller's post-apocalyptic *Land of the Golden Clouds* (1998), set in the future, which examines the challenges of inter-racial reconciliation that groups of people face when confronted with a common enemy. Mudrooroo's *Doctor Wooreddy's Prescription for Enduring the Ending of the World* (1983) returns to the past to address the question of white colonization more directly. The novel frames European settlement of Australia as the end of the world for Australian indigenous groups in Tasmania, whose interaction with the white colonists results in the death of their culture and ultimately the entire race. Mudrooroo's work thus reflects the historical events of the nineteenth century. Some characters in the novel demonstrate a passive acceptance of the catastrophe: "He consoled himself with the thought that it must be the times" (24), which is an attitude that recurs frequently:

Mangana, he had heard, on hearing of his wife's murder, had only shrugged his shoulders and muttered: "It is the times." His words summed up the general mood of the community. No one had any trust in the future and they accepted a prophecy that passed among them: fewer babies would be born to take the place of the adults dying ever younger; fewer babies to be born, to be weaned, to die—and this meant fewer mature adults to keep and pass on the traditions of the islanders. Thus it was, and it was the times. Everyone knew this and accepted it. Wooreddy alone knew more. He knew that it was because the world was ending. (Mudrooroo, 1983: 9)

Yet Mudrooroo's work is one example of the way that writers can use apocalypse in science fiction as critique. His work retells historical events and thus acts as a protest against dominant versions of history that construct European colonization as a benign experience. In novels such as this, the themes and imagery of apocalypse—catastrophe, death, the end of the world—are deeply appropriate for the subject matter.

Conclusion

Apocalyptic scenarios in literary science fiction are therefore appealing for several reasons. The theme of catastrophe in science fiction texts is flexible enough to symbolize a range of issues and anxieties, and in some cases, the articulation of these issues may alleviate the fear of real-life catastrophe. Yet the key attraction of apocalypse for science fiction writers lies in its ability to function as a literature of interrogation. After all, biblical apocalypse, so influential on contemporary secular apocalyptic fictions, was deeply concerned with the promise of future freedom from violent regimes. Thus, much as science fiction itself can aim to reveal the future and change perspectives, apocalyptic themes provide a powerful framework for writers to address a range of issues. While there is the potential for apocalypse to enable oppressive rhetoric and practices, it can also allow science fiction writers to invent a new world in which to challenge and change prevailing cultural constructions. Given that their settings are often dystopic, such science fiction texts often present negative depictions of society, essentially operating as critiques of present-day politics and shadowing more optimistic future visions. Minority groups may also use apocalypse to highlight injustices and reject dominant ideologies and instead imagine a new and better world. Science fiction writers may canvass social, environmental and ethical issues, using dark futures to speak against present society and critique current practices. Apocalypse, then, proves useful for a range of political stances in literary science fiction.

Notes

1.   For instance, one newspaper titled its special edition following the 2004 Asian tsunami "Tsunami Apocalypse" (2005: 1), and superimposed the headline over a picture of the debris and wreckage, while the back page had pictures of wounded and lost children accompanied by the headline "Children of the Apocalypse" (14). Inside the section, other headlines associate the disaster with religious imagery: "The earth shook, the sea rose up and there was death on a biblical scale" (9), and "A deep-rooted psychological satisfaction in linking natural disaster with human excess" (13). In the weeks following the tsunami, newspaper letter pages contained debates about the disaster, the possible role of people in its cause (scientific, moral, political failures), and God's existence. Similar responses and debates occurred after the 11 September 2001 terrorist attacks on the USA, while people often refer to the attacks on Jews in the Second World War as the Holocaust—a term also denoting an apocalyptic event.

2.   Lyman Tower Sargent (1994: 9) has characterized the dystopia as "a non-existent society described in considerable detail and normally located in time and space that the author intended a contemporaneous reader to view as considerably worse than the society in which that reader lived". Many studies have canvassed the subject of utopia and dystopia in considerable detail. See, for instance, Sargent (1994), Moylan (2000), and Baccolini and Moylan (2003). For a discussion of utopia, dystopia and apocalypse, see Fredric Jameson (2005: 199).

3.   Berger (1999: xiii) argues that Kermode's "sense of ending" has in fact "given way to visions of after the end, and the apocalyptic sensibilities both of religion and of modernism have shifted toward a sense of post-apocalypse". He writes that apocalypses are breaks in time and that because life continues even after real-life apocalypses have occurred, this leaves a perspective of post-apocalypse, post-catastrophe.

4.   Morris (1962) points out that readers commonly interpret the apocalyptic writing of Revelation in four different ways. The preterist perspective interprets the text in terms of the historical context, viewing "all the visions as arising out of conditions in the Roman Empire of the 1st century AD", while the historicist view considers that the visions offer a "continuous story" of history from the time of writing until Christ's return (Morris, 1962: 1094). Futurist interpretations relate the events to the future, although this can be problematic in that such views "removed the book entirely from its

historical setting" (Morris, 1962: 1095). Morris (1962: 1095) labels the fourth interpretation the "idealist" or "poetic" view, and argues that it reads Revelation's imagery purely in symbolic terms as representative of God's victory and "insists that the main thrust of the book is concerned with inspiring persecuted and suffering Christians to endure to the end". He suggests that an accurate reading of Revelation takes all four views into consideration.

5.   *Terminator Gene* (Irvine, 2003) features the catastrophic failing of the New Orleans levees after a severe storm, Hurricane Jemma. Irvine's novel was published in 2003, two years before the real-life events of Hurricane Katrina and the flooding of New Orleans occurred. In the novel, "the emergency response here [in New Orleans] is first class" (295), and following the disaster, the characters praise the immediate and liberal reaction of the Government (464). In contrast, the government agency responses after Hurricane Katrina were widely criticized for their apparent delay.

6.   Readings of Revelation as a message specifically concerning the Roman Empire, however, may overlook the text's wider implications. Revelation is part of an overall narrative coherence throughout both the Old and the New Testaments in a line of prophetic tradition that is strongly intertextual and interdependent. The ambiguity, allegory and symbolism in Revelation and its openness to multiple interpretations would appear to discourage a reading of the text only in terms of the threat of the Roman Empire. Revelation also closely follows in the tradition and themes and visions of prior prophecies in the Old Testament—for example, Daniel and Isaiah—that were not necessarily speaking to the Roman Empire, although some Biblical commentators read Daniel in relation to Rome (Whitcomb, 1962: 292). The long-term perspective of the prophetic tradition in the Testaments suggests that overly narrow interpretations can be problematic. However, even if the Roman Empire was not the only target of Revelation, Goldman's point about the imperialist discourse remains valid and significant, for earlier biblical apocalypses in Daniel, for instance, are very much concerned with empires and invasion and are critical of imperialism.

References

Margaret Atwood, *Oryx and Crake* (London: Bloomsbury, 2003).
Raffaella Baccolini and Tom Moylan (eds), *Dark Horizons: Science Fiction and the Dystopian Imagination* (New York: Routledge, 2003).
James Berger, *After the End: Representations of Post-Apocalypse* (Minneapolis, MN: University of Minnesota Press, 1999).
Paul Brians, *Nuclear Holocausts: Atomic War in Fiction 1895–1984* (Kent, OH: Kent State University Press, 1987).
Simon Brown, *Winter* (Pymble, NSW: HarperCollins, 1997).
Malcolm Bull (ed.), *Apocalypse Theory and the Ends of the World* (Oxford: Blackwell, 1995a).

————. "On Making Ends Meet." In Bull (ed.), *Apocalypse Theory*, 1995b, pp. 1–17.

————. *Seeing Things Hidden: Apocalypse, Vision and Totality* (London: Verso, 1999).

Norman Cohn, *The Pursuit of the Millennium: Revolutionary Millenarians and Mystical Anarchists of the Middle Ages* (1957) (revised edn London: Pimlico-Random House, 1993).

Richard Dellamora, *Apocalyptic Overtures: Sexual Politics and the Sense of an Ending* (New Brunswick, NJ: Rutgers University Press, 1994).

Jacques Derrida, "Of an Apocalyptic Tone Recently Adopted in Philosophy", Trans. John P. Leavey, Jr. *Oxford Literary Review* 6.2 (1984), pp. 3–37.

J.D. Douglas (ed.), *The New Bible Dictionary* (London: The Inter-Varsity Fellowship, 1962).

Northrop Frye, *Anatomy of Criticism: Four Essays* (1957) (New York: Atheneum, 1969).

Francis Fukuyama, *The End of History and the Last Man* (New York: Bard-Avon Books, 1998).

Marlene Goldman, *Rewriting Apocalypse in Canadian Fiction* (Montreal: McGill-Queen's University Press, 2005).

Van Ikin and Terry Dowling, Introduction. In Van Ikin and Terry Dowling (eds), *Mortal Fire: Best Australian SF* (Rydalmere, NSW: Coronet–Hodder and Stoughton–Hodder Headline, 1993) pp. vii–xviii.

Ian Irvine, *The Last Albatross*. The Human Rites Trilogy (2000) (East Roseville, NSW: Earthlight-Simon & Schuster, 2001).

————. *Terminator Gene*. The Human Rites Trilogy 2 (East Roseville, NSW: Earthlight-Simon & Schuster, 2003).

————. *The Life Lottery*. The Human Rites Trilogy 3 (Pymble, NSW: Pocket-Simon & Schuster, 2004).

Rosemary Jackson, *Fantasy: The Literature of Subversion* (London: Methuen Press, 1981).

Edward James, "Rewriting the Christian Apocalypse as a Science-Fictional Event." In Seed (ed.), *Imagining Apocalypse*, 2000, pp. 45–61.

P. D. James, *The Children of Men* (London: Faber and Faber, 1992).

Fredric Jameson, *Archaeologies of the Future: The Desire Called Utopia and Other Science Fictions* (London: Verso-New Left, 2005).

Catherine Keller, *Apocalypse Now and Then: A Feminist Guide to the End of the World* (Boston, MA: Beacon Press, 1996).

Frank Kermode, *The Sense of an Ending: Studies in the Theory of Fiction with a New Epilogue* (1967) (New York: Oxford University Press, 2000).

David Ketterer, *New Worlds for Old: The Apocalyptic Imagination, Science Fiction, and American Literature* (Garden City, NY: Anchor-Doubleday, 1974).

Krishan Kumar, "Apocalypse, Millennium and Utopia Today." In Bull, *Apocalypse Theory*, 1995, pp. 200–24.

Richard Matheson, *I Am Legend* (New York: Fawcett, 1954).

Cormac McCarthy, *The Road* (New York: Alfred A. Knopf, 2006).

Andrew McGahan, *Underground* (Crows Nest, NSW: Allen & Unwin, 2006).

Sean McMullen, *Souls in the Great Machine*. The Greatwinter Trilogy 1 (1999) (New York: Tor-Tom Doherty, 2002).

————. *The Miocene Arrow*. The Greatwinter Trilogy 2 (2000) (New York: Tor-Tom Doherty, 2003a).

————. *Eyes of the Calculor*. The Greatwinter Trilogy 3 (2001) (New York: Tor-Tom Doherty, 2003b).

Andrew McNab, "I Peter: Commentary." In F. Davidson (ed.) *The New Bible Commentary*, 2nd edn (London: The Inter-Varsity Fellowship, 1962), pp. 1130–43.

Walter M. Miller, Jr., *A Canticle For Leibowitz* (1959) (New York: Bantam Spectra-Random House, 1997).

L.L. Morris, "Book of Revelation." In Douglas (ed.), *The New Bible Dictionary*, 1962, pp. 1093–95.

Tom Moylan, *Scraps of the Untainted Sky: Science Fiction, Utopia, Dystopia* (Boulder, CO: Westview Press, 2000).

Mudrooroo [Colin Johnson], *Doctor Wooreddy's Prescription for Enduring the Ending of the World* (1983) (Melbourne: Hyland House, 1994).

Stephen D. O'Leary, *Arguing the Apocalypse: A Theory of Millennial Rhetoric* (New York: Oxford University Press, 1998).

Robert Plank, "The Lone Survivor." In Rabkin, Greenberg and Olander (eds), *The End of the World*, 1983, pp. 20–52.

Eric S. Rabkin, Martin H. Greenberg and Joseph D. Olander (eds), *The End of the World* (Carbondale, IL: Southern Illinois University Press, 1983).

Lyman Tower Sargent, "The Three Faces of Utopianism Revisited." *Utopian Studies* 5.1 (1994): 1–37.

David Seed, "Aspects of Apocalypse." In Seed (ed.), *Imagining Apocalypse*, 2000a, pp. 1–14.

David Seed (ed.) *Imagining Apocalypse: Studies in Cultural Crisis* (Basingstoke: Macmillan Press, 2000b).

Mary Shelley, *The Last Man* (London, 1826).

Nevil Shute, *On the Beach* (London: Heinemann, 1957).

Susan Sontag, "The Imagination of Disaster" (1965). In S. Sontag, *Against Interpretation and Other Essays* (New York: Anchor-Doubleday-Bantam Doubleday Bell, 1990), pp. 209–25.

George R. Stewart, *Earth Abides* (Boston, MA: Houghton-Mifflin, 1949).

"Tsunami Apocalypse" *Sydney Morning Herald* 1–2 January 2005, weekend special edn, pp. 1–14.

George Turner, *Beloved Son* (London: Faber and Faber, 1978).

W. Warren Wagar, *Terminal Visions: The Literature of Last Things* (Bloomington, IN: Indiana University Press, 1982).

W. Warren Wagar, "The Rebellion of Nature." In Rabkin, Greenberg and Olander (eds), *The End of the World,* 1983, pp. 139–72.

Archie Weller, *Land of the Golden Clouds* (St Leonards, NSW: Allen & Unwin, 1998).

H. G. Wells, *The War of the Worlds* (London, 1898).

J.C. Whitcomb, Jr., "Book of Daniel." In Douglas (ed.), *The New Bible Dictionary,* 1962, pp. 290–93.

Gary K. Wolfe, "The Remaking of Zero: Beginning at the End." In Rabkin, Greenberg and Olander (eds), *The End of the World,* 1983, pp. 1–19.

Lois Parkinson Zamora, *Writing the Apocalypse: Historical Vision in Contemporary US and Latin American Fiction* (Cambridge: Cambridge University Press, 1989).

Films Cited

Children of Men (Dir: Alfonso Cuarón, 2006)
The Day After Tomorrow (Dir: Roland Emmerich, 2004)
I Am Legend (Dir: Francis Lawrence, 2007)
Supervolcano (Dir: Tony Mitchell, 2005)

An End Times Virtual "Ekklesia"
Ritual Deliberation in Participatory Media

Robert Glenn Howard

Introduction

Believing that they were acting in a way much like "first century Christians," David (a professional psychologist and convert to evangelical Christianity) told me that he and his wife Brenda used the Internet to enact their *"ekklesia."* For David, "any time people are together—two or more are gathered in His name: there you are! You're the ekklesia!" Rejecting the need for religious institutions, David described how his online communication replaced the function of a brick-and-mortar church:

> There is no real reason you have to show up at a denomination or every Sunday show up at this certain location in the city or else you're a reprobate. And I think it's absolutely viable for the "church", if you understand what I mean by that: the ekklesia; to meet on the Internet. And I have seen it happen a lot. And that's pretty much where we hold our church. (Brenda and David, 1999)

In the New Testament, the word "church" is translated from the Greek word *"ekklesia."* Ekklesia referred to the congregation associated with a particular synagogue. As Christianity evolved, both the Catholic and Eastern Churches emphasized the importance of institutional leadership. Over time, institutional structures began to be synonymous with the communities that they supported. Ultimately, this institutional power was embodied in the physical brick-and-mortar buildings and "church" came to refer to the institutions of Christianity instead of the community they engendered.

David, however, was imagining the older meaning of "church:" the people who comprise a congregation. While individuals may not have always needed an overarching institution to be a "church" in this sense, such institutions function to spread shared knowledge through institutional documents, religious leaders, and community-based organizations. As those ideas are shared, they become the glue that holds the congregation together. When Brenda and David "hold church" online, their religious expression creates a new kind of ekklesia. Though this ekklesia is enacted by its members, it is unlike any ancient congregation because it lacks both a specific geographic place and any authorizing institutional affiliation. A leaderless and placeless community, it is "virtual". Because it is virtual, its very existence rests on the continual performance of shared ideas by those who imagine themselves as comprising its human congregation.

Many individuals use the Internet to supplement activities and commitments associated with their brick-and-mortar churches (Hoover et al., 2004). Because these behaviours seem largely to lack significant ritual or social interactivity, researchers have struggled to define what constitutes the "religious" online (Campbell, 2006). Sustained qualitative research demonstrates that some individuals do engage in religious social behaviour online. For example, neo-pagans have been found to gather in chat rooms and conduct online rituals (Cowan, 2005: 121). In another case, online texts invite the believers to engage in the ritual performance of a "Sinner's Prayer" and then subsequently engage in email exchanges about their experiences (Howard, 2005b). Locating online religious behaviours like these, Glenn Young has suggested that researchers have not paid enough attention to the performative qualities of online religious communication (Young, 2004).

This chapter documents individuals for whom the performance of online discourse has largely replaced brick-and-mortar-based religious ritual practices. For them, no central organization or location undergirds their sense of shared identity. Instead, they recognize each other as participating in a shared social formation when they use the Internet to share information about a particular form of contemporary Protestant belief: apocalypticism in the so-called "End Times" form (O'Leary, 1994; Strozier, 1994; Howard, 1997; Wojcik, 1997; Hendershot, 2004). For them, the ritual performance of online information sharing about the "End Times" enacts a religious community. Because this community has no physical existence beyond its emergence in performance, it must be sustained by open-ended communication practices. I have termed these practices "ritual deliberation".

To document ritual deliberation, ethnographic data are deployed to locate group performances of online communication about the End Times. Tracing the basic form of the End Times narrative in media discourse, it is seen to emerge in mass media during the early

1970s. Next, out of a sample of 200 blog entries, examples of ritual deliberation about the End Times are located. Then, those examples are contextualized in the surrounding web of Websites and blogs that are the virtual locations where this ekklesia is performed. In the end, it is important to consider the implications of this web because its emergence suggests that the ability to limit diversity made possible by network technologies is seen as a benefit by participants in the discourse. This limiting tendency is a result of the individual choices everyday believers are making about how they deploy network media.

Ritual Deliberation and the End Times Narrative

The set of ideas that came together to offer the resources of shared meaning that make ritual deliberation about the End Times possible can be traced back to the growing influence of communication technologies over the course of the twentieth century (Marsden, 1980: 4ff; Harris, 1998: 3ff). During the early twentieth century, American Protestants became increasingly polarized. By 1915, Protestant denominations in the United States were deeply divided into more liberal and more conservative camps over how literally the Bible should be understood (Marsden, 1980: 117ff). This division had been fuelled by a series of annual conferences on biblical study held between 1883 and 1887. At these conferences, a network of conservative evangelicals developed a set of ideas deemed fundamental to Christian belief. These fundamentals included a literal approach to the Bible, evangelism, spiritual rebirth, and the most distinctive: the belief in an approaching Second Coming of Christ (see Marsden, 1980: 77ff; Moore, 1994: 184ff; Harris, 1998: 24 and 25ff).

When evangelical mass media began to emerge first on the radio and later on television, it emerged wedded to a consumer market. Motivated to use new communication technologies to share their message, conservative evangelical institutions were confronted with high broadcasting costs. By emphasizing a simple message that many different believers could support, they successfully began to raise funds by soliciting donations directly from their audience (Moore 1994; Schultze 2003; Howard, 2009). This message emphasized a simple, literal, and emotional understanding of the Bible. Using it, successful evangelists like Billy Graham, Pat Robertson and Jerry Falwell developed media empires. With these empires, the mass media audience of evangelical Christians formed a huge new market.

In 1970, a mass-marketed evangelical book produced for consumption by this audience sold 7.5 million copies and became the bestselling non-fiction book of the decade (excluding the Bible itself): Hal Lindsey's literalist interpretation of biblical prophecy as foretelling Cold War politics titled *The Late Great Planet Earth* (Wojcik, 1997). During the 1980s, Lindsey published many successful books, hosted his own television show, and developed a significant following. Building on this success, Baptist minister Tim LaHaye updated Lindsey's ideas in the form of evangelical fiction. With his co-writer Jerry Jenkins, LaHaye published the first in series of novels called *Left Behind* in 1995. By May of 2004 (when the *Left Behind* series was completed), LaHaye appeared on the cover of *Newsweek* proclaiming that the combined sales of the 12 books had topped 62 million (Hendershot, 2004).

This conservative Protestant mass media successfully courted a large non-denominational audience by placing its emphasis on an overtly emotional personal relationship with the divine and simple relatively literal interpretations of the Bible. Without contradicting any specific Protestant doctrines, the mass media audience of Protestant Christians could be large enough to support a huge industry of evangelical media products. As a byproduct, however, this evangelical media spread a coherent narrative interpretation of Biblical prophecy across institutional lines.

Looking at *The Late Great Planet Earth*, Hal Lindsey presents a model that defined the popular understanding of the End Times. With the controversial addition of the "secret Rapture" instead of an open "pre-Tribulational" Rapture (bodily ascension of born-again Christians to Heaven near the End of Time), Lindsey's basic narrative would be largely reproduced in the *Left Behind* series, and would persist in a myriad of variants online. In 1970, Lindsey's narrative could be reduced to the following schematic narrative:

1. rise of New Roman Empire as European Common Market, before 1988;
2. the establishment a world governing body led by Antichrist;
3. Antichrist sides with world government and Israel against Russia;
4. Antichrist dies of head wound, but miraculously recovers;

5. Antichrist is worshipped as a god;
6. 666 tattoo on forehead or palm established as economic mark of European Common Market;
7. rebuilding of Temple in Jerusalem;
8. Arab, other African states, and the Soviet Union attack Israel;
9. Antichrist destroys Soviet Alliance with a nuclear attack;
10. China attacks forces of Antichrist;
11. one third of world destroyed by nuclear weapons;
12. Christ returns to protect faithful, "secret Rapture";
13. mass conversion of Jews;
14. Armageddon;
15. establishment of "atomic material" paradise for 1,000 years;
16. resurgence of Antichrist put down by Christ;
17. return of "faithful to heaven with Christ". (Lindsey 1970)

Nearly 40 years later, a Website detailed an "End Times Prophecy" portraying functionally the same scenario (*Endtime Bible Prophecy*, 2008). First noting that Israel was re-established in 1947 and took control of Jerusalem in 1967, the page on the *Endtime Bible Prophecy* Website describes a variety of "Signs of the End" including "Earthquakes", "False Messiahs" and "Wars and Rumors of Wars". It goes on to assert that the Rapture or "the instantaneous removal of God's people from the earth" will occur just before the, "SEVEN-YEAR PERIOD OF DANIEL BEGINS". Then it offers the following basic schematic of events:

1. "Seven-year covenant or peace treaty with Israel is confirmed by the Antichrist";
2. "Antichrist is revealed";
3. "Rebuilding of the Third Temple in Jerusalem";
4. "War";
5. "Mark of the Beast is required on all people to buy or sell";
6. "Resurrection of the Beast/Antichrist after a fatal wound" marks the "TRIBULATION MIDPOINT (3½ years after the peace treaty with Israel)";
7. "Breaking of the covenant with Israel by the Antichrist";
8. Persecutions of Christians Begins;
9. "Death"—"One-fourth of the world's population (new Christians and Jews) are killed by the Antichrist/Beast with the sword and with starvation";

10. "Signs in the Sky" "(Great Earthquake, Bloody Moon, Black-out of the Sun, Meteors falling, Mountains and Islands moving, Sky splits apart)";
11. "144,000 of the tribe of Israel are sealed";
12. "Hail and Fire Destruction of all the grass and 1/3 of trees. Meteor falls into the Ocean destroying 1/3 of ships and sea life," and "Wormwood falls from the Heavens causing fresh water to become bitter," and "Eastern army of 200,000,000 men kill 1/3 of mankind";
13. Gathering of the Antichrist, kings and, armies of the world in final battle of "Armageddon";
14. "Second Coming" which results in the "Beast and False Prophet thrown into the Lake of Fire" and the "Destruction of the armies by the word of God";
15. millennial reign of Christ where "Christ rules on Earth";
16. "Judgment of Nations";
17. "NEW HEAVEN AND EARTH". (*Endtime Bible Prophecy,* 2008)

Lindsey's claim of a "secret Rapture" becomes one of the central deliberative issues among End Time believers. Debating when and how the Rapture will occur, some argue it will come before the violence predicted for the "Tribulation" period, some say during, and others hold that it will happen at the end. The timing of the Rapture, however, is just one issue about which individuals deliberate. For example, Lindsey's numbers 4, 5, 6 and 7 correspond directly to *Endtime Bible Prophecy*'s numbers 5, 6 and 7. However, neither interpretation can definitively answer who will be the Antichrist, where she or he will come from, or how her or his power will be exercised. There is agreement, however, that there will be an Antichrist, she or he will be assassinated and rise from the dead to be worshipped as if divine, and subsequently force everyone to take "the Mark of the Beast". Of course, no one is quite sure what that "Mark" will be or when it will be enforced.

In a similar way, while there is disagreement between the two timelines about when the Temple in Jerusalem will be rebuilt (number 7 for Lindsey and number 3 for *Endtime Bible Prophecy*), there is no doubt that it will occur. Ritual deliberation can arise from this narrative precisely because while these events are themselves not disputable, exactly who, how and when they will occur is. With access to news media content, new data can be inserted into the narrative and its validity discussed. While the narrative structure is largely rigid, it is highly plastic in the details. As a result, it is able to assimilate a wide range of potential specific new details without threatening its religious or theological import (Howard, 2006).

Before the advent of Internet communication, believers could watch television news, read newspapers and magazines looking for signs that indicated the fulfilment of prophecy. Through their church or other local institutions, they would have been able to locate a only few others with their interests. They might have generated interest by organizing lay Bible studies or meetings, but these geographically based communities would have been relatively small. For them, this limited access to shared ritual action could not generate any sizeable community.

However, the online environment that emerged in the 1990s transformed the possibilities for individuals interested in this set of beliefs. Online, individuals could not only rapidly access far more news sources than ever before, they could locate and interact with individuals who shared this interest in world events and biblical prophecy without being limited by geographic proximity. Online, these people formed networks of communication. In these networks, they engage in everyday conversations that speculate about an imminent End Times (Howard, 1997, 2000, 2009).

With the continual consumption of information about specific (but constantly changing) world events, believers deliberate together online. This deliberation does not necessarily seek to discover new facts or come to any final shared decisions. Instead, it seeks to exchange and consume ideas within a shared ideological frame. In this sense, it is a performative ritual. Enacting this ritual, individuals enact the shared nature of their ekklesia, and that sharing gives this virtual ekklesia its only existence. Because there are no geographic locations, institutions, or leaders, it constantly has to build itself up from the informal expression of everyday adherents. The Internet has transcended bricks and mortar to make this bottom-up construction possible on a scale not previously available.

In this ongoing everyday online communication, social control bubbles upward from the vernacular or "everyday" religious practice. At the "lived" or "vernacular" level, shared religious belief emerges not from religious institutions (Primiano, 1995; Howard,

2005a). Instead, it is learned and relearned in undifferentiated and countless moments in the ongoing flow of social interaction. Unlike the documents that form doctrines, the informal discourse of individuals manifests the creative diversity of personal expression. From this diversity, individuals can enact the shared markers that join them in their "church". One way this is done online is through the deployment of the Internet medium generally termed "blogs".

Heralded as marking a new era of "participatory culture," the number of web pages considered "blogs" exploded in the years after 2002 (Jenkins, 2006). In July of 2002, 3 per cent of Internet users reported having their own blog. By November of 2005, that number had jumped to 10 per cent. At that time, 27 per cent read other people's blogs and 19 per cent of teenage internet users maintained their own blogs (Lenhart, 2005; Pew, 2005). Since then, it has been estimated that 70,000 new blogs and about 700,000 new posts to existing blogs are appearing every day (Technorati Data, 2006).

This explosion has fuelled and been fuelled by a growing diversity of media forms. Famously termed "Web 2.0" by computer media CEO Tim O'Reilly, these forms were made possible by innovations on the original HTML computer language that Tim Burners-Lee created in 1992 (O'Reilly, 2005). After 2002, these more robust computer languages made it easier for web-users to add and change website content. From wikis, to social networking, to photo sharing, to blogs themselves, these new participatory forms of Web-use occur across network locations to create new and complex webs of vernacular communication (Howard, 2008, 2009). Emerging out of what is considered the first digital genre on the Worldwide Web, "web logs" were part of the content that was considered characteristic of personal "home pages" (Howard, 2005b). In 1999, several companies released software designed to automate Website creation in an effort to harness the growing popularity of so-called "weblogs." The most successful of these ventures was the "Blogger" software of *Blogger.com* (Blood, 2004).

In exchange for placing third party advertising on the personal Websites it hosted, *Blogger.com* offered a service that made it very easy for even computer novices to put personal content online. The software was primarily designed to put diary-like entries on a Website. The popularity of its software allowed *Blogger.com* to define the basic features of the new genre of "blogs". Primary among these was the reverse dated entries by a single author. Secondarily, was a

"Comments" section included after each entry. These comments sections allowed audience members to post responses to the blogger's entries (Blood, 2004).

To locate ritual deliberation about the End Times in online vernacular communication for this chapter, specific blog entries and comments sections have been collected and compared. In order to find those entries, the terms "End Time", "End Times", "Endtime" and "Endtimes" were searched in two common search engines on 28 June 2007. For the sample set, the top 100 hits from each of the two search engines were combined to create a collection of 200 specific Webpages. For this chapter, I have chosen a series of these pages that exemplify the way very different individuals can enact a shared virtual ekklesia based on ritual deliberation. Despite their differences, these examples demonstrate that the online communication of these individuals generates a web of communication that is emergent from their online performance of ritual deliberation.

Deliberating the End Times in Participatory Media

Because it is typically free for individuals to post text, graphic or video media on their blogs, individuals often use these media to make personal statements that may or may not generate an interested audience. Using search engines such as *Google Blog Search* or *Technorati*, individuals can locate others with similar interests based on key words associated with the End Times narrative. When the conditions are right, these individuals can use participatory media to generate their virtual ekklesia through the performance of ritual deliberation.

With 20 entries, *666 Mark of the Beast 666* was the most prevalent blog in the sample set. Run by "Joshua", the site uses a modified version of the *Wordpress.com* blogging software. Set on a black background, the text of the blog is blood red. Using no graphic or video content, it featured its title across the top followed by a "Welcome!" statement. Along the left side, the site deploys the *Wordpress* software to create a search engine for its blog entries. Readers can also browse the entries based on specific topics: "News", "Prophecy", "Mark of the Beast", "Antichrist", "Satanism" and "Catholic Times" (Joshua, 2008). Below that, the audience can access the entries by date going back two years.

The reverse dated entries themselves are in the central pane of the site, and they were comprised primarily of links to news stories suggestive of End Times predictions or other writings about the End Times collected from around the Web. In its "Welcome!" statement, the site clearly associates its discourse with the End Times by announcing it is a Website:

> Dedicated to the study of the End Times, the Rapture, the Tribulation, and the Prophecies in Revelation. We believe that Bible prophecy is to be understood in a literal way and the expressed view of this site is of a pre-millennial return of Christ and pre-tribulational Rapture of the Church. Therefore, this website is dedicated to bring fellow believers the latest news, stories, events and signs that brings us closer to the End Times. (Joshua, 2008)

666 Mark of the Beast 666 exemplifies the most common way the blog medium was deployed in the examples found in the in the sample set. Here, a single individual or small group uses blogging software to communicate their ideas outward to an audience of passive receivers. In this form, the medium does not encourage deliberation. In the case of *666 Mark of the Beast 666*, there were very few comments in the comments sections of the many blog entries. Still, *666 Mark of the Beast 666* is deliberative in a weak sense because its entries are almost exclusively comprised of material performatively reframed as potential new details in the End Times narrative.

In blogs, this performance is typically the action of cutting and pasting or linking to mainstream news media stories elsewhere online. Often with few elaborations, the frame set by the blog as being, "to bring fellow believers the latest news, stories, events and signs" redefines and redeploys whatever content has been collected from around the Web. This new frame is the End Times narrative. This information reframing constitutes the weak form of online ritual deliberation because it functions to draw otherwise more general information into the vernacular web of communication emergent from a shared belief in the End Times narrative. Another blog that appeared in the sample, *Jesus Christology,* presents an example of a blog that was moderately open to deliberation. In this case, a stronger form of ritual deliberation emerges as individuals publicly responded to each other in the comments sections of the blog entries.

A 35 year old male living in Georgia, *Jesus Christology*'s "Job" was drawn to the End Times ekklesia through what he considers a "spiritual warfare" experience. A life-time sufferer from severe asthma, Job relied on an inhaler. As he describes it, "Because of the longtime overuse of the asthma medicine, I reached the point where it did me virtually no good anymore." When he discovered that his son might also suffer from asthma, he began a regime of fasting in an effort to bring the power of the divine to bear on his health problem. His religious fasting gave him, "revelations of things concerning prophecy, discernment, and spiritual warfare" (Job, 2008b).

Job described his belief that, "Satan knew that my moment of truth was coming and thought that filling me with doubt, fear, failure, and desperation would cause me to crumble when it came." However, Job did not crumble. Instead, in an inspired moment, he threw his inhaler into the trash. Witnessing the event, Job's wife threw her eyeglass in the trash, and their toddler threw his favourite toy in the trash. "And so we all ran around the house praising God, all three of us!" Job was inspired by this experience to create his own amateur ministry online. This ministry took the form of the *Jesus Christology* blog (Job, 2008b).

Specifically rejecting church institutions, Job hopes his ministry will help individuals avoid what he sees as the failure of church institutions. Job believes that during the Tribulation period the world will witness God, "pouring out his wrath upon and scattering the church". Job writes:

> God is about to judge the church, and when that judgment comes it will be better to be outside the church than to be a sinner in it! [...] I pray that I will allow God to use me in this ministry and all those who have similar ministries, such that all who receive this and similar teachings will be spared God's wrath, be part of God's remnant, and do his will. In the name of Jesus Christ, Amen. (Job, 2008c)

Believing that Satan and his demons are leading both Christians and non-Christians astray, Job's focus is spiritual warfare. As he describes it, "spiritual warfare is fighting against and overcoming demons, or former angels that have been cast out of God's Kingdom and now follow Satan, with the power and Name of Jesus Christ". As is common among individuals involved in spiritual warfare, individuals associated with non-Christian traditions also become targets. According to Job, spiritual warfare must target humans, "who (whether knowingly or not) work for Satan with the assistance of demons: witches, satanists, devil worshippers, idolators, etc." (Job 2008d).

One of these individuals turned out to be the 2008 US Democratic presidential candidate, Barack Obama. While many of Job's posts are largely just linking and forwarding articles like those of *666 Mark of the Beast 666*, others encourage audience engagement. Job's cues for his audience to respond result in the blog becoming a location for strong-form ritual deliberation. One example of this cued deliberation is in a blog entry posted on 26 January 2008 entitled: "Does Anyone Know The Number Of Barack HUSSEIN Obama's Name?" In this entry, Job writes:

> It would seem that one would have to somehow translate Barack HUSSEIN Obama to either Arabic, Aramaic, Hebrew, Latin, or Greek first and then just add up the position of the letters in the alphabet. [...] Don't get me wrong, I really do not think that Obama is the anti-Christ. It is just that we have to keep our eye on all these unifying charismatic figures. (Job, 2008e)

This post is openly deliberative because its title is a question. With this question, it actively it encourages the participation of others who might be able to translate Obama's name and "add up" the letters. This encouragement elicits nine comments from five individuals in Job's audience. In these comments, there are two requests to engage in a discussion of the matter in private. There is an attempt to apply the long held association between Ronald Wilson Regan's name and 666 to Obama, and there is the following comment posted by "Someone":

> Barack Hussein Obama=666, here's why:
> Barack=6
> Hussein=7
> Obama=5
> (all possible combination)
> 567
> 576
> 657
> 675
> 756
> 765
> ——
> 3,996(total)/6=666
> (Job, 2008e)

While the responses to the initial blog entry about Obama subsided after this response, the concern about Obama did not. On 14 February 2008, Job posted another entry about Obama titled: "NO WE CAN'T! BARACK HUSSEIN OBAMA IS A FALSE CHRIST!" This post asserts that Obama is part of the new Satan-inspired threat termed "the religious left". The post attacks Obama's church, the United Churches of Christ, as "one of the most liberal". It states that Obama's church in Chicago is "pastured" [*sic*.] by a "racist". The post then goes on cite the "revival-like" atmosphere surrounding Obama's political campaign. Claiming to have predicted "a 'faux revival'" earlier that year, the post implores its audience saying: "I am challenging you? today to decide who YOU are going to follow, B. Hussein Obama, the most ?recent false messiah, or Jesus Christ, the true Messiah!!!" (Job, 2008f)

This blog entry resulted in the most comments on any open blog in the sample set. With these 21 comments, the site functioned as a location for ritual deliberation. However, it also drew the attention of outsiders, and these outsiders hampered that deliberation. Six of the 21 comments were curt and hostile. The very first comment set the tone writing, simply, "You're about five kinds of @#$%^&$." This was followed by a short barrage of similar statements. Then "Independent Conservative", a long time commenter on the site, addressed Job directly writing: "Job, it looks like the Obama fans are worse than the Romney fans [another presidential candidate at that time]. Proving Obama is a false christ, that many see as their hope." Then Job replied:

> Oh, most of these fellows are being sent here by this anti-Christian blog that linked to my site [. . .] They are having real fun with my spiritual warfare content in particular as you might guess. Ah well, at least they are being exposed to the gospel of Jesus Christ crucified and raised from the dead. (Job, 2008f)

On that "anti-Christian blog", the blogger posted a copy-and-pasted text of one of Job's posts about Obama (Edroso, 2008a). Then, in the comments section of that post, individuals colluded to disrupt Job's blog saying: "I say we make this Job person's life a waking nightmare" (Edroso, 2008b). Once the disruption dissipated, however, 14 more posts continue to explore the possibility that Obama is a "false christ" (Job, 2008f). Somewhat ironically, the outsiders who attacked Job's blog seemed to never realize that Job actually did not write the document at all. Instead, it was yet another cut-and-pasted piece of content written by a professional minister named Bill Keller who runs a well-known Christian site called *Liveprayer.com* (Keller, 2008).

This example suggests that outsiders hostile to the End Times narrative can hamper public ritual deliberation. In turn, that suggests that when a blog is able to limit the influx of non-believers, it is more likely to become a virtual location for ritual deliberation. One clear example of this more deliberative blog environment appeared in the sample set as *RaptureAlert.com* (Mickey, 2008a). Dating back to 2003, Michael, the builder of *RaptureAlert.com,* started a *Blogger.com* blog in 2008 to augment his site (Mickey, 2008b).

A 44 year old retired police officer in the Southeastern United States, Michael posts to *RaptureAlert.com* almost daily. Unlike *666 Mark of the Beast 666* or even *Jesus Christology*, Michael elicits far more comments from his audience than any other blog appearing in the sample set. A typical exchange occurring on the site is that from 15 February 2008 titled: "A Rumbling in The Middle East". This post generates 16 comments. In this entry, Michael firsts refers to his post from the previous day saying, "In light of yesterday's commentary and the potential implications of recent events in the Middle East, I have to admit I got chills when I read of a magnitude 5 earthquake rattling Lebanon and neighboring countries today" (Mickey, 2008c).

The day before, he wrote an entry titled "The Middle East: Back To The Brink". In that post, he recounts the recent slaying of the leader of Hezbollah's "second in command" in Damascus. As a result of the attack, Hezbollah issued a statement "declaring 'open war' on Israel". Michael asks, "A prelude to Gog-Magog?" Citing Matthew 26: 6, he places this attack into the End Times narrative and finishes his 963 word analysis writing, "The end times drama continues ..." (Mickey, 2008d).

When the earthquake in Lebanon occurred the day after his post, Michael wrote, "Just another earthquake here in the last days or a harbinger of things to come? Only the Lord knows but I'll bet the air in and around Israel could practically be cut with a knife right now." A classic invitation to ritual deliberation among participants in the End Times ekklesia, it is deliberative because it posits a question. Further, the question it posits is about a typical End Times world news item: an earthquake. Beyond that, it is a news item relating to the area most important to the End Times narrative: the Middle East. Although the invitation is from a blogger that initiates and controls the discussions on his site, it is to an audience that is comprised of individuals who share belief in the basic End Times narrative. Many of these individuals respond immediately by expression support. The first example is "jo anna":

> WOW! I hadn't heard about this one yet. I heard about the 2 in Greece yesterday, but not this one. I've also been reading how lake Mead is drying up and then with the the problems Georgia and Florida are having and the HUGE push about global warming! And of course all that's going on war wise in the middle east. My heart is racing at how close we could be to going home! I am so ready to be with Jesus and done with this place! Oh how I pray people accept Christ quickly before it's too late! (Mickey, 2008d)

With the ritual deliberation started, Michael responds saying: "Amen, Jo Anna! A lot is going on and on a variety of fronts. Broadening the spectrum a bit, do you realize we have had FOUR campus shootings in the United States in one short week?" Then ten different people in 14 more posts consider nine different world events reported by various news organizations as other indicators that the beginning of the End Time wars is near at hand. These events include, Russian president Vladimir Putin, "making threats against western Europe", "FOUR campus shootings in the United States in one short week" and Lake Mead (a popular lake resort area in the Western United States) "drying up". The deliberation climaxed as one commenter wrote in all capitals: "I AM SO LOOKING FORWARD TO A FRONT ROW SEAT TO THE MAJOR BUTT KICKING SATAN IS GOING TO GET SOON!" (Mickey, 2008d).

After this crowning vernacular expression of shared belief, a commentor suggested that they pray for those dead and injured in the Lebanese earthquake. That plan then developed into an agreement to pray for one of the commentors' relative's infant son who was going in to have a biopsy the next day (Mickey, 2008d). As this example makes clear, *RaptureAlert.com* proved a good place for individuals interested in the End Times to engage in its characteristic behaviour: ritual deliberation.

The suitability of this location for ritual deliberation based on the End Times is no accident. A regular commenter on a variety of forums, Michael is very a savvy Internet user who is careful to maintain deliberative communication. Before even creating a blog, he chose to engage his audience in deliberation about the choice. He recounts the story in his 6 February 2008 post titled, "To blog!":

As most of you are aware, I have been trying to assess the desire of my readers to have an opportunity to leave comments in relation to the content of the site as once was the case. Based on over 1,500 visits to the page I set up for polling, it seems that some 70% of those polled either want an option to blog or don't care if there is one. Approximately 30% of the site's readers would prefer not to have a blog option. (Mickey 2008e).

In addition to polling his audience about the idea of starting a blog, Michael asked if the blog should be, "open for anyone to post their thoughts". Apparently, many in his audience suggested that he use a, "Christian forum on the web". However, because Michael didn't want to make people register before commenting, he decided to use the far more well-known and secular *Blogger.com* service. In his post describing his decision, he expressed concern that if outsiders are allowed to post to the new blog, his audience of believers will have, "to contend for the faith vigorously in some instances". Instead he decides it is best if:

Anyone to be able to comment (even anonymously) and for those comments to be moderated by me prior to posting. That will result in some delays, periodically, in posted comments appearing on the blog but it seems the only safe way for the blog to go forward without a good portion of the site's bloggers being uncomfortable. We'll take things as they come and see how it goes. (Mickey, 2008e).

In this way, Michael creates a safe place for ritual deliberation by limiting the voices able to be heard in the discussion to only those that support belief in the End Times.

Civil Society and the Problem of the Virtual Ekklesia

In the 1990s, utopian claims about Internet use gave some researchers cause to hope that the exclusionary beliefs and intolerance associated with Christian fundamentalism would fade away in the online environment (Brasher, 2001; Howard, 1997). Since then, however, studies have shown that intensely held religious belief allows individuals to deploy network technologies in ways that filter out the voices of those who might offer alternate or dissenting ideas (Howard, 2005c, 2005d, 2006). The web of communication emergent from ritual deliberation about "The End Times", suggests that the virtual *ekklesiae* made possible by the Internet may actually enable intolerance.

As network media empower individuals to act more out of their own volition as they construct religious communities, some of those individuals choose to engage in exclusionary communication behaviours. Without the forces of geography or the institutions that have traditionally mediated conflicts arising from that geography, individuals are able to filter out the diversity that could challenge their religious convictions. As Heidi Campbell has noted, individuals involved in religion online can choose to engage in "self-regulated forms of socialization" (2005: 188).

Unyoked from geography or institutions, a virtual ekklesia is comprised of weakly linked individuals (Wellman and Guilia, 1999; Csermely, 2006). These individuals are weakly linked in the sense that they share few if any material resources and seldom seek shared action beyond expressing their ideas to each other. As a result, the virtual ekklesia is freed from the geographic factors associated with living in proximity and sharing material resources. For its congregants, the only pressing need for cooperation is in the actual sharing of the beliefs themselves. The ability to pick and choose with whom to share religious information allows individuals to by-pass the forces of "civil society". As Harris Breslow has described it, "civil society" can be imagined as a discursive space in which, "all may congregate where subjective identity and social membership are made palpably obvious" (1997: 254).

While Internet technologies have freed individuals from institutional control, this radically individualized form of communication may undermine the valuable role social institutions have traditionally played in creating and maintaining the spaces for public deliberation. Cass Sunstein has argued that, "The public forum represents one area of law in which the right to free speech demands a public subsidy to the speakers" (2001: 28). As Sunstein has argued, the freedom to speak is twofold.

One sort of freedom is the freedom to express one's personal opinion. However, the ability to express one's self is expanded by access to the knowledge of the diversity of possibilities for expression available. Thus, the freedom to speak is enlarged by the freedom to hear the diversity of others speaking. When social institutions bring divergent voices together in the public of the "civil society", the sheer diversity of alternative opinions challenge the voicing of absurd or intolerant claims. Claiming that a political candidate should not be voted for because she or he is "the Antichrist" is an acceptable argument for only a tiny sector of society. Confronted with a more diverse audience voicing more broadly acceptable reasoning, claims based on narrowly "self-regulated" belief are challenged by the voice of the majority.

The virtual ekklesia does not foster these broad audiences, however, because it connects individuals based exclusively on their own desire to share information about topics of their choosing. This radical freedom to "self-regulate" enables some individuals to engage in communicative behaviours that deny social institutions their traditional ability to create and maintain public locations for the exchange of ideas. It is true that institutions can and often do enforce homogeneity, and virtual ekklesiae can help individuals overcome this hegemonic power. However, the practice of online ritual deliberation about the End Times suggests that some individuals are using that freedom to limit their own exposure to new, divergent, and possibly empowering ideas. This limiting factor is a product of how individuals choose to deploy the Internet in their everyday lives. With increasing freedom to engage religiosity outside of institutions or the spheres of discourse they have traditionally created, individuals must take particular care not to abuse their new power by choosing exclusion and intolerance over diversity and compassion.

References

B. E. Brasher, *Give Me That Online Religion* (San Francisco, CA: Josey-Bass Publishing, 2001).

Brenda and David, Interviewed by the author, Helena, MO, 17 October 1999.

H. Breslow, "Civil Society, Political Economy, and the Internet." In S. G. Jones (ed.) *Virtual Culture: Identity and Communication in Cybersociety* (London: Sage Publications, 1997), pp. 236–57.

H. Campbell, "Internet and Cyber Environments." In D. A. Stout (ed.) *Encyclopedia of Religion, Communication, and Media* (New York: Routledge, 2006), pp. 177–82.

H. Campbell, *Exploring Religious Community Online: We are One in the Network* (New York: Peter Lang Publishing, 2005).

D. E. Cowan, *Cyberhenge: Modern Pagans on the Internet* (New York: Routledge, 2005).

P. Csermely, *Weak Links: Stabilizers of Complex Systems from Proteins to Social Networks* (New York: Springer Verlag Publishers, 2006).

R. Edroso, "Speaking in Tongues," *Alicublog,* 12 February 2008. <http://alicublog.blogspot.com/2008/02/speaking-in-tongues.html> (2008a).

R. Edroso, "Comments," *Alicublog.* 15 February 2008, <http://www.haloscan.com/comments/edroso/213531270659411955/> (2008b).

Endtime Bible Prophecy, "Endtime Prophecy Time Line." In *Endtime Bible Prophecy*, URL: <http://home.flash.net/~venzor/outline.htm> accessed 1 February 2008).

H. A. Harris, *Fundamentalism and Evangelicals* (Oxford: Clarendon Press, 1998).

H. Hendershot, *Shaking the World for Jesus: Media and Conservative Evangelical Culture,* (Chicago, IL: University of Chicago Press, 2004).

S. M. Hoover, L. Scofield Clark and R. Lee, "Faith Online: 64% of Wired Americans Have Used the Internet for Spiritual or Religious Information," *Pew Internet and American Life Project,* <http://www.pewInternet.org/reports/toc.asp?Report=119> (2004).

Robert Glenn Howard, "Apocalypse in your In-Box: End-Times Communication on the Internet," *Western Folklore* 56 (1997), pp. 295–315.

Robert Glenn Howard, "On-Line Ethnography of Dispensationalist Discourse: Revealed versus Negotiated Truth." In Jeffery K. Hadden and Douglas Cowan (eds) *Religion on the Internet*, New York: Elsevier Press, 2000), pp. 225–46.

Robert Glenn Howard,. "A Theory of Vernacular Rhetoric: The Case of the 'Sinner's Prayer' Online," *Folklore* 116 (2005a), pp. 172–88.

Robert Glenn Howard, "Toward a Theory of the World Wide Web Vernacular: The Case for Pet Cloning," *Journal of Folklore Research* 42 (2005b), pp. 323–60.

Robert Glenn Howard, "The Double Bind of the Protestant Reformation: The Birth of Fundamentalism and the Necessity of Pluralism," *Journal of Church and State* 47 (2005c), pp. 91–108.

Robert Glenn Howard, "Sustainability and Radical Rhetorical Closure: The Case of the 1996 'Heaven's Gate' Newsgroup Campaign," *Journal of Communication and Religion* 28 (2005d), pp. 99–130.

Robert Glenn Howard, "Sustainability and Narrative Plasticity in Online Apocalyptic Discourse After September 11, 2001," *Journal of Media and Religion* 5 (2006), pp. 25–47.

Robert Glenn Howard, "Electronic Hybridity: The Persistent Processes of the Vernacular Web," *Journal of American Folklore* 121 (Spring) (2008a), pp. 192–218.

Robert Glenn Howard, "The Vernacular Web of Participatory Media," *Critical Studies in Media Communication* (December) (2008b), pp. 490–512.

Robert Glenn Howard, "Enacting a Virtual 'Ekklesia:' Online Christian Fundamentalism as Vernacular Religion," *New Media and Society*: forthcoming, (2009).

Job, "A Brief List Of Reasons Why Christians Should Not Support Barack HUSSEIN Obama," 14 February 2008, *Jesus Christology Earnestly Contending For The Faith Once Delivered To The Saints Jude 1:3*, <http://healtheland.wordpress.com/category/anti-christ/> (2008a).

Job, "Testimony Time," 1 February 2008, *Heal the Land Ministries*, <http://www.healtheland.bravehost.com/Archives/Devos/TestimonyTime.htm> (2008b).

Job, "Purpose," 1 February 2008, *Heal the Land Ministries*, <http://www.healtheland.bravehost.com/General_Docs/Purpose.htm> (2008c).

Job, "Spiritual Warfare." 1 February 2008, *Heal the Land Ministries*, <http://www.healtheland.bravehost.com/General_Docs/Subdirec/SpiritualWarfare.htm> (2008d).

Job, "Does Anyone Know The Number Of Barack HUSSEIN Obama's Name?" 26 January 2008, <http://healtheland.wordpress.com/2008/01/26/does-anyone-know-the-number-of-barack-hussein-obamas-name/#comments> (2008e).

Job, "NO WE CAN'T! BARACK HUSSEIN OBAMA IS A FALSE CHRIST!" 14 February 2008, *Heal the Land Ministries*. <http://healtheland.wordpress.com/2008/02/14/no-we-cant-barack-hussein-obama-is-a-false-christ/> (2008f).

H. Jenkins, K. Clinton, R. Purushotma, A. J. Robison and M. Weigel, Confronting the challenges of participatory culture: Media education for the 21st century, retrieved 19 January 2007, from http://www.digitallearning.macfound.org/site/c.enJLKQNlFiG/b.2108773/apps/nl/content2.asp?content_id=%7BCD911571-0240-4714-A93B-1D0C07C7B6C1%7D&notoc=1 (2006).

Joshua, "Welcome to 666 Mark of the Beast," In *666 Mark of the Beast 666*, 1 February 2008, <http://www.666markofthebeast.com/> (2008).

B. Keller, "Today's Daily Devotional," *Live Prayer: The First Global Prayer Meeting*, 1 February 2008, <http://www.liveprayer.com/today.cfm> (2008).

E. Larsen, "CyberFaith: How Americans Pursue Religion Online." In *Pew Internet and American Life Project*, URL (accessed 1 November 2005): <http://www.pewInternet.org/pdfs/PIP_CyberFaith_Report.pdf> (2001).

A. Lenhart and M. Madden, "Teen content creators and consumers", accessed 6 January 2006, from http://www.pewinternet.org/pdfs/PIP_Teens_Content_Creation.pdf (2 November 2005).

G. Marsden, *Fundamentalism and American Culture: The Shaping of Twentieth Century Evangelicalism, 1870–1925*, (New York: Oxford University Press, 1980).

M. Mickey, "The Blog," 1 February 2008, *RaptureAlert.com: The Blog*. <http://rapturealert.blogspot.com/> (2008a).

M. Mickey, "RaptureAlert.com: Sounding the alarm that Jesus Christ is coming soon!" 1 February 2008, *RaptureAlert.com,* <http://rapturealert.blogspot.com/> (2008b).

M. Mickey, "A Rumbling in The Middle East," 15 February 2008. *RaptureAlert.com: The Blog,* <https://www.blogger.com/comment.g?blogID=7527279812767969161&postID=410073931187569533> (2008c).

M. Mickey, "The Middle East: Back To The Brink," 14 February 2008, *RaptureAlert.com: The Blog*. <http://rapturealert.blogspot.com/2008/02/middle-east-back-to-brink.html> (2008d).

M. Mickey, "To blog!" 14 February 2008, *RaptureAlert.com: The Blog*. < http://rapturealert.blogspot.com/2008/02/to-blog_06.html> (2008e).

R. L. Moore, *Selling God: American Religion in the Marketplace of Culture* (Oxford: Oxford University Press, 1994).

S. D. O'Leary, *Arguing the Apocalypse: A Theory of Millennial Rhetoric* (New York: Oxford University Press, 1994).

T. O'Reilly, "What is web 2.0: Design patterns and business models for the next generation of software," *O'Reillynet,* accessed 10 November 2006 from <http://www.oreillynet.com/lpt/a/6228> (2005).

Pew, January 2005, daily tracking survey, accessed 6 January 2006, from http://www.pewinternet.org/datasets/Jan%202005%20tracking%20topline.zip (11 February 2005).

L. N. Primiano, "Vernacular Religion and the Search for Method in Religious Folklife," *Western Folklore* 54 (1) (1995), pp. 37–56.

C. B. Strozier, *Apocalypse: On the Psychology of Fundamentalism in America,* (Boston, MA: Beacon Press, 1994).

Q. J. Schultze, *Christianity and the Mass Media in America: Toward a Democratic Accommodation,* (East Lansing, MI: Michigan State University Press, 2003).

C. Sunstein, *Republic.com*. Princeton, NJ: Princeton University Press, 2001).

Technorati Data, "About Technorati", accessed 6 January 2006, from http://www.technorati.com/about/ (6 January 2006).

B. Wellman and M. Gulia, "Virtual Communities as Communities: Net Surfers Don't Ride Alone." In M. A. Smith and P. Kollock (eds) *Communities in Cyberspace* (New York: Routledge, 1999), pp. 167–94.

D. Wojcik *The End of the World as We Know It: Faith, Fatalism, and Apocalypse in America,* (New York: New York University Press, 1997).

G. Young, "Reading and Praying Online: The Continuity of Religion Online and Online Religion in Internet Christianity." In L. Dawson and D. Cowan (eds) *Religion Online: Finding Faith on the Internet* (New York: Routledge, 2004), pp. 93–106.

Index